The Practice and Politics of Fiat Finance

The Practice and Politics of Fiat Finance

North Carolina in the Confederation, 1783-1789

***by* JAMES R. MORRILL**

The University of North Carolina Press
Chapel Hill

Manufactured in the United States of America
Printed by Seeman Printery, Durham, N. C.
Library of Congress Catalog Card Number 71-80920

To Carolyn, Ashley, and Whitney

Contents

PART I

NORTH CAROLINA STATE FINANCE

I. *The North Carolina Economy*

The period immediately following the end of the Revolution was one of recovery and adjustment for the North Carolina economy: recovery from the destructiveness and disruption that the war had imposed upon agriculture, manufacturing, and commerce; and adjustment to the new conditions of trade brought about by the state's political and economic independence. North Carolina's agricultural production revived rapidly, and during the postwar years the state's exports reached unprecedented proportions.[1] The amount of corn exported in 1788, for example, totaled nearly 160,000 bushels, compared to 127,000 bushels in 1768; 16,000 bushels of peas left the state's ports in 1788, compared to less than 3,000 bushels in 1768. Wheat exports declined after the war, but

1. Charles Christopher Crittenden, *The Commerce of North Carolina, 1763-1789* ("Yale Historical Publications," No. 29 [New Haven: Yale University Press, 1936]), pp. 157-58. The statistics and general conclusions regarding exports, imports, and tonnage which are cited above, pp. 3-4 are found *ibid.*, pp. 160-61. Detailed statistics on North Carolina exports are in the British Public Records (photostats), Southern Historical Collection, The University of North Carolina at Chapel Hill. Detailed information regarding exports, imports, clearances, and entrances for the postwar period is in the Treasurers' and Comptrollers' Papers, Ports, State Department of Archives and History, Raleigh. For contemporary comments upon North Carolina exports see William Attmore, *Journal of a Tour to North Carolina*, ed. by Lida Tunstall Rodman ("The James Sprunt Historical Publications," Vol. 17, No. 2 [Chapel Hill: North Carolina Historical Society, 1922]), p. 29 and *passim*; and Robert Hunter, Jr., *Quebec to Carolina in 1785-1786*, ed. by Louis B. Wright and Marion Tinling (San Marino: Huntington Library, 1943), p. 266 and *passim*. For treatment of exports and general economic conditions during the late colonial period see Harry Roy Merrens, *Colonial North Carolina in the Eighteenth Century: A Study in Historical Geography* (Chapel Hill: The University of North Carolina Press, 1964) and Lawrence Lee, *The Lower Cape Fear in Colonial Days* (Chapel Hill: The University of North Carolina Press, 1965).

3,000 barrels of flour were shipped in 1788. Although less pork was exported, fish became a more important item. Rice and potatoes, insignificant exports before 1775, attained some significance after the Revolution. Naval stores, while suffering something of a decline because of the loss of British bounties, remained major articles of export, especially to the northern states. The shipment of lumber products became more important than during the colonial period. The number of shingles, for example, jumped from 6,000,000 in 1768 to nearly 20,000,000 in 1788; staves and headings from 2,750,000 to 4,250,000; boards and scantling from 3,250,000 board feet to nearly 6,000,000 board feet. Although these increases of lumber exports were quite marked, the greatest increase of any export was that of tobacco. In 1768 a total of only 360,000 pounds had left the state's ports, while in 1788, with European markets directly available, exports of tobacco reached almost 6,000,000 pounds, about half of it going to Great Britain.

The increased exports, accompanied by the postwar influx of foreign and American products, stimulated activity in the state's commercial centers. The total vessel tonnage putting into North Carolina's ports approximately doubled that of the late colonial period. As before the war, about 40 per cent of the tonnage consisted of coasting vessels. British tonnage dropped from about 30 per cent to about 10 per cent of the total North Carolina trade. Trade with the West Indies increased, with most of that commerce going to and coming from the non-British West Indies. The types of imports from the West Indies, and from Europe and the northern states, remained basically the same as before the Revolution. In summary, although the postwar period did witness a great increase in tobacco exports, a greater trade with the non-British West Indies, and fewer exports to Great Britain, the coming of independence did not radically alter the products or channels of North Carolina commercial life. Thus the commerce of the period was essentially a continuation of colonial development.[2]

2. Crittenden, *Commerce*, p. 162.

The generally high production of North Carolina agriculture, the increase in many of the state's exports, and the general bustle of the state's ports must not be accepted, however, as proof that the postwar years were ones of great profits. Although the period has been described as one of prosperity,[3] an examination of contemporary evidence establishes that, behind the encouraging but misleading statistics, North Carolina's economy suffered from a number of problems that made the state's agricultural, manufacturing, and commercial life far less prosperous than appearances indicate.

The most fundamental handicap besetting the economy of eighteenth-century North Carolina was the injurious but inescapable overcommitment to agriculture. This overcommitment forced the people to import almost all the manufactured products that they desired or needed, and, during the postwar years, caused the foreign and domestic markets for North Carolina produce to become glutted and therefore frequently unprofitable. The very export statistics that have been cited as proof of prosperity are, in fact, figures that reveal the problems of overproduction and diminishing economic returns. Eager to acquire the imports that the war had long denied them, the farmers and planters of North Carolina and of the other American states sought to maximize their own production; after purchasing items from merchants who were all too ready to give extensive credit, a grower was all the more interested in obtaining the greatest possible yield. The disastrous consequences of overproduction can be illustrated by the plunging price of the state's chief export, tobacco. At Petersburg, Virginia, North Carolina tobacco was bringing 34*s.* to 34*s.* 6*d.* Virginia currency per hundredweight in early 1785; by the end of that year it could command only 22*s.* to 23*s.*; during 1786 it never rose above 24*s.*; all during 1787 and

3. Crittenden's study uses the word "prosperity" in the title of the chapter covering the period 1783-89. For the same view that the postwar years were prosperous ones for the southern states in general, see Forrest McDonald, *E Pluribus Unum* (Boston: Houghton Mifflin Company, 1965), pp. 84, 104. McDonald describes North Carolina's economy as "bustling and booming" throughout the 1780's.

1788 it hovered around 22*s.* 6*d.* to 23*s.*; in 1789 it hit a low of 18*s.* At other markets the decline of tobacco prices was as sharp and prolonged as that at Petersburg.[4] The persistently low prices for tobacco harmed not only the growers but also domestic merchants who had bought and sold on credit and who usually paid their own debts with tobacco and other produce. Thus the sharp increase in tobacco exports, far from being an indication of prosperity, was in fact a phenomenon that in many cases gave small comfort and smaller financial returns to growers and merchants alike.

Although prices for other agricultural products did not drop as precipitously as did the price of tobacco, agricultural prices were generally low,[5] not only because the markets were amply supplied, but also because these products, when compared to manufactured imports, simply did not have a high value proportionate to weight and bulk. The difficulties of transportation, moreover, made the handling of North Carolina agricultural produce a cumbersome and

4. The price of tobacco at Petersburg, Virginia, may be traced almost weekly in the correspondence of David Buchanan, merchant of Petersburg, to Richard Bennehan, merchant of Orange County, North Carolina, in the Cameron Family Papers, Southern Historical Collection. Additional evidence of low tobacco prices is legion. See, for example, letters from other correspondents to Richard Bennehan, *ibid.* Also from the Southern Historical Collection: Judge Pollock to Edward Jones, July 28, 1785, John De Berniere Hooper Papers; James Bourget to Mr. and Mrs. Strudwick, January 4, 1786, Strudwick Papers. See also the following correspondence in Alice Barnwell Keith and William Henry Masterson, eds., *The John Gray Blount Papers* (3 vols.; Raleigh: State Department of Archives and History, 1952-65), I: Thomas Blount to John Gray Blount, August 30, 1783, p. 95; September 2, 1783, pp. 99-100; Hugh Williamson to John Gray Blount, September 26, 1783, p. 113; Thomas Blount to John Gray Blount and Thomas Blount, November 7, 1785, p. 229; Jean Jacques Berard to John Gray Blount and Thomas Blount, July 26, 1788, p. 414; William McDaniel to John Gray Blount, August 17, 1788, p. 418.

5. For the prices of agricultural produce other than tobacco, together with complaints about the glutted markets and low prices, see the following selected sources from the Southern Historical Collection: Samuel Johnston to ———, October 4, 1788, Hayes Collection (microfilm), reel number four; Justin Foote to Ebenezer Foote, October 26, 1789, Edenton Papers; ——— to "Ned," April 24, 1784, Abraham Rencher Papers; Anthony Diggs to Samuel Simpson, April 19, 1789, Simpson-Bryan Papers.

costly process that further reduced the margin for profit.

The generally low prices offered for the tobacco and other crops of North Carolina could partially be attributed to the poor quality of much of the produce.[6] Although the state did have inspection laws, the inspections were often less careful than those of other states. The exportation of poor-quality produce tarnished the state's commercial reputation and generally contributed to North Carolina's economic difficulties.

Despite the general overproduction during the years 1783-89, the harvests in North Carolina were not consistently bountiful. Conditions of weather or blight created local and occasionally state-wide scarcities of corn, tobacco, and other produce.[7] While such crop failures might to some degree relieve the glutted world markets, the failures could prove disastrous to indebted farmers, planters, and merchants whose only mode of remittance consisted of agricultural products.

The difficulties and disadvantages associated with the economy of eighteenth-century North Carolina did not preclude, of course, the possibility of making a comfortable livelihood. If a farmer or planter were willing to resist the

6. See the many letters from David Buchanan to Richard Bennehan, Cameron Family Papers, Southern Historical Collection. See also, Charles Johnson's resignation as a delegate in Congress, Walter Clark, ed., *The State Records of North Carolina* (16 vols.; Winston, Goldsboro, and Raleigh: State of North Carolina, 1895-1906) [volumes numbered consecutive to William L. Saunders, ed., *The Colonial Records of North Carolina* (10 vols.; Raleigh: State of North Carolina, 1886-90)], XVIII, 774. Also, memorial of the town of Wilmington to the General Assembly, 1784, Legislative Papers, LI, May 11 folder, State Department of Archives and History, Raleigh.

7. Petition from the inhabitants of Tar River to Governor Richard Caswell, January, 1786, Governors' Papers, Series II, Box III (Caswell), State Department of Archives and History, Raleigh. Petition of the commissioners of the town of Wilmington to Governor Richard Caswell, Governors' Papers, XIV, 133. See also, the *Fayetteville Gazette*, October 12, 1789 (microfilm), North Carolina Collection, The University of North Carolina at Chapel Hill. See the following at Duke University: Samuel Crafton to ———, September 15, 1789, Samuel S. Downey Papers; William Hooper to James Iredell, March 15, 1784, James Iredell Papers; petition from the town of Edenton to Governor Richard Caswell, January, 1786, Richard Caswell Papers.

temptations of overgenerous credit and if he were content to lead a simple agrarian life without most of the luxuries of more industrialized and urbanized societies, he might lead a reasonably comfortable life free from the terrors of indebtedness and the shadows of bankruptcy.[8] Such a person, however, would have relatively little purchasing power and could do little to stimulate the domestic economy.

The state's manufactured exports, consisting largely of forest products, also traveled to markets that generally were oversupplied. In foreign ports vessels carrying lumber, staves, scantling, and shingles could usually be found in abundance, a fact that increased the frustration and reduced the proceeds of North Carolinians who had all too few export possibilities.[9] The unfortunate results of overproduction were reflected also by the low prices commanded by naval stores. Before initial postwar demands were satisfied at Philadelphia, for example, a barrel of tar sold for as much as thirty shillings; the price declined sharply, however, and in mid-1787 hovered at nine to eleven shillings per barrel.[10] At Portsmouth, Virginia, a barrel of tar brought twenty-four shillings in August, 1783; in 1787 the price stood at seven to eight

8. The best contemporary expression that this writer has found of such a life is that written by P. G. Roulhac to his mother, March 1, 1786 (copy), Ruffin-Roulhac-Hamilton Papers, Southern Historical Collection.

9. Keith and Masterson, eds., *Blount*, I: Thomas Blount to John Gray Blount, September 11, 1783, p. 105; Thomas Williams to John Gray Blount, August 12, 1784, p. 173; Tyler & Mumford to John Gray and Thomas Blount, November 20, 1784, p. 183; Thomas Williams to John Gray Blount, December 8, 1784, p. 186; John Cowper to John Gray Blount, March 23, 1787, p. 273; William McDaniel to John Gray Blount, August 17, 1788, p. 418; T. Brice to John Gray Blount, September 5, 1788, p. 423; Abner Neale to John Gray Blount, January 1, 1789, p. 450; William Blount to John Gray Blount, March 25, 1789, p. 469; James Barr to John Gray & Thomas Blount, July 11, 1789, p. 492. As with all exports, particular market conditions at a given time occasionally enabled a load of forest products to bring a good price, but the general trend was toward oversupply and low prices.

10. *Ibid.*: James Barr to John Gray Blount & Company, August 7, 1783, p. 81; Flahavan & Willcox to John Gray Blount and Thomas Blount, May 2, 1787, p. 296; James Barr for Stuart & Barr to John Gray Blount, August 11, 1787, p. 334.

shillings.[11] A barrel of pitch commanded thirty to thirty-two shillings at Philadelphia in the fall of 1783, declining to twenty-five shillings by year's end. At the same port during 1787 pitch sold for twelve to thirteen shillings per barrel, and it was reported in December, 1788, that the current Philadelphia price of fourteen shillings per barrel was the highest in two years.[12] Turpentine sold for as much as forty shillings per barrel at Philadelphia in the autumn of 1783; three years later the price stood at slightly over twelve shillings, with little improvement thereafter.[13] At Portsmouth, Virginia, turpentine brought thirty-two shillings per barrel in August, 1783; in March, 1787, the price per barrel was between eight and nine shillings.[14] The depressed prices for naval stores transcended all seasonal considerations and clearly reveal the glutted markets that are also abundantly attested to by contemporary correspondence. Writing from London, for example, a North Carolina merchant lamented that Great Britain had enough naval stores in its ports to last three years and that those items would not presently sell at any price.[15] So saturated were the domestic markets that the arrival of additional naval stores could drop the price sharply. At New York such arrivals lowered the price of pitch from twenty shillings per barrel to fourteen shillings within a matter

11. *Ibid.*: Thomas Blount to John Gray Blount and Thomas Blount, August 20, 1783, p. 86; John Cowper to John Gray Blount, January 30, 1787, p. 243; March 15, 1787, p. 265; March 23, 1787, p. 273; April 7, 1787, p. 278; May 2, 1787, p. 297; July 15, 1787, p. 321.

12. *Ibid.*: Thomas Blount to John Gray Blount, September 9, 1783, p. 102; September 23, 1783, p. 109; James Barr to William Blount, December 16, 1783, p. 141; Flahavan & Willcox to John Gray & Thomas Blount, May 2, 1787, p. 296; James Barr for Stuart & Barr to John Gray Blount, August 11, 1787, p. 334; Stuart & Barr to John Gray and Thomas Blount, December 12, 1788, p. 444.

13. *Ibid.*: James Barr to John Gray Blount & Company, August 7, 1783, p. 81; James Barr for Stuart & Barr to John Gray Blount, August 11, 1787, p. 334.

14. *Ibid.*: Thomas Blount to John Gray Blount, August 20, 1783, p. 86; John Cowper to John Gray Blount, March 15, 1787, p. 265; March 23, 1787, p. 273.

15. *Ibid.*; Thomas Blount to John Gray Blount and Thomas Blount, November 7, 1785, p. 229.

of three weeks; ten days thereafter the current price was twelve shillings.[16] The entrance of three vessels loaded with naval stores could drastically reduce prices at Philadelphia.[17] Altogether, the surplus production, the cost of handling and transporting the bulky products, the relatively low value of each unit, and the poor quality of some of the goods combined to limit or eliminate the profits to be made from forest manufacturing. The opportunity for significant profits did not exist.

Other than a modest shipbuilding industry and the manufacture of some molasses along the coast, little secondary manufacturing was conducted within the state. The sparseness of the population together with the vastness of the land, the difficulties of transportation, the shortage of skilled labor, the lack of investment capital, and the shortage or lack of many natural resources—in short, the conditions of eighteenth-century North Carolina—precluded the establishment of a manufacturing base that could produce the luxuries and necessities demanded by the people of the state. In an age that was becoming increasingly conscious of the benefits of industry, North Carolina was simply not in the position to develop that industry. The result was that North Carolinians imported products of more total value than the sum value of the state's exports. The extensive use of credit furthered the unfavorable balance of trade and quickened the drain of specie from the state. Given the people's determination to have the products of industry, the only solution to the state's financial problems lay in the significant development of industry within North Carolina.[18] Such development could lie

16. *Ibid.*: Abishai C. Thomas to John Gray Blount, November 15, 1789, p. 515; December 9, 1789, p. 519; December 19, 1789, p. 523.

17. *Ibid.*: Thomas Blount to John Gray Blount, September 11, 1783, p. 103; September 23, 1783, p. 109.

18. Contemporaries realized this fact, of course, but achieving significant industrialization was another matter. See Hugh Williamson, *Letters from Sylvius* ("Historical Papers of the Trinity College Historical Society," Series 11 [Durham: Trinity College Historical Society, 1915]), p. 7 and *passim*.

only in the distant future, when conditions should have greatly changed from what they were in the eighteenth century.

As previously indicated, the small commercial class, attached to and dependent upon the great agricultural base of the economy, suffered in full measure from all the difficulties afflicting the agrarians. The lack of intrinsically high-value domestic products to exchange for imports, the difficulties of transportation, the shortage of specie resulting from the unfavorable balance of trade, the absence of significant domestic manufacturing—these factors placed serious limitations upon domestic commerce and the opportunities for profit therefrom. A natural restriction upon direct trade with Great Britain and Europe was the shallow and irregular coastal waters of North Carolina. Since the state's merchants were forced to import most foreign goods by land or by coasting vessels from other states, the margin of profit for North Carolina's mercantile element was reduced all the more, and the drain of specie was accelerated.

Although most of the obstacles to commerce were beyond the merchants' control, the mercantile elements brought some of their difficulties upon themselves. Freed from British commercial regulations and anxious to explore the opportunities that peace provided, North Carolina merchants, in common with those of other states, over-extended themselves. The temptations of easy credit and the hopes for quick profit proved all too alluring, and many merchants purchased more manufactures on credit than they had reasonable hopes for selling at a profit. As their creditors began to press them, the merchants desperately sought to meet their obligations by remitting ever more produce (which further glutted the market and depressed prices) and, as we have seen, by offering their customers easier credit terms. Thus the spiral of indebtedness and credit continued, ending frequently in bankruptcy.[19] When alarmed foreign creditors began to cut back

19. See, for example, Robert Williams to Joseph Leech, ——— 15, 1788, David Miller Carter Papers, Southern Historical Collection; bill of sale

on credit terms,[20] the difficulties of the indebted American merchants increased. Had the mercantile class of North Carolina been more realistic about the opportunities for profit, many of the bankruptcies of the postwar years could have been avoided.

A fundamental limitation facing North Carolina entrepreneurs was the lack of any domestic business opportunity that offered the possibility of a substantial and reasonably prompt profit. The absence of any such opportunity forced merchants either to export their investment capital[21] or to invest their money in the one great resource that the state had to offer—land.[22] While some speculators did profit from westward migration during the period, the limited population prevented the value of much land from appreciating significantly or at all and thus often made the investment a sterile one. Nevertheless, since the modest profits of commercial enterprise made diversification of investment almost a necessity, many merchants tied up part of their resources in the frequently unprofitable purchase of land.

Faced with these inherent and inescapable disadvantages and saddled with their own over-optimism and resulting over-indebtedness, many North Carolina merchants found the business road a rough and often disastrous one during the

---

dated May 13, 1787, Mary Farrow Credle Papers, Southern Historical Collection.

20. Keith and Masterson, eds., *Blount*, I: Thomas Blount to John Gray Blount and Thomas Blount, August 25, 1785, pp. 210, 211; September 5, 1785, pp. 213-15; October 18, 1785, pp. 224, 226.

21. See the following in the Hayes Collection (microfilm), reel number four, Southern Historical Collection: agreement between Samuel Johnston and two New York merchants, dated July 30, 1787; William Lowther to Samuel Johnston, July 13, 1787; Samuel Johnston to Alexander Elmsly, June 20, 1784.

22. This writer has examined all the deeds and bills of sales in all the private collections of the period which are found at Duke University and the Southern Historical Collection. The overwhelming majority of these indentures involve the sale and purchase of land. For a clear statement of the unprofitability of some land investments, see Richard Caswell to Winston Caswell, May 3, 1784, Richard Caswell Papers, Southern Historical Collection.

late 1780's.[23] To be sure, some of them made a profit by careful management of diversified activities,[24] but, as contemporaries realized,[25] under existing conditions an economically independent North Carolina was unable to yield significant commercial profits or support a sizable mercantile class.

In summary, many limitations restricted the development of a vigorous and profitable economy in eighteenth-century North Carolina. The natural barriers to direct oceanic trade, the lack of highly valuable resources, the sparseness of the population, the very limited manufacturing, the unfavorable balance of trade with the resulting shortage of specie, the scarcity of domestic investment opportunities—these factors were inescapable disadvantages during the 1780's. The overextension of credit and the saturation of world markets with North Carolina produce further contributed to conditions that created a period far more economically difficult than export statistics would indicate at first glance. With the states loosely united under the Articles of Confederation, North Carolina possessed economic independence, but the state was in no position to reap great economic advantages from that independence. Within the framework of an underdeveloped

23. The accountant examining the books of John Huske & Co. for the years 1783-87 stated that the firm had suffered a "considerable loss." See the John Huske and James Hogg Business Ledger, Duke University. William Borritz, a merchant of Wilmington, lost thousands of pounds. See Account of Bell, Smith & Co. and William Borritz with James Paterson, Cupola House Papers (microfilm), reel number one, Southern Historical Collection.

24. John Dickey, merchant of Rowan County, made a modest profit of somewhat less than one hundred pounds during the six months period July-December, 1786. John Dickey Ledger, Duke University. Richard Bennehan of Orange County made a "net gain" of £2,550 on a total investment of about £9,650 during the year June 1, 1785, to June 1, 1786. Cameron Family Papers, XI, Southern Historical Collection. Bennehan was one of the more successful inland merchants. A readable secondary study of mercantile success through diversification is William Henry Masterson, *William Blount* (Baton Rouge: Louisiana State University Press, 1954).

25. John B. Lohier to Herman Brimmer, April 4, 1786, Herman Brimmer Papers, Duke University. P. G. Roulhac to his mother, March 1, 1786 (copy), Ruffin-Roulhac-Hamilton Papers, Southern Historical Collection.

economy, the government of North Carolina sought to carry on the functions of government, liquidate its domestic and foreign debts, remedy the shortage of money, and discharge its financial obligations to the United States. Existing conditions during the period 1783-89 made each of these objectives a sizable challenge.

II. The Domestic Debt

The unfavorable balance of trade during the postwar years was a phenomenon that had afflicted North Carolina throughout its history. The enduring scarcity of specie had been serious before the Revolution, but the shortage had become critical as the state had struggled to finance the war effort. Without specie resources or substantial military assistance from the United States government, North Carolina had been compelled to resort to deficit financing and thus had incurred a large domestic debt consisting of two basic components: paper currency issued as legal tender upon the faith and credit of the state; and certificates of various types that the state pledged itself to redeem with money. During the postwar period the redemption of the debt was, predictably, a matter of important public and private concern.

The wartime resort to paper currency had been a natural and familiar course of action, for upon numerous occasions during the colonial period the scarcity of money had prompted the North Carolina government to emit fiat currency.[1] The war currencies, declared legal tender in the payment of all public and private debts but devoid of any support except the faith and credit of the state, had boldly proclaimed that the government would redeem the paper with specie. The specie redemption pledge had been no more than legal fiction designed to bolster the currency's market value, for, as everyone had fully realized, the government had no foreseeable prospect of redeeming the currency with gold or silver. Although North Carolinians had no alternative but to reconcile

1. The most detailed coverage of North Carolina colonial emissions is that found in Charles Jesse Bullock, *Essays on the Monetary History of the United States* (New York: Macmillan Company, 1900).

themselves to the impossibility of specie redemption, the public expected the currency to be retired by other means.

Basically there were two views as to what would constitute acceptable redemption alternatives. One argued that since specie was regretably not available, some other form of valuable, tangible property would have to be employed. Maintaining that the state possessed insufficient resources to redeem the currency in that manner, other persons were prepared to accept or promote reduction of the currency debt by means of devaluation, retirement of old emissions by new emissions, and withdrawal of currency through taxation. During the Revolution the latter two fiat redemption policies had been attempted in an effort to improve the currency's reputation,[2] but the financial necessities of war had rendered the measures ineffective and had only led to additional currency emissions. As redemption expectations had faded and as new emissions had appeared, public confidence in the paper—and hence its market value—had sharply declined. Market depreciation, in turn, had made further emissions all the more frequent and sizable. Caught in this cycle of emission and depreciation, the North Carolina legislature had directly emitted a total of $6,850,000 between 1775 and the end of 1780.[3] By the latter year the currency had depreciated so

2. The 1777 Assembly had levied a sinking tax, but the tax had been small and the small amounts that it raised had probably been recirculated because of the great need for money. In 1778 the Assembly had provided that the currency issued that year should be used to retire currency already in circulation, but such redemption had been repeatedly postponed because of the same need for money. Walter Clark, ed., *The State Records of North Carolina* (16 vols.; Winston, Goldsboro, and Raleigh: State of North Carolina, 1895-1906) [volumes numbered consecutive to William L. Saunders, ed., *The Colonial Records of North Carolina* (10 vols.; Raleigh: State of North Carolina, 1886-90)], XXIV, 134-35, 184-87, 217-18, 331, 382.

3. Saunders, ed., *Colonial Records*, X, 194, 533; Clark, ed., *State Records*, XXIV, 184-87, 255-57, 320-22. An incorrect listing of wartime emissions is found in Hugh Talmage Lefler, *History of North Carolina* (2 vols.; New York: Lewis Historical Publishing Company, 1956), I, 236. Lefler states that the emission of 1776 was $500,000, whereas it was actually $250,000; Lefler mistakes bounty certificates issued in 1781 for a currency emission. The amounts issued directly by the legislature were as follows: 1775—$125,000; 1776—$250,000;

greatly that, in order to meet the increased British threat to the southern states, the Assembly had granted the governor and council the broad authority to issue whatever amounts of legal tender currency "the exigencies of the State may require."[4] Acting under this authority, the governor and council had issued "large sums" amounting approximately to $13,000,000, thus bringing the total nominal value of wartime emissions to the vicinity of $20,000,000.[5] The currency had proved useful in helping to finance the war effort,[6] but the state had acquired a currency debt of unprecedented and enormous proportions. To the extent that the state might fail to retire the currency at nominal value—some would say with tangible property—the currency debt would be repudiated.

1778—$2,125,000; 1779—$1,250,000; 1780—$3,100,000. The emission acts of 1778, 1779, and 1780 stated in pounds the amount to be issued, but the bills were expressed in dollar denominations. The author has converted pound value to dollar value for the sake of clarity and consistency.

4. Clark, ed., *State Records*, XXIV, 321.

5. U.S. Congress, House. Representative Burges, debating the amounts due by North Carolina to the United States for the settlement of war expenses, maintained that North Carolina had emitted $20,000,000 currency during the Revolution. 4th Cong., 2nd sess., January 4, 1797, *Annals of Congress* (42 vols.; Washington: Gales and Seaton, 1834-56), VI, 1800. In the settlement of accounts between North Carolina and the United States, the state's agents knew that "large sums" had been issued by the governor and council and requested that the state's records be searched for information to help them determine the amount. Letter, no date and unsigned, Treasurers' and Comptrollers' Papers, Military Papers, LXVII, State Department of Archives and History, Raleigh. Burges' figure of $20,000,000 was probably based on the results that the author has been unable to locate except as reflected in Burges' statement.

6. The war forced the states and Congress to emit copious amounts of fiat currency, and North Carolina Federalists later were prepared to admit that the war currencies had been useful in financing the war. Jonathan Elliot, ed., *The Debates, Resolutions and Proceedings, in Convention, on the adoption of the Federal Constitution* (3 vols.; Washington: Jonathan Elliot, 1827-30), III, 89. Historians have tended to emphasize the disadvantages of paper emissions and to minimize or ignore the paper's contribution to financing the war. For important interpretations and re-evaluations of fiat currency policy, see E. James Ferguson, *The Power of the Purse: A History of American Public Finance, 1776-1790* (Chapel Hill: The University of North Carolina Press, 1961). Ferguson's views are summarized above, pp. 25-26.

The most comprehensive method of repudiation lay in devaluation of the currency from its legal tender status to some fraction of its original legal value, but this policy was opposed by persons who considered the government's honor and reputation to be at stake in maintaining and redeeming the currency at its legal tender value. Other individuals argued that the debt's size and the currency's market depreciation made devaluation of the currency the only logical policy to pursue.

Market depreciation had indeed confronted the state with cruel dilemmas. With varying degrees of dismay the citizenry had watched the currency depreciate in their hands, and creditors had resented that the law required its acceptance at nominal value. The money's legal tender status had contributed greatly to inflation, not only harming private interests but also reducing the purchasing power of government revenues. Thus both private and public considerations had militated in favor of abandoning the currency as legal tender. Another set of factors had given the Assembly pause, for to legislate devaluation of the currency would be to repudiate much of the currency debt, to reduce the amount of money in circulation, and perhaps to accelerate the depreciation of existing and future fiat currency. In the opinion of many persons, the dilemma's most equitable solution lay in the enactment of a scale of depreciation which would progressively lower the currency's legal value by chronological increments. During the Revolution several states had adopted such scales, and in 1781 Congress had urged all states to do so, but North Carolina had resisted such broad currency repudiation.[7] As depreciation had become increasingly severe, however, the Assembly had grudgingly begun to devalue the currency in an unsystematic and piecemeal fashion.

The first legal distinction between specie and North Caro-

7. In 1781 Congress had called upon the states to make allowance for depreciated currency paid to the respective Continental Lines. In 1782 the North Carolina General Assembly had endorsed the principle, but, as we shall see, the scale was not established until 1783. Clark, ed., *State Records*, XXIV, 419-20, 485-88.

lina currency had been made in the fall of 1779, when the Assembly had enacted that all debts incumbent upon confiscated property were to be discharged in specie or in currency at the rate of £175 "current money of North Carolina" to £100 sterling.[8] In a major concession to market depreciation, the Assembly had provided in 1780 that specie certificates issued by county commissioners could be redeemed not only with specie but also with the market value equivalent in state (or continental) currency.[9] This redemption policy had been confirmed in 1781, during which year the legal status of currency had been altered for several specific purposes. Claims against the state for purchased or impressed goods were thereafter to be determined in specie or in the exchange value (that is, the nominal amount of currency needed to purchase a given amount of specie) of the currency at the time the state obtained the goods. The same principle was to apply to the collection of imposts. Public salaries were to be paid in specie or in the "true value of such specie in the currency of the State." Although none of these measures had specified the procedure by which the market value was to be determined, the Assembly had revealed its general intent by requiring that the courts decide the currency equivalent of certain specie fines, a solution consistent with colonial practice.[10] Thus during 1781 rather extensive currency repudiation had begun, and in that same year the Assembly, emboldened by the heady experience, had made precise devaluations by requiring that certain public monies and fees be collected at the rate of two hundred dollars currency to one dollar specie.[11] By the end of 1781, then, North Carolina had yielded significantly, if selectively, to the facts of market

8. *Ibid.*, p. 264.

9. *Ibid.*, pp. 345-46.

10. *Ibid.*, pp. 375, 380, 389, 409-10. Reflecting the depreciation of the currency, the governor's salary had been set at £2,200 in 1778, £6,000 in 1779, and £13,000 in 1780. In 1781 the Assembly had abandoned currency designations for the salary and had established it at £750 specie.

11. *Ibid.*, pp. 398-400, 408.

depreciation and the government's inability to retire the currency at par.

During 1782 the Assembly had extended its patchwork policy of currency repudiation. Fees and public monies formerly to be collected at two hundred to one were to be collected instead at the rate of eight hundred dollars currency to one dollar specie. Salaries paid to public officials and confiscated property sold by the state were also to be valued at the rate of eight hundred to one.[12]

It is manifest that by the end of 1782 North Carolina currency had acquired a confusingly mixed status. For all private and some public purposes (including taxation) it was still legal tender; for other public purposes it had a legal value of eight hundred to one. The mixed legal status of the currency, the severity of its market depreciation, and the universal violation of the Tender Acts—including by juries in the awarding of debt judgments—all gave rise to the demand for a more comprehensive, consistent, and equitable adjustment to market depreciation, that is, for a scale of depreciation. Whatever the arguments or necessities for the enactment of such a scale, the proposal was a painful one to many persons because it involved an acknowledgment that the state could not redeem the debt in any manner except after greatly reducing the currency's legal value.

The General Assembly that convened at Hillsborough on April 18, 1783, was prepared to make that painful acknowledgment. Two legislative elements opposed, for very different reasons, the devaluation of the currency: legislators representing debtor preference for legal tender fiat money; and staunch fiscal conservatives who, despite their dislike for fiat currency, were unprepared to support the abrogation of a public contract. A comfortable majority in each house, however, saw no alternative to repudiation and thus supported a scale of depreciation bill that was introduced, significantly enough, by the assemblyman from the commercial center of Edenton. Acknowledging that the rapid depreciation had led

12. *Ibid.*, pp. 426, 444, 445-46.

to difficulty in the adjustment and settlement of debts within and outside the state courts, the act established for the currency a descending scale of value from March, 1777, to December, 1782, ending with a value of eight hundred for one. The act prescribed that since plaintiffs (creditors) would receive far less than the true value of the debts if the debts were paid in currency at nominal value, juries should evaluate in specie all pending debt judgments, which judgments should be converted into currency according to the scale. The act provided also that debtors who had offered the currency as legal tender after March 21, 1777, should file an affidavit that the sum so offered had been equal at the time of tender to the debt or damage demanded, according to the market depreciation at that time. If such an affidavit were not provided, the plaintiff, that is the creditor suing for recovery, should proceed with his suit as usual under the laws. No creditor who before March 21, 1777, had refused to receive payment in currency should be entitled to have the depreciation made good to him. The depreciation act suspended the statute of limitations on debt suits from July 4, 1776, to June 1, 1784, so that creditors who had been prevented by the war or deterred by depreciation from suing for recovery should have an opportunity to sue under the new scale. The act specified also that nothing in the act should be interpreted as enabling persons under the confiscation acts to sue for the recovery of debts.[13] By enacting the scale of depreciation, the General Assembly recognized the currency's severe market depreciation and sought to do all possible justice to creditors by stabilizing and standardizing the rate and degree of that depreciation. The legal establishment of eight hundred for one in all future transactions did nothing, however, to enhance the reputation of the state, for the government had originally promised to redeem the currency at its nominal value with specie.

Upon the bill's third approval in the House, Archibald Maclaine, one of the irreconcilable conservatives, entered a

13. *Ibid.*, pp. 485-88.

formal protest upon the following grounds: that the law conflicted with the fourth article of the treaty of peace with Great Britain, which article provided that creditors on either side should meet with no lawful impediment to the recovery of the full value in sterling money of all bona fide debts; that the law, a "breach of national faith," would bring North Carolina into contention with the other states of the United States as well as with Great Britain and would disgust European nations that had become the guarantees of the treaty; that this "manifest injustice" deprived honest men of their property by establishing the future value at eight hundred for one; that the law was retroactive and thus violated the state constitution by having a clause that declared null and void all legal actions undertaken prior to the war by men who later came under the confiscation acts; that the law was unconstitutional also because it deprived men of property by "new and unheard of ways"; and that the law destroyed commercial confidence and damaged foreign trade by undermining the reputation of the currency and of the state government.[14] Maclaine's protest ran counter to the majority sentiment that notorious depreciation should best be recognized and systematized since it could not be remedied.[15]

14. *Ibid.*, XIX, 350-51.

15. The scale of depreciation was successfully employed for public purposes, but it failed to bring order to the realm of private transactions. The vague wording of the act enabled creditors to maintain that currency payments already made should be revised to meet the new scale and that contracted but unpaid debts from the colonial period should be paid according to the scale. To the relief of debtors, the state courts held that the scale did not apply to payments made prior to the enactment of the scale, that the scale applied only to obligations assumed and unadjusted after depreciation had begun in 1777, and that, in settling wartime debts, payments should be made according to a rate of depreciation for the year in which the debt was contracted. Debtors wished to interpret the act so as to pay off specie debts with the currency at the rates prescribed by the scale. The courts maintained, however, that the scale of depreciation applied only to the year it was passed, 1783, not to any previous years and not to future years. In the absence of legislative prohibition, ruled the courts, juries could settle all cases of depreciation between currency and specie after 1783. A favorite method of adjusting depreciation came to be the

While carrying the onus of debt repudiation, the devaluation of the currency greatly facilitated, of course, the government's efforts to retire the paper money. Specie redemption, even at the currency's drastically reduced value, remained patently impossible, but the state came to employ other redemption methods familiar to the eighteenth century. An effective mode lay in accepting the old currency in partial payment of the annual property tax, a policy that gave holders at least some benefit and that was the absolute minimum opponents of fiat financing were prepared to accept. The revenue acts of 1783 through 1785 contained such provision.[16] A far different type of tax—a fiat measure bitterly resented in some quarters—was the sinking tax, that is, a special property tax levied specifically and exclusively to retire the state's domestic debt. Because of opposition to a tax that gave the holder nothing in exchange for his payment, the 1783 Assembly rejected a sinking tax bill that would have retired old currency at the rate of eight hundred to one; but the burden of the debt led the Assembly beginning in 1786 to enact heavy annual sinking taxes payable in old currency at its legal rate (or in components of the certificate debt).[17]

Another method of retiring old currency lay in exchanging it (at the rate of eight hundred to one) for newly emitted legal tender currency, a fiat redemption method that fiscal conservatives likened to a regenerating, many-headed monster that defied extermination.[18] Of £200,000 legal tender

---

practice of allowing damages for withheld interest equal to the difference between the depreciation fixed by the scale and the actual market depreciation. William Kenneth Boyd, *The Federal Period, 1783-1860* (New York: Lewis Publishing Company, 1919), pp. 7-8.

16. Clark, ed., *State Records*, XXIV, 477, 648-49, 658, 731. The tax enacted in 1783 gave the taxpayer the option of paying up to two-thirds of the property tax in old currency. The acts of 1784 and 1785 provided that one-half could be paid in such manner.

17. *Ibid.*, XIX, 324, 362; XXIV, 802, 885, 952; XXV, 7-8; Richard Caswell to William Caswell, May 4, 1783, *ibid.*, XVI, 959. Although the Assembly did not specify that old currency would be received in payment of excise taxes, imposts, and other taxes, it appears that the old currency was accepted in payment of such taxes. Old currency received in such manner may or may not have been recirculated.

18. Hugh Williamson, *Letters from Sylvius* ("Historical Papers of Trin-

fiat currency emitted by the Assembly during the postwar period, less than £28,000 ($70,000) was designated to retire old emissions[19]—comparative restraint that gave no comfort to opponents of fiat policy. Despite their distaste for fiat redemption methods, however, most hard-money men were unprepared to actually employ the state's chief tangible assets, confiscated property and western land, to retire the state currency because, as we shall see, the use of these resources to redeem the certificate debt was a more alluring policy. Thus the wartime currency, despite occasional laments, was delivered into the hands of fiat redemptioners almost without a struggle.[20]

The repudiation of 1783 together with the postwar property taxes—especially the sinking taxes inaugurated in 1786—took giant strides toward exterminating the currency debt. Between 1783 and 1789 somewhat over $15,000,000 nominal value of old currency was retired.[21] When one allows for the large amount of circulating currency that had been lost, defaced, or destroyed through the years, it becomes clear that well over three-fourths of the existing wartime currency debt had been withdrawn from circulation by the end of 1789.

Following North Carolina's ratification of the Constitution of the United States and the federal assumption of the state's remaining certificate debt, the Assembly abandoned fiat re-

---

ity College Historical Society," Series 11, [Durham: Trinity College Historical Society, 1915]), p. 35. Williamson was actually comparing the issuing of new certificates for old as a many-headed monster, but the remark was as appropriate to such currency policy.

19. Clark, ed., *State Records*, XXIV, 475-78. The postwar emissions of 1783 and 1785 are discussed in detail above, pp. 57-99.

20. The uses and attempted uses of western land and confiscated property are treated above, pp. 28-29, 31, 35-40.

21. At each Assembly a committee was appointed to destroy the old currency that had been retired since the previous Assembly had adjourned. These reports are not altogether complete, nor are they always clear. It appears, however, that the committees between 1783 and 1789 certainly destroyed $15,281,350 nominal value and perhaps somewhat more. For the committee reports, see the following in the Legislative Papers, State Department of Archives and History, Raleigh: LVI, May 25 folder; LIV, November 8 folder; LXII, December 10 folder; LXXIV, January 3 folder; LXXVI, December 21 folder; LXXXII; LXXIX.

demption of the currency and employed tangible property previously reserved for retirement of state certificates. In November, 1790, the sinking tax was terminated and public land was made purchasable with specie or state currency.[22] While the latter policy was designed primarily to honor the postwar currencies, old currency was accepted at the legal rate of eight hundred to one. Once fiat redemption had been abandoned, retirement proceeded more slowly but steadily. By 1797 North Carolina had reduced its debt to the vicinity of $430,000 nominal value, the great bulk of which undoubtedly consisted of old currency.[23]

The assessment of North Carolina's currency redemption policy must include an appraisal of several views set forth by E. James Ferguson in his significant study of public finance entitled *The Power of the Purse.* Chiding hard-money historians for their unfavorable interpretations of eighteenth-century currency finance, Ferguson argues that fiat policy was a traditional and logical solution to the continuous money shortage resulting from an unfavorable balance of trade and an absence of credit institutions; that until the unprecedented expenses of the Revolution, most colonies had issued currency with restraint so that the paper enjoyed widespread support, even among mercantile, creditor elements; that this widespread support stemmed from the fact that, under existing conditions, no alternative to fiat policy was possible; that Americans did not expect the currency to be redeemed with specie but rather resigned themselves to its retirement through taxation or other means; and that Americans did not generally consider the currency (or certificates of public debt) to be a

22. Clark, ed., *State Records*, XXV, 77, 79.

23. U.S. Congress, House. Representative Blount's speech on the debt owed to the United States by North Carolina as a result of the settlement of wartime accounts. 4th Cong., 2nd sess., January 4, 1797, *Annals of Congress*, VI, 1802. In the early 1790's North Carolina's agents to settle accounts with the United States were of the opinion that North Carolina's wartime emissions had been largely retired. See Abishai Thomas' Answers to a List of Questions, n.d., Treasurers' and Comptrollers' Papers, Military Papers, LXVIII, State Department of Archives and History, Raleigh.

sacred contract but instead looked upon it as a necessary medium that, in effect, served as a tax upon the public as the currency underwent the process of depreciation.[24] Ferguson's interpretation is important to an understanding and appreciation of early financial policy and suggests that in North Carolina, as elsewhere, the public supported currency repudiation with resignation if not enthusiasm. North Carolina's postwar policy indicates that Ferguson's interpretation is essentially correct, but, as Ferguson himself acknowledges,[25] North Carolina's wartime fiat policy had proved unusually burdensome as over-extensive and unsupported emissions, combined with the consequent lack of public confidence, had rendered the currency worthless and wrought great property losses. Thus, while North Carolinians (with a few hard-money exceptions) were prepared to accept legal devaluation and retirement through taxation as the only feasible way of eliminating the enormous currency debt, that resignation was accompanied by an unusual degree of disappointment and disillusionment with the whole wartime currency experience. To a degree the sense of disenchantment and frustration was directed toward the United States government, which had failed to aid the state significantly during the war and thus had left North Carolina largely to its own resources—or lack of them.[26] It may be safely said that the losses and grievances resulting from North Carolina's wartime fiat currency policy contributed to the antifederal sentiment found within the state during the postwar years.

While wrestling with the problem of retiring the currency debt, the Assembly grappled with the equally vexatious matter of redeeming the state's certificate debt. Consisting of several basic types of certificates, the debt had been incurred as the depreciating currency had proved inadequate to meet

24. Ferguson, *Power of the Purse*, Chaps. I and II, *passim*.

25. *Ibid.*, pp. 11, 12, 15, 17.

26. U.S. Congress, House. Representative Burges' speech concerning the debt owed by North Carolina to the United States. 4th Cong., 2nd sess., January 4, 1797, *Annals of Congress*, VI, 1800. This speech clearly reveals the resentment toward the United States.

the government's wartime needs. Issued in exchange for or in lieu of money, the certificates carried a redemption pledge, and, as in the case of the currency debt, the certificate debt would be repudiated to the extent that the certificates were not redeemed at par in the promised manner.

One component of the certificate debt consisted of currency certificates, the vast majority of which neither bore interest nor specified a redemption date. These certificates, which, as the name indicates, pledged the state to redemption with currency, had first been issued in 1781 in an effort to bring order out of the chaotic manner in which certificates had previously been issued. Beginning in 1778 the Assembly had authorized various officials—militia commanders, militia brigade quartermasters, contractors for the state's Continental Line, and even individual soldiers—to issue certificates for the purchase or impressment of guns, provisions, clothing, and other materials needed for the armed struggle.[27] Uniformly bearing no interest, these certificates had possessed little else in common, for the Assembly's failure to prescribe certificate forms had led to a multitude of varieties. Adding to the diversity and leading to inequity, the law had required that the value of purchased or impressed goods be determined by local freemen. The Assembly's lack of explicit directions, moreover, had produced many certificates specifying currency value, others indicating specie value, and yet others stating sums without currency or specie designation. Inadequate bookkeeping procedures had compounded the confusion. Because the decentralized and disorganized manner of issuing certificates had created limitless opportunities for error, injustice, and fraud, the Assembly in the spring of 1780 had created a state board of auditors, which, among other tasks, was to examine the validity of claims against the state, that is, to examine the validity of certificates possessed by the public.[28] In February, 1781, an Assembly resolution had ex-

27. Clark, ed., *State Records*, XXIV, 155, 157, 194-95, 360, 371, 385, 416.

28. *Ibid.*, pp. 325-26. Another function of the board is given above, p. 132.

pressly empowered the board of auditors to issue new certificates to replace all valid certificates that had previously been issued by authorized officials.[29] Also in early 1781 the Assembly had supplemented the state board with district boards of auditors, upon which were conferred the same functions possessed by the central board. The same act had prescribed a price list to guide the boards, and the wording of the act had implied that the redemption of the new certificates—at some unspecified date—would be in state currency. The certificates were to bear 10 per cent interest only if the original holder should retain them at least until March 1, 1782.[30] These currency certificates—or "auditors' certificates," as they were popularly known—thus brought a degree of uniformity to a portion of the certificate debt. Although for years haphazard bookkeeping obscured the total amount issued by the boards, the state comptroller reported to the 1789 Assembly that, "as accurately stated as is practicable," the nominal value of state currency certificates issued by the boards and other officials totaled £8,437,538/4/8 (approximately $21,000,000).[31]

Issuing certificates was one matter, redeeming them another. As the work of the boards had gradually and only partially revealed the enormity of the certificate debt, and as the redemption medium—state currency—had approached worthlessness, the Assembly had felt compelled to reduce the size of the debt by the fiat method of repudiation. In an act of 1782 declaring that currency certificates could be used to purchase confiscated property, the Assembly had established that currency certificates issued through July 14, 1781, were to be accepted at the rate of 150 dollars currency to one dollar specie, while those issued after July 14, 1781, were to be received at the rate of eight hundred dollars currency

29. Clark, ed., *State Records*, XVII, 792.

30. *Ibid.*, XXIV, 373-75. Originally seven in number, with some districts having more than one board, the boards were increased to ten in 1782. *Ibid.*, pp. 442-44. For additional activity of the boards, see above, pp. 132-33.

31. Comptroller's Report, Treasurers' and Comptrollers' Papers, Military Papers, LXVII.

to one dollar specie.[32] By combining the repudiation with the use of confiscated property as a redemption medium, the Assembly sought to salvage something of its own and the certificates' reputation and provide holders with something tangible in exchange for their reduced certificates. The scale of depreciation established in 1782 for currency certificates was consistently employed thereafter for all purposes of government. Also, in 1781, the Assembly had terminated the issuing of currency certificates, a step consistent with the cessation of currency emissions. Thereafter the state was to make purchases with certificates specifying redemption with specie "or the value thereof in the circulating currency, agreeable to the par of exchange at the time said certificates are paid." The boards of auditors were to issue only certificates pledging redemption with specie "or the true and real value of the amount of such specie in the currency of the State."[33]

These specie certificates, together with others issued by different authority, were designed primarily as an escape from the depreciated currency and were a second basic component of the certificate debt. As indicated in the discussion of the currency debt, specie certificates had first been employed in 1780, when county commissioners had been authorized to issue, in payment for foodstuffs, certificates promising redemption in Spanish milled dollars "or in Continental or State currency, equal in [exchange] value to such Spanish milled dollars. . . ."[34] The authority to issue specie certificates had soon thereafter been extended to other officials.[35] Agreeable to the various acts under which they were authorized, specie certificates issued by the boards and most specie certificates issued in payment carried an annual interest of 6 per cent. Other specie certificates bore no interest when issued, but it appears that most certificates issued by individual officials were presented to the boards of auditors for examination and

32. Clark, ed., *State Records*, XXIV, 426.
33. *Ibid.*, pp. 375, 389.
34. *Ibid.*, pp. 345-46.
35. *Ibid.*, pp. 375, 389, 403, 407, 422.

exchange for new, interest-bearing certificates.[36] At war's end, therefore, most specie certificates in circulation were those of the boards of auditors. As in the case of currency certificates, no approximation of the specie certificate debt was obtained until 1789, when the comptroller reported "as accurately . . . as practicable" that the boards and other officials had issued a total of £1,575,756/14/9 (about $3,900,000) specie certificates.[37] Because these certificates were attached to hard money and because most of them bore 6 per cent annual interest and were transferable, specie certificates were preferred securities in the market. Having made them preferred, the Assembly had maintained them at par throughout the war.

A third element of the certificate debt consisted of bounty certificates issued in 1781 as an inducement to enlistment in the state's Continental Line. So greatly had the currency depreciated by that year that the amount authorized had been $26,250,000 nominal value, of which $20,430,000 had been issued.[38] These bounty certificates bore 6 per cent annual interest but were not prized in the market because they were attached to the currency. Despite the devaluation of currency certificates in 1782 and the devaluation of the currency early in 1783, bounty certificates legally retained their nominal value at war's end.

A fourth segment of the certificate debt was composed of

36. Adelaide L. Fries, "North Carolina Certificates of the Revolutionary Period," *North Carolina Historical Review*, Vol. IX, No. 3 (July, 1932), p. 232. Presentation of all types of certificates was legally necessary since the Assembly directed the boards not only to examine the legality of each certificate but also to determine if the amount specified was just in accordance with price guidelines established by the law. Not all noninterest specie certificates were turned in, however, and in 1784 a bill proposed to make such certificates bear the same interest as those which did. Above, p. 34.

37. Comptroller's Report, Treasurers' and Comptrollers' Papers, Military Papers, LXVII.

38. Clark, ed., *State Records*, XXIV, 372; "General Abstract of Claims of the State of North Carolina Against the United States," p. 11, Treasurers' and Comptrollers' Papers, Military Papers, LXVIII. Bounties had been paid to 2,724 men at an average of $7,500 per man. It was correctly anticipated that responsibility for bounty certificates would ultimately be accepted by the United States. Above, p. 131.

certificates issued in exchange for loans to the state. These loan certificates had first been authorized in 1779, when the Assembly had empowered the governor to receive loans up to the total amount of $500,000 and to issue therefor certificates bearing 6 per cent annual interest until redemption at some unspecified date. The act had not made explicit what type of money should be used for redemption, but because specie was so scarce and so valued, it was probably assumed that both the loan and the redemption would be in currency. Depreciating currency had proved a deterrent to loans, so the Assembly had sought to overcome public reluctance by allowing for the depreciation. An act of 1780 authorizing each of the state's treasurers to accept loans up to the amount of one million pounds had provided that certificates issued in exchange were to bear 5 per cent annual interest and were to be redeemed with allowance for currency depreciation.[39] The total value of loan certificates cannot be ascertained because of incomplete records. At the end of the war, loan certificates were preferred securities, but few appeared on the market because the original holders were comparatively prosperous individuals and thus were under no compulsion to sell them.

The final basic segment of the state's certificate debt consisted of certificates presented to the state's Continental Line in lieu of monetary payment. In 1782 one type of certificate, bearing no interest, had been declared redeemable with perishable categories of confiscated property; another type of 1782, also bearing no interest but allowing for depreciation according to a congressional scale of depreciation, was to be redeemed "as soon as the situation of the finances will permit."[40] Despite the non-interest feature, these certificates were sought after because one type could be exchanged for tangible property and the other allowed for depreciation. The certificates were available because most members of the Line were impoverished by the end of the war and were

39. Clark, ed., *State Records*, XXIV, 282, 347.

40. *Ibid.*, p. 420. Payment of the Line as a factor in state-federal relations is treated above, pp. 169-90.

compelled, frequently with bitterness, to sell their hard-earned certificates at a small fraction of nominal value.

The preceding five categories—currency certificates, specie certificates, bounty certificates, loan certificates, and payment certificates to the Line—were the components of the certificate debt that pressed heavily for redemption. Wartime efforts at retiring the debt had met with limited success. When the state had first resorted to certificates, the Assembly had set deadlines by which time a particular issue of certificates was to be redeemed with money. As the demands of war and the currency depreciation had invariably compelled the government to ignore the deadlines, the Assembly had resorted to indefinite redemption dates—often with a statement about retirement when finances would permit—and to the employment of other redemption means. One such alternative had been the acceptance of certificates in partial or complete payment of money taxes, sometimes at a reduced rate if tendered prior to a certain date. More broadly, loan certificates had been declared equivalent to money for all public purposes. As we have seen, confiscated property had been employed beginning in 1782 to retire currency certificates (at greatly reduced legal value) and certificates issued to the Continental Line.[41] At war's end the great majority of devaluated currency certificates and of the other elements of the certificate debt remained in circulation. The task of formulating effective redemption policies fell to the postwar Assemblies.

Those postwar policies had to be addressed not only to certificates extant at the end of the war but also to specie certificates and final settlement certificates issued after the Revolution. The latter certificates were authorized by an act of 1783 and were designed to give a measure of justice to the back-pay demands of the state's Continental Line and to attach the loyalties of the Line to the state. Bearing specie value, final settlement certificates carried 6 per cent annual interest and were assignable, factors that made them preferred

41. *Ibid.*, pp. 157, 346, 347, 368, 371, 374, 385, 388, 403, 407, 416, 420.

securities.[42] While the claims of the Line went undisputed, considerable debate arose over the postwar practice of issuing specie certificates to private individuals for goods and services provided to the state during the Revolution. Simple justice, on the one hand, argued that the state should pay certificates to its creditors; a number of legislators maintained, on the other hand, that the state could not indefinitely continue accepting claims because prolongation would encourage fraud, prevent ascertainment of the total certificate debt, and thus confuse and postpone a final settlement of wartime accounts between North Carolina and the United States.[43] Hoping to expedite settlement with its creditors and thereby to avoid these problems, the Assembly set a deadline for presenting claims against the state; but as the deadline approached, it was, on several occasions, extended for another year, and the Assembly maintained until late 1789 boards of auditors to receive and settle (with specie certificates) wartime claims against the state.[44] The Assembly's decision to continue accepting claims is only partly attributable to a desire to do justice to the state's creditors; speculators stood to gain as additional specie certificates (and final settlement certificates) appeared on the market during the postwar years.

That speculators should try to shape certificate policy is manifest. Arrayed against them were those persons who felt that speculators were profiteering as hard times forced original holders to sell, at greatly reduced value, certificates that represented wartime sacrifice. The frequently bitter antipathy toward speculators had to be qualified, however, by an inescapable dilemma: the government's honor and the interests of the speculators were inextricable. Another consideration was

42. *Ibid.*, p. 477. The payment of the Line and its political implications are covered above, pp. 169-90.

43. The settlement of accounts between North Carolina and the United States is treated above, pp. 132-68.

44. *Ibid.*, pp. 442-44, 499-500, 686, 896-97, 956. Also see pertinent information in the Legislative Papers: LII, May 24 folder; LIX, December 15 folder; LXXV, November 23 folder; LXXX.

that certificates lay also in possession of original holders and others who did not speculate actively.

Although speculators wielded significant, sometimes decisive legislative influence in the period following the war, their efforts to capitalize on the certificate debt were not always successful. In the fall of 1784, for example, they failed in an effort to profit by having the Assembly improve the legal status of currency certificates. A bill introduced at that time proposed to reduce all currency certificates of whatever origin to specie according to the scale of depreciation enacted in 1782; to have the reduced certificates bear the same interest rate as other specie certificates; and to have older specie certificates that did not carry interest bear the same interest (6 per cent) as those that did.[45] The measure's chief feature proposed, in effect, that currency certificates—already devalued by the confiscation act of 1782—be exchanged for interest-bearing specie certificates. Speculators would have been the chief beneficiaries, while the government's financial burdens would have increased by the amount of the interest. Antispeculator sentiment was sufficient to defeat the bill upon second reading in the House, and no further efforts were made to improve the status of currency certificates.

If rebuffed concerning currency certificates, speculators persisted in their efforts to profit from the government's redemption policies; and indeed most public creditors and many other public-minded individuals were concerned that the state redeem the certificate debt as honorably as possible, that is, without further devaluation and with tangible property. These persons lamented or accepted as a painful necessity the 1782 devaluation of currency certificates, and they viewed similarly the 1784 devaluation of bounty certificates to a rate of eight hundred dollars currency to one dollar specie.[46] Grieved by these massive repudiations and aware that specie redemption was impossible, those individuals who stood to gain and/or considered the debt a sacred obligation

45. Bill in Legislative Papers, LVII, November 3 folder.
46. Clark, ed., *State Records*, XXIV, 556.

advocated redeeming the remaining certificate debt with the state's chief tangible assets: confiscated property and public land. Those persons who favored fiat redemption measures—whether because of disinterested convictions or because they did not stand to gain from redemption with property—proposed certificate redemption by means of taxation, further devaluation, or exchange of old certificates for new currency or new certificates. During the postwar years both groups achieved victories in the formulation of redemption policies.

As we have seen, the Assembly in 1782 had established confiscated property as a medium to redeem currency certificates (at reduced legal value) and certain certificates issued to the Continental Line. Postwar Assemblies, faced with a large domestic debt and pressed by other financial problems and by speculative interests, lengthily debated the question of how to employ confiscated property remaining in the state's possession. When several considerations prompted the 1783 Assembly to emit currency, that Assembly—to the disappointment of certificate speculators—set aside confiscated property exclusively as a fund to retire the new currency.[47] At the spring Assembly of 1784, however, speculators and others who gave priority to the certificate debt managed to defeat legislation that would have empowered certain individuals to sell confiscated property to redeem the 1783 currency.[48] The controversy gained momentum at the fall Assembly of 1784. A bloc within the Senate proposed that a variety of certificates for militia and continental service be accepted in payment of confiscated property, but the proposal was rejected by a vote of fifteen to twelve, undoubtedly on the basis that such policy would severely undermine the currency. The bill that left the Senate constituted a compromise between the two factions, for it specified that confiscated property could be purchased with new currency or final settlement certificates (at nominal value) issued to the

47. *Ibid.*, p. 478. See above, pp. 59, 60, 71, 77-78, for treatment of the postwar currencies and their relation to confiscated property.

48. The defeated bill is in Legislative Papers, LVI, undated folder.

Continental Line. Speculators were not altogether pleased with the measure because final settlement certificates were not numerous when compared with other types and because the policy would encourage members of the Line to retain their certificates. Reflecting speculators' dissatisfaction, the House voted forty to fourteen to amend the bill so that confiscated property could be purchased with specie, new currency, and (the more numerous) specie certificates at nominal value. By a vote of seventeen to twelve the Senate insisted on its own version, and the House yielded by the margin of twenty-nine to twenty-six.[49] Abandoning their efforts to have specie certificates accepted in payment, speculators adjusted their tactics to conform with the prevailing sentiment that members of the Line should be given preference. At the 1785 Assembly it was piously argued that the Line was so deserving that all types of certificates issued to its members should be accepted at nominal value in payment for confiscated property, a position that ignored the fact that speculators had long ago snatched up earlier certificates issued to the impoverished Line. The appeal to sentiment proved irresistible, and the Assembly resolved, by large majorities, that confiscated property could be purchased with new currency (including an emission authorized by this same 1785 Assembly), with currency certificates at their reduced legal values, and with all types of certificates (at nominal value) issued to the Continental Line.[50] Enacting the 1785 resolution into law,[51] the 1786 Assembly also received from the comptroller a report that the total value of confiscated property sold to that time stood at £200,752/9/10 (approximately $500,000) and that of that amount £119,881/4/4 (about $300,000) had actually been received in certificates at the comptroller's office.[52] A later report establishes that

49. Clark, ed., *State Records*, XIX, 466-67, 487, 824, 834-35; XXIV, 662.

50. *Ibid.*, XX, 115. Redemption of the Line's certificates was also politically motivated. Above, pp. 169-90.

51. *Ibid.*, XXIV, 803.

52. Comptroller's Report, Legislative Papers, LXXII, December 28 folder. In addition to the amounts cited in the text, £2,160 in coins

between 1784 and 1790 confiscated property sales totaled £284,452/4 (about $711,000).[53] The general shortage of money and the availability of certificates make it likely that payment was received in certificates in almost all cases. Thus to the benefit primarily of speculators, members of the Line, and creditors to the Line, the certificate debt was somewhat reduced by confiscated property.

Confiscated property was an important asset to the state, but North Carolina's greatest resource was its public land—particularly that vast amount located in the western regions. Land speculators were anxious that the western land be made available for purchase, and because many of these same individuals were certificate speculators they advocated that certificates be accepted in payment. Such policy could be justified, of course, on the noble grounds that the market value of certificates would be increased and that the debt would be honored and reduced by tangible property. Another possibility was to sell the land for revenue, but the shortage of money deprived the argument of considerable weight. Because great potential wealth was involved, the matter of western land quickly appeared at the 1783 Assembly. Sponsored by speculators who sought to employ their previously acquired securities,[54] an act of that year opened a land office for the sale of western land at the rate of ten pounds per hundred acres, with payment to be made in specie, in specie certificates at nominal value, or in currency certificates and other certificates at their legal rates.[55] There were

---

had been received and £11,060/4 value of property had been sold on five years credit. These same figures appear in the Legislative Papers of the 1787 Assembly, but the total amount received at the comptroller's office had risen to £122,755/13/11. See *ibid.*, LXXVI, December 12 folder, and LXXIX, December 19 folder.

53. Hugh Talmage Lefler, ed., *North Carolina History Told by Contemporaries* (Chapel Hill: The University of North Carolina Press, 1934), p. 112.

54. William Henry Masterson, *William Blount* (Baton Rouge: Louisiana State University Press, 1954), pp. 70-74, covers the influence of speculators behind the western land act.

55. Clark, ed., *State Records*, XXIV, 479. Boyd, *Federal Period*, p. 12, mistakenly writes that in 1783 the land office was opened to redeem the emission of 1783.

persons who, for several reasons, regretted that the land was not employed to raise revenue,[56] but the influence of speculators had predominated. During the next year specie certificates were feverishly sought (thereby increasing their market value), and great quantities of land were entered in the land office.[57]

The frenzied speculation was abruptly terminated when the Assembly, on May 25, 1784, closed the land office.[58] Antipathy toward speculators undoubtedly influenced the decision, but there were other, more powerful forces behind the move. The Assembly contained a number of men who advocated cession of the state's western lands to the United States as a means of strengthening the national government. In addition, a number of western landowners had become convinced that their lands would appreciate in value more rapidly if the authority of the United States replaced that of North Carolina in the transmontaine area. Also, because under the Articles of Confederation the war debt of the United States was to be apportioned among the states on the basis of land, cession offered a way to reduce North Carolina's portion of that debt.[59] All these considerations combined to produce the closing of the land office and cession of the state's western land to the United States upon several conditions, one of which was that incomplete land warrants could be completed.[60]

During the land office's brief life a significant proportion of

56. Hugh Williamson to Governor Samuel Johnston, September 29, 1789, Governors' Papers, XVII, 82, State Department of Archives and History, Raleigh. As covered above, p. 51, Williamson wished that the state had collected revenue so that continental securities could have been purchased. The state's need of money was manifest.

57. For a vivid description of speculators' search for specie certificates, see Masterson, *William Blount*, pp. 78-80. Private correspondence relating to the search are found in Alice Barnwell Keith and William Henry Masterson, eds., *The John Gray Blount Papers* (3 vols.; Raleigh: State Department of Archives and History, 1952-65), I. Also, see Richard Caswell to William Caswell, May 4, 1783, Clark, ed., *State Records*, XVI, 959-60.

58. Clark, ed., *State Records*, XXIV, 563-64.

59. Masterson, *William Blount*, pp. 84-86. Above, p. 138.

60. Clark, ed., *State Records*, XXIV, 563-64.

the state's debt had been retired, but, as often proved to be the case in the eighteenth century, public finances were in such disarray that years passed before an accurate account could be obtained. A subcommittee reported to the 1786 Assembly that a total of 4,393,945 acres had been entered in the land office, amounting in certificates to £439,394/10 (about $1,100,000). Of these amounts, warrants had actually been issued for 3,221,928 acres, amounting to £322,192/16 (roughly $800,000) in certificates.[61] Several more years passed before the entry taker's accounts were settled, the delay caused primarily by fraud within the land office. An official working on the accounts reported in October, 1789, that an exact total of 4,464,195½ acres had been entered in the land office, evaluated at £446,419 ($916,000) in certificates.[62]

Far from proving of benefit to speculators, the cession act passed in the spring of 1784 had unanticipated consequences that threatened the interests of speculators and the sovereignty of the government of North Carolina. Certain western elements, encouraged by the cession act and by Congress' general policy of establishing new states, declared into existence the State of Franklin.[63] Although they stressed that the new government would recognize North Carolina land titles in the region, the pretensions of the Franklinites threatened uncompleted titles and the future prospects of North Carolina speculators. Thus the campaign for the fall Assembly of 1784 centered upon the cession act, with nationalist, western, and antispeculator elements opposing repeal.[64] Advocates of repeal triumphed, and the Assembly withdrew the cession without mentioning the major reason for its action.[65] Gradually thereafter the Franklin movement disintegrated.

61. Comptroller's Report, Legislative Papers, LXXIII, January 5 folder.

62. George Doherty to Francis Child, October 21, 1789, *ibid.*, LXXXVIII.

63. Masterson, *William Blount*, p. 92 and *passim*.

64. *Ibid.*, p. 93.

65. Clark, ed., *State Records*, XXIV, 678-79. The stated reasons for repeal were that the United States had not assumed financial responsibility for North Carolina expeditions against the Indians dur-

With western land again available, speculators fought to reopen the land office. The 1786 Assembly considered a bill that proposed to sell western land at the rate of fifteen pounds per hundred acres, payable in specie certificates at nominal value and currency certificates at their legal values, for the purpose of discharging the interest and principal of the certificate debt.[66] The House passed the bill three times, but upon final reading the Senate laid the measure over until the next Assembly. At that next Assembly, of 1787, the bill was reintroduced only to be defeated in the Senate by a vote of nine to thirty.[67] Despite pleas that the certificate debt cried for redemption, the 1789 Assembly rejected another bill to open a western land office. Also rejected in 1789 was a bill to cede the territorial rights of the land west of the "Great Iron and Stone Mountains" to the residents thereof, to erect a distinct state there, and to open a land office to dispose of unappropriated lands in the new state so as to sink the specie certificates and paper money of North Carolina. A third defeated bill proposed to do the same thing without ceding the western land.[68] The unwillingness to reopen the western land office during the late 1780's stemmed from several factors: first, the conviction that as the state's chief resource, western land could most beneficially be employed as a source of revenue; second, resentment against speculators, who were the chief beneficiaries of certificate redemption policy; third, the growing awareness that western land, disposed of at rates that would enable original holders and small investors to obtain acreage, could not come near retiring the certificate debt; fourth, the insistence of fiat men that the

ing the war, that other states had failed to make similar cessions, that other states had not approved a constitutional amendment granting Congress an impost, and that Massachusetts and Connecticut were extending their western land claims.

66. Bill in Legislative Papers, LXVII, December 4 folder.

67. Clark, ed., *State Records*, XX, 200, 434. An effort to rescind the repeal of the cession act was also defeated, indicating that political forces were on dead-center. Masterson, *William Blount*, pp. 138-39.

68. Clark, ed., *State Records*, XXI, 271, 648-49; bills in Legislative Papers, LXXXVII.

sinking tax inaugurated in 1786 should be the means of extinguishing the certificate debt.

As we have seen, the retirement of certificates through taxation had begun during the war. The established policy of allowing the taxpayer to pay a portion of his property tax in certificates was continued through 1786. During the postwar years certificates were accepted at their various legal rates, that is, specie certificates at nominal value, currency certificates according to the 1782 scale, and bounty certificates (after 1784) at eight hundred to one. Although persons—especially speculators—who held the debt to be a sacred trust grumbled that this policy failed to redeem certificates with tangible property, retirement by this method at least enabled the taxpayer to avoid paying the entire tax with money. Records are fragmentary, but evidence indicates that the amounts of certificates drawn in by this form of taxation were not great when compared to the enormous certificate debt.[69] By the meeting of the 1786 Assembly it was becoming increasingly obvious that the employment of confiscated property, western land, and existing tax policy had not brought the certificate debt near the point of extinction. This awareness plus a great desire to have done with the debt led the 1786 Assembly to inaugurate a major device of fiat policy—a mandatory sinking tax. Opponents of fiat policy bitterly resented such a tax because it offered the holder nothing in exchange for his certificates; and, of course, speculators were particularly injured even though they could sell their certificates at something of a profit as taxpayers were forced to procure certificates in order to pay the mandatory tax.

The property tax acts for 1787, 1788, and 1789 each contained two distinct and equal property taxes, one payable in currency or specie to meet the needs of government and

69. To illustrate the relatively small amounts retired by means of the optional tax, one might examine the report of a committee to the 1786 Assembly on the returns of revenue officials. The report states the following amounts received: £2,070 in loan certificates; £819/3/5 in specie certificates; £64,306/6 in currency certificates; and £41,311/14/3 in certificates that the committee did not identify.

the other payable in certificates to sink the certificate debt.[70] One justification forwarded for levying the high-rate, mandatory certificate tax was that the policy encouraged the transfer of certificates between individuals and thereby more evenly distributed the domestic burden of the war which the certificates represented, that is, more widely distributed the burden of the certificates' depreciation.[71] Transfer was indeed accelerated as persons without certificates had to acquire them to pay the tax; the increased activity, in turn, somewhat raised the market value of the certificates,[72] a fact that must have been of minimum comfort to speculators who would have much preferred purchasing tangible property to selling their securities at a nominal profit for depreciated legal tender currency. Whatever the merits or injustices of the mandatory certificate tax, it did take significant strides toward retiring the debt. Although the records are obscure and again incomplete, it appears that upwards of a half million pounds value of specie certificates (retired at nominal value) and several million pounds nominal value of currency certificates (retired according to the 1782 scale) were withdrawn from circulation.[73]

70. This is the same sinking tax, mentioned above, pp. 23, 24, that was payable in currency as well as certificates.

71. Johann David Schoepf, *Travels in the Confederation*, ed. and trans. by Alfred James Morrison (2 vols.; Philadelphia: William J. Campbell and Company, 1911), II, 130-31. Schoepf wrote in 1784, before there was a mandatory sinking tax, but his remarks apply to the later mandatory tax. Mistakenly under the impression that a mandatory tax was law in 1784, he may have actually overheard arguments in favor of establishing such a tax.

72. *Ibid.*, p. 131. Schoepf states that certificates had little market value until the government started receiving them for taxes.

73. A committee at the 1789 Assembly reported the following amounts destroyed from the comptroller's office: £113,636 loan office certificates (retired at nominal value); £855,263/6/3 specie certificates, including interest (retired at nominal value); £1,871,360/3/7 currency certificates at nominal value (retired at reduced value). Legislative Papers, LXXXIX. A copy of the report is in the Lenoir Family Papers, Southern Historical Collection, The University of North Carolina at Chapel Hill. It may also be found in the *State Gazette of North Carolina*, December 10, 1789 (microfilm), North Carolina Collection, The University of North Carolina at Chapel Hill. The report does not in-

A fourth redemption method was government purchase of certificates with postwar fiat currency, the type of policy that conjured up visions of that many-headed monster. As previously mentioned, a total of £200,000 was emitted during the postwar period, of which amount perhaps as much as £64,000 was apparently employed in such purchase.[74] The sums involved were relatively small, but the policy itself must have been particularly depressing to the opponents of fiat policy.

During the postwar years, then, five means—sale of confiscated property, sale of western land, employment of taxes, purchase with fiat currency, and repudiation (of bounty certificates)—were used to reduce the certificate debt. The debate over whether to seek redemption by tangible property or fiat means revolved both around the self-interest of those who stood to gain or lose from the various redemption possibilities, and around the issue of whether the debt was a sacred obligation involving the state's honor or a financial burden to be distributed among the population as the certificates were taxed or devalued out of existence. The latter view ultimately prevailed, although not before a portion of the debt had been retired by confiscated property and western land.

An important facet of the controversy associated with retirement methods was the debate over whether the government should devaluate specie certificates or continue to accept them at nominal value. These certificates deserved special consideration because they had been reduced to specie value, but many persons could not reconcile themselves to the fact that speculators could acquire the certificates in the market at a fraction of their face value and

---

dicate the manners in which the certificates were retired. The text statement regarding redemption by the sinking tax is the result of taking into account the various reports dealing with confiscated property, western land sales, and certificates issued and destroyed.

74. Clark, ed., *State Records*, XXIV, 722-25. U.S. Congress, House. Speech of Representative Williamson of North Carolina. 1st Cong., 2nd sess., March 30, 1790, *Annals of Congress*, II, 1489. The postwar emissions of 1783 and 1785 are discussed in detail above, pp. 57-99,

then receive full value for them in the purchase of western land (up to May 25, 1784, and potentially thereafter) and until 1787 (and potentially thereafter) in the partial payment of money taxes.[75] A possible solution to the dilemma lay in distinguishing between original and subsequent holders so that the latter would receive only a fraction of the value that the original holder could obtain. A bill to make such a distinction was considered by some legislators in 1783,[76] but the measure was not introduced, probably for several reasons: first, because the bill, if enacted, would have been difficult or impossible to administer; second, because it would have injured non-speculating creditors; third, because speculators could have been expected to oppose it bitterly; fourth, because the government's pledge was associated with all certificates; and fifth, because some critics of specie certificate policy felt that it would be unfair to award full value even to original holders, since appraisers for goods and services provided to the state had overvalued the goods and services in anticipation that the specie certificates being issued would subsequently depreciate.[77]

The most obvious possible alteration of specie certificate policy, and one that did find some legislative support, was to reduce the legal value of all specie certificates. Resistance at the Assembly proved formidable, for repudiation would injure original holders as well as speculators and would especially impair the government's reputation because the certificates were attached to specie. Thus in 1783 the Assembly turned back the proposal that a sinking tax allow a person to pay twenty shillings value of specie certificates in lieu of

75. Members of the Continental Line, whose certificates bore specie value, were especially embittered that creditors and speculators could easily acquire their hard-earned certificates. See petition of Orange County residents to the General Assembly, Legislative Papers, LXVI, November 28 folder. See also, a letter signed "One of the People" in the *North Carolina Gazette*, September 2, 1784 (microfilm), North Carolina Collection.

76. Charles Johnson to Richard Benningham, May 5, 1783, Clark, ed., *State Records*, XVI, 961.

77. The latter point is made in "One of the People."

four shillings currency.[78] In 1788 the Assembly rejected a tax measure that would have allowed the taxpayer to pay one shilling currency in lieu of a greater amount of specie certificates, with the currency to be set aside to retire other certificates.[79]

In 1789, however, the Assembly, after much debate, devalued all certificates carrying specie value and further devalued certificates that had previously been reduced. The act required that state certificates of all descriptions be brought to the treasury on or before January 1, 1791, where they were to be exchanged according to their various legal rates for new specie certificates. The holder of an old certificate was to receive three certificates in exchange: one for the interest due (if any) on the old certificate; one for one-third of the principal of the old certificate; and one, bearing interest from January 1, 1790, for the two-thirds balance of the principal of the old certificate. As a fund to redeem the certificates for one-third the principal, the law set aside all unappropriated revenue from the land tax for 1787 and 1788 and from tonnage fees and imports for 1787, 1788, and 1789 up until the United States should start to collect the duties in the state (North Carolina having recently ratified the constitution).[80] While thus providing for monetary redemption of part of the certificate debt, the law repudiated much of that debt by stating that the one-third certificates should be redeemed at the treasury at the rate of four shillings "cash" for twenty shillings value of the new certificates. This repudiation reduced the principal of the debt by more than one-fourth[81] and was especially significant because it embraced specie certificates. The fate of the remaining debt was made clear by the same act: the certificate sinking tax, now payable also in new currency at the rate of four shillings

78. Bill in Legislative Papers, XLVIII, May 8 folder. The sinking tax proposal, as previously mentioned, was itself defeated.

79. Clark, ed., *State Records*, XX, 587-88.

80. *Ibid.*, XXV, 7-9.

81. That is, 80 per cent of one-third of the certificate debt was repudiated.

currency for twenty shillings specie certificates, was to be continued annually upon property until the debt was extinguished. Incorporating both repudiation and a sinking tax, the measure clearly marked the triumph of fiat policy. Not even the monetary-redemption feature could be considered as a concession to the opposition, for the provision was included as a useful means to recirculate the postwar currency presently in the treasury.[82]

Opponents of fiat policy struggled furiously if futilely at the 1789 Assembly. They attempted to have specified monies in the treasury as of January 1, 1790, set aside to redeem specie certificates at nominal value and other certificates at their legal rates; they sponsored a resolution directing the treasurer to make monetary redemption, with depreciation allowance, of all loan certificates issued under the act of 1780; and, as the repudiation-sinking tax bill neared passage, they made a last-ditch effort to make the payment of certificates optional on part of the monetary tax upon property.[83] Defeated at all points, these men could only protest and lament as the fiat forces carried the day. Their bitter disappointment is reflected in the formal protest of eight senators to the passage of the bill, a protest based on the following grounds: that in settling accounts with the United States the state would receive full value for certificates for which the holders would receive only one-fifth value; that reducing the value of specie certificates would undermine public confidence in the government; that such policy would impair the obligation of contracts and thus violate the Constitution of the United States; that it would injure the Continental Line; that it would punish persons who had contributed to the war effort while it benefitted the disaffected who had not contributed; and that it would primarily injure original holders be-

82. Archibald Maclaine to James Iredell, November 26, 1789, December 22, 1789, John Griffith McRee, ed., *Life and Correspondence of James Iredell* (2 vols.; New York: D. Appleton and Company, 1867-68), II, 274, 276.

83. Bill fragment, Legislative Papers, LXXXVI; resolution, *ibid.*, LXXX; bill to redeem the domestic debt, *ibid.*, LXXXVI.

cause (the protest argued) most certificates still lay in the hands of original holders.[84] The protest insisted that devaluation stemmed not from antipathy toward speculators, as the bill's proponents claimed, but from a desire to escape the debt; and that the devaluation would not injure speculators because they had already exchanged their certificates for western land. In truth the western land office, as we have seen, had been closed since 1784 and had retired far less than a majority of specie certificates; also, sentiment against speculators, which had always been present and genuine, had, in fact, reached somewhat of a crest in 1789. This antagonism and the actions of the 1789 Assembly regarding the certificate debt can best be appreciated in the light of two related and converging factors: first, in 1789 the Assembly received the first comprehensive report on size and nature of the state's certificate debt; second, in 1789 the state's certificate debt reached its greatest influence as an ingredient of North Carolina's financial relations with the United States. These two factors must now be examined.

Since 1784 the Assembly had been seeking a detailed account of the certificate debt, to include its size, its components, and the interest and due-dates of each type of certificate. So confused and incomplete were the records that for years various officials could only confess their ignorance, mutter vaguely and unofficially that retired certificates "in number are amazing," and make rough estimates that usually conflicted with other rough estimates.[85] The inability of the government to determine its own certificate debt stemmed from a number of factors, among which were the haphazard and decentralized manner of issuing certificates, especially early in the war; the confusion and destruction attendant to the Revolution; the unsystematic methods of bookkeeping characteristic of the eighteenth century; and the nomadic existence of state government during and after the war. At the urgent insistence of the 1788 Assembly the

84. Clark, ed., *State Records*, XXI, 726-27.

85. *Ibid.*, XVIII, 281; XIX, 663; XXI, 144-45; XXII, 1020. Governor Richard Caswell to William Blount, June 7, 1786, *ibid.*, XVIII, 646.

comptroller prepared the first comprehensive report on the certificate debt, a report that, as we have noted, was "as accurately stated as is practicable." Presented to the 1789 Assembly, the comptroller's report announced the following: North Carolina commissioners and boards of auditors had issued a grand total of £1,575,756/14/9 (about $3,900,000) specie certificates and £8,437,538/4/8 (approximately $21,-000,000) currency certificates. Of these amounts the state had retired, as of the end of 1789, the totals of £940,672/13/2 ($2,350,000) specie certificates at nominal value and £7,-231,987/16/7 ($18,500,000) nominal value of currency certificates at the specie value of £30,311/10/2. In summary, of the £10,013,294/6/3 nominal value certificates issued by North Carolina, the state had retired the nominal amount of £8,172,659/19/9. Considering specie certificates at nominal value and currency certificates at their reduced value, the state had issued certificates to the specie value of £1,614,-105/5/0, of which a total of £970,984/3/4 had been redeemed. The outstanding domestic certificate debt stood, therefore, at a specie value of £643,121/1/8, which with interest totaled £874,644/13/2.[86]

The 1789 Assembly was sobered by the realization that the specie value of the unredeemed debt, together with interest, approximately equaled the specie value that had been retired; and by the fact that the bulk of the outstanding debt consisted of specie certificates rated at par. With most confiscated property already sold, with western lands ceded to Congress by act of the 1789 Assembly, and with the public weary of the debt, the 1789 Assembly, as we have seen, decided to enact repudiation and to continue the sinking tax.

The second consideration that led the Assembly to promote certificate retirement by repudiation and taxation was the debt's sensitive role in state-federal relations. That role consisted of two related aspects: first, the final settlement of wartime accounts between North Carolina and the United

86. *Ibid.*, XXII, 1020; Comptroller's Report, Treasurers' and Comptrollers' Papers, Military Papers, LXVII.

States; second, the prospect of the assumption of state debts by the United States. These features of state-federal relations were brought into combination by North Carolina's ratification of the constitution, an event that occurred during the meeting of the 1789 Assembly. The ratification struggle also involved the question of the state's debt and must be examined prior to a discussion of final settlement and assumption.

During the extended debate over North Carolina's ratification of the constitution, the state's certificate debt had proved to be a vital issue—far more so than the continental certificate debt that played such a positive and important role in a number of other states. Because North Carolina had already absorbed most continental certificates that had lain in the hands of its citizens[87] and because out-of-state speculators were continuing to grab much of the remainder,[88] the number of continental securities held by North Carolinians was inconsequential—a fact which, as Charles Beard puts it, "must have had a very deadening effect on the spirit of the movement for ratification."[89] While the continental debt was significant in a negative sense, that is, by its absence, the presence of a large unredeemed state debt exerted a positive influence. Ratification followed by federal assumption and redemption of North Carolina's certificates was a sequence by which the holders of that debt stood to gain; and despite the scarcity of contemporary evidence and the purchase of North Carolina certificates by outside speculators, it is reasonable to conclude that a number of North Carolinians, including individuals attending the ratification conventions, were speculating in state certificates.[90] At the July,

87. North Carolina's policy with regard to continental securities is covered in detail above, pp. 132-90, *passim*.

88. Masterson, *William Blount*, p. 173; Ferguson, *Power of the Purse*, pp. 267-68. Intense out-of-state speculation in continental certificates within North Carolina began in late 1789.

89. Charles Austin Beard, *An Economic Interpretation of the Constitution of the United States* (New York: Macmillan Company, 1913), p. 287.

90. See, for example, George Nicolson to John Gray Blount, August 24, 1788, Keith and Masterson, eds., *Blount*, I, 420.

1788, Hillsborough Convention, which was safely controlled by Antifederalists, the matter of North Carolina's certificate debt had been employed to oppose ratification. Exploiting the widespread antagonism toward speculators, Antifederalists had warned (with the powers of prophecy) that North Carolina's ratification would lead to federal assumption of the state debt and hence to the emolument of men who had purchased the debt at a fraction of its nominal value. Taking another tack and capitalizing upon the manifest inability of the state to honor its debt fully and immediately, Antifederalists had argued that if ratification occurred, the constitution's provision that contracts could not be impaired would compel North Carolina to redeem its domestic certificates at face value. In response to these assertions Federalists had replied that the constitution referred only to contracts between individuals and did not give the federal government the power to interfere with the public securities of any state. Unpersuaded, Antifederalists had insisted that a precondition for North Carolina's ratification would be a constitutional amendment prohibiting direct or indirect congressional interference with any state's liquidation of its own public securities. The Federalists, who wished the convention to propose amendments only subsequent to ratification, also suggested a list of amendments, but, indicating to some extent the influence of speculators in the state debt, the list contained no reference to the domestic debt.[91] Thus at the 1788 Convention, the certificate debt of North Carolina had been of great concern to both advocates and opponents of ratification.

Following the 1788 Convention's faliure to ratify the constitution, the state's certificate debt continued to loom as a major factor in the continuing debate over ratification. Painfully aware that the debt was a formidable obstacle to ratification, Federalists nevertheless generally shrank from the

91. Elliot, ed., *Debates*, III, 168, 169; Clark, ed., *State Records*, XXII, 22, 23-24. The secondary work on the ratification struggle is Louise Irby Trenholme, *The Ratification of the Federal Constitution in North Carolina* ("Studies in History, Economics and Public Law," No. 363 [New York: Columbia University Press, 1932]).

idea of eliminating the debt (and the obstacle) by repudiation or taxation. Their reluctance was founded both on the view that the debt was a sacred trust and also because a number of them were certificate speculators. In the midst of their dilemma the Federalists seized upon a plan that conceivably could have enabled the state to discharge its debt at par and thus could have eliminated the barrier to ratification while salvaging the state's honor and securing the interests of speculators. Outlining that policy—already adopted by some other states—Hugh Williamson, a prominent North Carolina Federalist, urged Governor Samuel Johnston in September, 1789, to support the idea of having the state purchase depreciated continental securities on the market. These securities, when funded at par by the new United States government, would provide the money to redeem the state certificate debt and to discharge North Carolina's wartime debt to the United States. Williamson viewed as a serious error the state's past policy of redeeming state certificates (and currency) through taxation, the sale of western land, and the sale of confiscated property. Had North Carolina been using these means to gather revenue to purchase continental certificates, Williamson argued, the state treasury would already contain enough such certificates to effect the desired results.[92] At the 1789 Assembly, John Haywood, the state treasurer, implored the government to adopt the policy that Williamson suggested,[93] but the Assembly refused. That refusal was the result, in part, of the antagonism toward speculators and, in part, of the insurmountable fact that by 1789 few continental certificates were circulating in North Carolina. Intensifying speculation together with North Carolina's financial limitations, moreover, precluded the purchase elsewhere of significant quantities of continental certificates. Also, as we have seen, the majority of legislators positively favored fiat policy (repudiation and taxation) because tangible property was no longer available for certif-

92. Hugh Williamson to Governor Samuel Johnston, September 29, 1789, Governors' Papers, XVII, 82.
93. Memorial of John Haywood, Legislative Papers, LXXXVII.

icate redemption. Finally, the Assembly's decision to retire its debt by fiat policy could be attributed to North Carolina's ratification of the constitution and hence the active combining of the final settlement and assumption issues—aspects to be treated hereinafter.

Between July, 1788, and November, 1789, a number of factors worked to shift North Carolina to the Federalist position. The propaganda or educational efforts of influential Federalists, the reassuring effect of Washington's election as president, the real prospect of a bill of rights, the threat of commercial pressures by the United States against North Carolina, the generally discomforting prospect of being outside the Union—these considerations have been cited[94] to explain why the November, 1789, Fayetteville Convention, which like the Hillsborough Convention overwhelmingly represented real estate and contained insignificant continental security holdings,[95] decisively reversed the previous convention's position by voting 194 to 77 for ratification. Ratification by the Fayetteville Convention may also be partially explained by the prospect that North Carolina speculators in the state's certificates would stand to benefit from assumption of the debt by the United States. Such a conclusion must be strongly qualified, however, by two important developments: first, during late 1789 a number of out-of-state speculators, especially from New York, had been grabbing up the North Carolina certificate debt as they received inside information that assumption was imminent.[96] This fact meant that North Carolinians held less of the debt than in 1788 and thus stood to gain less from ratification. The second qualifying factor is that after ratification—a significant sequence—the Fayetteville Convention

94. Beard, *Economic Interpretation*, p. 236; Forrest McDonald, *We the People: The Economic Origins of the Constitution* (Chicago: University of Chicago Press, 1958), p. 317.

95. For property interests of members of the North Carolina conventions, see McDonald, *We the People*, pp. 318-21.

96. Ferguson, *Power of the Purse*, pp. 270-72, 285, 328. North Carolina's certificates could be procured cheaply, especially prior to the state's ratification of the constitution.

unanimously urged a constitutional amendment prohibiting Congress from interfering with each state's redemption of its own certificates.[97] The unanimity may have been the result of speculators' confidence that the proposed amendment stood no chance, but it is almost certain that the majority of the convention delegates held no state certificates. Antipathy toward speculators—especially toward those from other states—undoubtedly played a major role in bringing about the proposed amendment, and another powerful motive was the prospect that federal assumption of the debts of North Carolina and of the other states would work to the serious disadvantage of North Carolina. It remains now to examine that prospect.

A basic fact of which North Carolinians were painfully aware was that the state's domestic certificate debt, while large when compared with the state's resources, was small when compared with the debts of certain other states. Thus, if the United States assumed the state debts and subsequently levied taxes upon the states to discharge the total of the states' debts, North Carolina would be called upon to contribute more than she would benefit by being unburdened of her own debt. While state debts assumed by the federal government were to be charged against the individual states in their respective settlement of wartime accounts with the United States,[98] North Carolina—in common with other states having relatively small debts—feared that if assumption preceded final settlement, the states benefiting from assumption would endlessly forestall final settlement.[99] This fear was all the more felt because North Carolina (like other southern states) anticipated that it would be found a creditor to the United States at final settlement[100] (a belief that had

97. Clark, ed., *State Records*, XXII, 51-52.

98. Ferguson, *Power of the Purse*, pp. 307-25, *passim*, stresses that the states were to be charged with their assumed debts in their respective settlements with the United States.

99. *Ibid.*, 309, 310; Hugh Williamson to Governor Alexander Martin, March 6, March 20, May 13, 1790, Governors' Letter Books, X, 27-28, 31-32, 53, State Department of Archives and History, Raleigh.

100. Ferguson, *Power of the Purse*, p. 212; Hugh Williamson to Gov-

weakened opposition to ratification between the two conventions[101]). These considerations, compounded by the fact that increasing amounts of the state debt were falling into the hands of out-of-state speculators,[102] contributed to the 1789 Assembly's decision to adopt fiat redemption measures and to the unanimity of the Fayetteville Convention's call for a constitutional amendment that would have blocked assumption.

Vigorous efforts to block assumption until after final settlement were made on the national level by North Carolina's congressmen. Representative Hugh Williamson, especially, struggled valiantly to facilitate final settlement and to postpone assumption.[103] In the task Williamson was encouraged by Governor Alexander Martin, who labeled assumption an "iniquitous . . . measure . . . fraught . . . with ruin to this State."[104] Martin maintained that the state's creditors were "satisfied" with receiving four shillings in the pound under the 1789 state redemption policy, and he saw no reason why the federal government, which, he stressed, had no business interfering with state contracts, should "compel" a state certificate holder to receive twenty shillings in the pound.[105] Martin's commentary served only to emphasize that North Carolina's fight against assumption appeared to be unavailing and that the measure was about to become law. Representative John Steele undoubtedly expressed the general sentiment of North Carolina officialdom when he wrote that as-

ernor Alexander Martin, April 24, 1790, Governors' Letter Books, X, 29-30. Final settlement between North Carolina and the United States is covered above, pp. 132-68.

101. Trenholme, *Ratification*, p. 243.

102. As previously noted, during 1790 speculators became increasingly interested in state certificates, especially because the prospect of funding the continental debt was elevating the purchase price of congressional securities. Ferguson, *Power of the Purse*, pp. 270-72, 285, 327-29.

103. Hugh Williamson to Governor Alexander Martin, March 6, March 20, May 13, 1790, Governors' Letter Books, X, 27-28, 31-32, 53.

104. Governor Alexander Martin to Hugh Williamson, June 29, 1790, *ibid.*, p. 63.

105. *Ibid.*, p. 64.

sumption, "tho' a bitter draught for No Carolina, must be swallowed."[106] When the assumption bill became law in the summer of 1790, the 1790 Assembly had no alternative but to terminate the 1789 state redemption program of repudiation and taxation.[107] In his address to that Assembly, Governor Martin refused to elaborate upon the assumption of state debts; but while he said he must presume that "pure and equal justice" dictated the measure, his speech implied that assumption was, in his opinion, an invasion of state sovereignty.[108]

If the state was disappointed that assumption preceded final settlement, the fear that final settlement would never occur proved groundless. In a tedious but important process that shall be covered in a later chapter, final settlement between North Carolina and the United States was completed in 1793. Contrary to the state's hopes and anticipation, however, North Carolina was declared to be a debtor to the United States. Thus, both assumption and final settlement worked to North Carolina's disadvantage.

One's evaluation of the policies and retirement methods associated with the certificate debt depends, like one's evaluation of the currency debt, upon the assumptions and beliefs with which one approaches the facts and statistics. If one agrees with the handful of eighteenth-century fiscal conservatives that specie redemption at par or at least redemption at par with other tangible property constitutes the only valid and honorable redemption, one may conclude that by using confiscated property and western land the state honorably retired only slightly over 7 per cent of the certificate debt,

106. John Steele to Governor Alexander Martin, July 19, 1790, *ibid.*, p. 112.

107. Clark, ed., *State Records*, XXV, 77. In early 1790 notices had appeared in the state's newspapers that an office was open at Hillsborough as of March 1, 1790, to receive specie certificates and other certificates and to issue in exchange the new certificates. *State Gazette of North Carolina*, April 17, 1790 (microfilm), North Carolina Collection.

108. Governor Alexander Martin's address to the Assembly, November 2, 1790, Governors' Letter Books, X, 138.

excluding bounty certificates from consideration.[109] If one assumes that the state was obligated to redeem all certificates at full value, whether by fiat means or tangible property, and that the public expected and had the right to expect such redemption, one must conclude that North Carolina legitimately redeemed between 9 and 10 per cent of its certificate debt.[110] If one maintains, as Ferguson does,[111] that the people generally expected and accepted the legal devaluation of certificates and their retirement by sinking taxes, one may conclude that North Carolina honorably redeemed approximately 80 per cent of the certificate debt.[112] If one accepts this fiat interpretation and uses the reduced specie value of the currency certificates as established by the confiscation act of 1782, one may conclude that the state redeemed about 60 per cent of the certificate debt.[113] The postwar certificate policies of North Carolina clearly indicate that whether by conviction or for lack of alternatives, whether because of self-interest or disinterested motives, the majority of North Carolinians—the large majority—were prepared to promote and accept retirement of the certificate debt by fiat methods of repudiation and sinking taxes. To the satisfaction of most North Carolinians, then, the bulk of the certificate debt and of the currency debt as well were effectively and honorably retired. These mediums had done much to finance the war, and the public bore the expense of their depreciation, repudiation, and fiat redemption. Regardless of the abstract justice or injustice of its actions, the government of North Carolina had no realistic alternative during the 1780's.

109. That is, about £730,000 (£284,000 from confiscated property and £446,000 from western land) out of a total nominal value of £10,013,294/6/3 in certificates.

110. That is, the state redeemed £970,984/3/4 specie value out of a nominal value of £10,013,294/6/3 issued.

111. Ferguson, *Power of the Purse*, p. 10.

112. That is, the state redeemed £8,172,659/19/9 nominal value of certificates of a total of £10,013,294/6/3 nominal value issued.

113. That is, £970,984/3/4 specie value out of £1,614,105/5/0 specie value issued. This interpretation is followed by Marion Gregory and Donald Lennon, "The North Carolina Revolutionary Debt" (unpublished manuscript at the State Department of Archives and History, Raleigh), p. 38.

III. *Emission of Currency*

As revealed in the previous chapter, North Carolina came to emit fiat currency during the postwar period. This decision, supported unhesitantly by some legislators and reluctantly by others,[1] was reached in response to the severe shortage of money and the pressing financial demands upon government. Fiscal conservatives found themselves engaged in another struggle against fiat policy, and it is to the details of that struggle that we must now turn.

The General Assembly that convened at Hillsborough on April 8, 1783, was the first to face the manifold problems of postwar finance. With specie practically unavailable and with the war currencies dead, the Assembly's overriding task was to attempt the creation of an adequate, viable medium of exchange. In addition to this general problem, there was an immediate and specific need for currency: the undeniably just demands of the North Carolina Continental Line concerning arrears of pay. Paying the Line, in turn, was not only a matter of simple justice but also, as a later chapter shall reveal,[2] an important factor in state-federal relations as Congress sought to pay the Line with certificates and thereby

1. In later years men who had supported fiat emissions during and after the Revolution would claim that they had reluctantly done so only because they had believed the policy to be absolutely necessary in view of the shortage of money. See, for example, the statements made at the North Carolina Convention of 1788 as recorded in Jonathan Elliot, ed., *The Debates, Resolutions, and Proceedings, in Convention, on the adoption of the Federal Constitution* (3 vols.; Washington: Jonathan Elliot, 1827-30), III, 87, 155. As the present chapter will reveal, many persons supported the 1783 currency only because much of it went to pay the state's Continental Line, and it is reasonable to assume that at the Assembly the plight of the Line did much to assure passage of the emission bill.

2. Above, pp. 169-90.

increase the national debt and strengthen the bonds of union. When, therefore, representatives of the Line's officers presented to the 1783 Assembly a petition for pay,[3] most potential opposition to an emission melted away as the legislators sought to do justice to the Line and head off what they considered a dangerous trend toward centralization. It has been argued that another ingredient for emission was the desire of land speculators to create a ready medium by which real estate could be purchased in the western land office opened later by this same 1783 Assembly.[4] It is possible that some speculators at the Assembly did hope that the new currency—with which the assemblymen were to be paid[5]—could be used to purchase western land, but most speculators preferred to employ western land to retire state certificates, and, as we have seen, the act opening the western land office specified that specie and certificates alone would be received.[6]

While the Assembly was not prepared to use western land as a currency redemption resource, the legislators had to consider other redemption avenues to support public confidence in the new currency and hence its market value. The redemption debate within the Assembly continued, therefore,

3. Commissioners on behalf of the North Carolina Continental Line to the General Assembly, Legislative Papers, XLVII, April 30 folder, State Department of Archives and History, Raleigh.

4. William Henry Masterson, *William Blount* (Baton Rouge: Louisiana State University Press, 1954), pp. 68-69, 73-74.

5. *Ibid.*, p. 68, argues that the provision for payment of assemblymen was carefully included so as to gain support for the emission bill. Charles Jesse Bullock, *Essays on the Monetary History of the United States* (New York: Macmillan Company, 1900), pp. 193-94, contends that the primary motive behind the passage of the bill was the desire of the Assembly to be properly paid. Masterson's view may have merit, although his view that the chief motive was to provide money to purchase land is not, in this writer's opinion, a valid one. Bullock's interpretation ignores the genuine need for a circulatory medium as well as the pressing demand of the Line with its political overtones.

6. Walter Clark, ed., *The State Records of North Carolina* (16 vols.; Winston, Goldsboro, and Raleigh: State of North Carolina, 1895-1906) [volumes numbered consecutive to William L. Saunders, ed., *The Colonial Records of North Carolina* (10 vols.; Raleigh: State of North Carolina, 1886-90)], XXIV, 479. Above, p. 37.

between the advocates and opponents of fiat redemption. Probably because of public weariness with the old pretense of specie redemption, the emission act did not pledge that the currency would be redeemed with hard money. A number of legislators favored a sinking tax of two pence in the pound value of taxable property, which tax, it was maintained, could handily retire the 1783 currency within a few years.[7] The sinking tax bill was tabled,[8] however, and the Assembly instead provided, in the emission act, that all confiscated property was to be set aside exclusively as a fund to redeem the new currency.[9] The defeat of the sinking tax and the employment of tangible property were clear indications that even some fiat men were convinced that extraordinary steps were necessary to support the new currency; but, for several reasons, the allocation of confiscated property must be considered a policy designed for appearances rather than actual implementation. Speculators, as we have seen, preferred to use confiscated property (and western land) to retire certificates;[10] a number of legislators, if not a majority, preferred to employ fiat measures, as indicated by the introduction of the sinking tax bill; finally, the 1783 Assembly failed to establish procedures by which the confiscated property was to be sold to redeem the currency, and, as we have seen and shall again see, later Assemblies blocked such enabling legislation. The fact that the 1783 Assembly was more interested in appearance than substance is further indicated by

7. Richard Caswell to William Caswell, May 4, 1783, Clark, ed., *State Records*, XVI, 959. The original letter is in the Richard Caswell Papers, Southern Historical Collection, The University of North Carolina at Chapel Hill. Caswell stated that it was believed such a tax could retire not only the new currency (at face value) but also the old currency at the rate of eight hundred for one.

8. Clark, ed., *State Records*, XIX, 324, 362. The defeated bill is in the Legislative Papers, XLVIII, May 8 folder. The tax would have been levied upon polls and land and would have been payable in specie, new currency at par, old currency at eight hundred to one, and certificates at their legal rates. This is the same defeated sinking tax mentioned above, p. 23.

9. The emission act is found in Clark, ed., *State Records*, XXIV, 475-78.

10. Above, pp. 35-37.

another intriguing provision of the emission act: the annual property tax for revenue purposes was embodied in the emission act, a tax which the public might misconstrue (as has at least one historian) to be a sinking tax.[11] Thus, the emission act appeared to provide both a sinking tax and confiscated property as redemption methods, when, in fact, neither was inaugurated.

In addition to the matter of redemption policies there were other considerations affecting the reputation of the new currency. That an excessive amount not be issued (to reverse the policy associated with wartime emissions) was of great concern, balanced against which was the obvious fact that a very limited amount would be insufficient to meet the government's objectives. Faced with this perplexity, the Assembly debated emissions ranging from £60,000 to £80,000[12] before settling upon £100,000 as the sum that best resolved the dilemma.

Another effort to bolster the currency involved a series of conscious steps designed to disassociate the new money from the discredited war currencies and to associate it as closely as possible with specie. It was this same Assembly which, for several compelling reasons, enacted a scale of depreciation giving the old currency a future legal value of eight

11. Samuel A'Court Ashe, *History of North Carolina* (2 vols.; Raleigh: Edwards and Broughton Printing Company, 1925), II, 5. The act provided that any of the new currency received by the state treasurers in payment of the property tax should be held until further instructions from the Assembly. Because payment of the currency for any public purpose was not mandatory and because no instructions were ever given as to the disposal of the money received under the 1783 Assembly's direction, the provision of the emission act cannot be considered a sinking tax. Ashe concludes also that confiscated property was actually employed as of 1783 to retire the currency. As indicated above, pp. 35-36, confiscated property was not employed against the currency until 1785 and thereafter, and it probably retired little if any of the money.

12. Richard Caswell to William Caswell, May 4, 1783, Clark, ed., *State Records*, XVI, 959; Charles Johnson to Richard Benningham, May 5, 1783, *ibid.*, p. 961; Van Schellebeck and Mailhol to Jacob Blount, May 10, 1783, Alice Barnwell Keith and William Henry Masterson, eds., *The John Gray Blount Papers* (3 vols.; Raleigh: State Department of Archives and History, 1952-65), I, 56.

hundred to one as contrasted with the new currency's par value.[13] Further to distinguish new from old currency, the new emission's bills carried denominations of pound value rather than the traditional dollar values.[14] Also, a declared (though minor) purpose of the 1783 emission was to redeem old currency (at eight hundred for one), a provision that although it bespoke of many-headed monsters also gave the impression that a fresh start was being made as the new money supplanted the old. Having made these attempts at escaping the dim reputation of past currencies, the Assembly of 1783 boldly prescribed the value of the new money to various foreign coins.[15] These efforts to bolster public confidence promised to be of limited effectiveness, but the Assembly sought any methods that might lend a modicum of respect to the 1783 emission.

The passage of the emission act through the Assembly seems never to have been in doubt. Although the votes are not recorded in the Journals of the General Assembly, one legislator wrote privately in mid-May that the measure would undoubtedly become law.[16] Far more than any other factor, the claim of the Continental Line accounts for the emission of 1783 and the lack of serious opposition to it. Stating as its purposes the redemption of old currency and the payment of arrears to the Line, the act allocated £72,000 of the emission for the latter purpose. Each pound issued was declared the equal of 2.5 Spanish milled dollars, thus making the £100,000 legally equivalent to $250,000 and a Spanish milled dollar equal to eight shillings of the currency. The money was issued on the full faith and credit of the state and was declared legal tender in payment of all public and private debts. Thus, with the reluctant support of some legislators

13. This scale of depreciation, covered above, pp. 20-22, is found in Clark, ed., *State Records*, XXIV, 485.

14. As previously revealed, some of the acts emitting currencies during the Revolution had stated the total emissions in pound value, but the denominations had been issued in dollar values.

15. Clark, ed., *State Records*, XXIV, 486.

16. Charles Johnson to Richard Bennehan, May 14, 1783, Richard Bennehan Papers, Southern Historical Collection.

who saw no alternative to currency emission, the Assembly prepared to thrust its latest fiat creation upon the public.

Before turning to other matters, the 1783 Assembly took one last step to lend support to the new emission. Apparently under the conviction that a stay law would give the public time to adjust itself to the introduction of the new money, the Assembly suspended for one year all legal actions involving debts contracted earlier than May 1, 1783.[17] This act may have been designed additionally to give the impoverished members of the Line an opportunity to receive the new currency before additional suits for recovery were undertaken against them. In any event, debtors stood to benefit from the stay law, especially in view of the shortage of money. Some creditors undoubtedly favored the measure in order to await the fate of the currency in the market. Other creditors, however, waged a bitter and protracted debate against the bill's enactment,[18] and in so doing employed arguments bordering on the ingenious. No stay law was necessary, went one protest, because the currency's probable depreciation would serve the same effect by discouraging creditors from suing for debts that could not be collected at full value.[19] To enact a stay law, insisted another opponent, would be to lessen debtors' need for the currency and hence to accelerate the process of market depreciation; while, conversely, to allow executions for debt to continue would be to create great demand for the currency and thus to uphold its value.[20] A related argument was that the stay law would impede circulation of the currency.[21] These points unavailing, the Assembly was convinced that a stay law would ease the immediate problem of debtors—especially members of the Line—and would give the public, hopefully, time to ad-

17. Clark, ed., *State Records*, XXIV, 490-91.

18. James Hogg to James Iredell, May 17, 1783, Griffith John McRee, ed., *Life and Correspondence of James Iredell* (2 vols.; New York: D. Appleton and Company, 1867-68), II, 46.

19. Argument attached to stay bill in Legislative Papers, XLVIII, May 9 folder.

20. *Ibid.*

21. McRee, ed., *Iredell*, II, 63-64.

just itself to the currency and hence to stabilize the money's market value. As the 1783 Assembly adjourned, there were encouraging signs that important elements of the population were indeed prepared to support the new emission.

It must be emphasized that public reaction to the 1783 emission was not divided strictly along debtor-creditor or agrarian-mercantile lines. Agrarian elements—small farmers and large planters alike—had traditionally been indebted to merchants and hence during the colonial period had generally favored and secured fiat money; and certainly in 1783 many agrarian debtors, with malice toward the merchants,[22] eagerly awaited the new currency as a means to discharge their obligations cheaply. Posed against this eagerness, however, was bitter Revolutionary experience that qualified the attitude of many common people toward the prospect of another fiat emission. They, as the broad agrarian base of the state's economy, had inevitably been called upon to carry a great part of the war's financial burden, and the copious quantities of currency (and certificates) thrust into their hands had depreciated so rapidly and severely that they as well as their creditors had been badly injured. The memories of that wartime depreciation caused many people—debtors—to be deeply suspicious of the 1783 currency as it came into circulation.[23] Should it stabilize at something below par or should it depreciate slowly, it would offer debtors an opportunity to pay their debts with cheap money, but until the rate and degree of depreciation should become known, agrarian interests, to varying degrees, were cautious and skeptical.

More than upon any other single element, the fate of the currency depended upon the attitude of North Carolina merchants. As creditors to farmers and planters, and as men who

22. William Attmore, *Journal of a Tour to North Carolina*, ed. by Lida Tunstall Rodman ("The James Sprunt Historical Publications," Vol. 17, No. 2 [Chapel Hill: North Carolina Historical Society, 1922]), p. 40.

23. Johann David Schoepf, *Travels in the Confederation*, ed. and trans. by Alfred James Morrison (2 vols.; Philadelphia: William J. Campbell and Company, 1911), II, 129-30, 132.

had also suffered the ravages of wartime currency, the merchants generally deplored fiat currency in principle and in practice. While the majority of merchants therefore lamented the new emission act, there were several considerations that led some businessmen to look upon the currency with ambivalence, acquiescence, or even approval. One such consideration was the painfully obvious fact that mediums of exchange were in great shortage. Some merchants believed that fiat currency, if it could be stabilized in the market, offered the only feasible, acceptable remedy for that shortage. It was better to conduct business and collect debts with a reasonably stable though somewhat depreciated currency than to have those processes impeded or obstructed for lack of a sufficient circulating medium. If the currency could be stabilized, even at a point below par, the money, if carefully handled, could be circulated without loss and possibly even with advantage to merchants (and others as well).[24] So arguing, some merchants actively advocated and supported the idea of an emission. The 1783 emission bill was introduced at the Assembly by William Blount, a member of a prominent North Carolina mercantile family.[25] His brother John Gray Blount, one of the most active and successful merchants in the state, was a staunch friend of the currency before and after its emission, as were other merchants.[26]

Another factor that qualified the attitude of some merchants was that while they were creditors to many persons, they themselves were debtors to other merchants of the state and, more often, to mercantile interests outside North Carolina. A number of North Carolina merchants, in fact, came

24. Masterson, *William Blount*, p. 77, points out that William Blount had a thorough mastery of the values of the various currencies and certificates, which mastery enabled him to handle the mediums without loss and even with profit.

25. Clark, ed., *State Records*, XIX, 307.

26. Archibald Maclaine to James Iredell, November 26, 1789, McRee, ed., *Iredell*, II, 274; Van Schellebeck and Mailhol to Jacob Blount, May 10, 1783, and John Gray Blount and Thomas Blount to Hugh Williamson, December 20, 1783, Keith and Masterson, eds., *Blount*, I, 56, 142.

to dare their out-of-state creditors to sue for recovery in the postwar fiat currency.[27]

It must be remembered also that the matter of paying the Continental Line—both in itself and for its political implications—cut across economic lines and in so doing swung many hard-money men, as we shall see, behind the 1783 emission. All these considerations meant that while many debtors rejoiced and many creditors shuddered at the appearance of postwar fiat currency, many of the lower class were less than enthusiastic and many "respectable" members of society favored the emission.[28] One's position regarding the currency would depend upon a number of variables.

The attitude of the majority of merchants is clearly revealed by the actions of the citizens of the commercial center of Edenton. At a town meeting of August 1, 1783, a resolution expressing great concern about paper money generally was almost unanimously adopted. The town pledged, nevertheless, that it would support the new emission because the money was primarily designed to aid the Continental Line; but at the same time the meeting earnestly entreated the Assembly to emit no further paper. The assemblymen from the town and county were instructed to work for the early redemption and destruction of the paper so that public confidence and thus the money's value might be maintained. Having pledged themselves to support this particular emission, the residents of Edenton were quick to point out that, in their opinion, paper money generally had pernicious consequences: it could not be used outside the state; it paid nothing on the continental debt; and through the inflation of domestic prices and the destruction of confidence, it discouraged foreign trade.[29] Having emphasized its general opposition to fiat money but its acceptance of the 1783 emission in

27. Memorial of William Attmore to the General Assembly, Legislative Papers, LXXXIII.

28. That "respectable" elements of society had originated the 1783 emission is reported in Schoepf, *Travels*, II, 131-32. Other evidence to this effect has already been cited.

29. McRee, ed., *Iredell*, II, 60-66.

particular, Edenton formed an organization to support the value of the new currency.[30] Wilmington sought to emulate Edenton,[31] and the residents of Hillsborough were reportedly also ready to support the money.[32] Merchants who joined these organizations pledged themselves to accept the paper at nominal value in accordance with the law. At least initially the money was often accepted freely, and mercantile cooperation was sufficiently widespread to induce Governor Alexander Martin to write privately in the fall of 1783 that faith in the currency was "pretty well established" between merchant and planter.[33]

Martin's cautious optimism was not without some basis, but public confidence in and acceptance of the currency was by no means universal; at the time of the governor's statement depreciation had already begun. Those areas with close economic ties with other states were especially disdainful of the money, for it could not be used outside North Carolina in commercial transactions. Inhabitants of the Roanoke River–Halifax region, for example, usually sold crops for specie at Petersburg, Virginia, and thus had little use for the currency; in the summer of 1783 many of these individuals streamed to New Bern to buy large quantities of goods before the money depreciated in their hands.[34] This kind of onslaught was capable of undermining the confidence and determination—if such existed—of local merchants, and in the face of the Halifax invasion at least two New Bern stores, in violation

30. Archibald Maclaine to James Iredell, August 25, 1783, *ibid.*, p. 70. The original letter is in the James Iredell Papers, Duke University. The Iredell Papers at Duke University and the Charles E. Johnson Collection at the State Department of Archives and History contain the letters found in McRee's *Iredell.* McRee's editing makes an examination of these two collections highly desirable.

31. Archibald Maclaine to James Iredell, August 25, 1783, McRee, ed., *Iredell*, II, 70.

32. William Blount to John Gray Blount, November 6, 1783, Keith and Masterson, eds., *Blount*, I, 127.

33. Alexander Martin to John Gray Blount and Thomas Blount, September 27, 1783, *ibid.*, p. 113.

34. Schoepf, *Travels*, II, 129-30.

of the law, refused to accept the 1783 currency.[35] The refusal of one or two merchants tended to influence other merchants, even those who had favored the emission. Upon hearing of events at Halifax and New Bern, William Blount, who, it will be recalled, had introduced the emission bill, began to fear losses from depreciation and decided to pass along the currency as rapidly as possible by forming contracts specifying payment in the money.[36] Thomas Blount, partner to John Gray Blount, also began shying away from the 1783 currency.[37]

To the westward also the money was less than joyously received. Noting in October, 1783, that depreciation had begun, the Moravians of Salem were caught between their determination to abide by the law and their desire to avoid financial loss, a dilemma all the more painful because they could not use the currency in their extensive commerce with Philadelphia and Charleston. After several months of watchful waiting to see what the currency's fate would be, they adopted, in December, 1783, the policy of accepting the money at nominal value in their stores from persons outside the community, but preventing the circulation of the paper among the residents themselves. As for that currency coming into the town, the Moravians set aside sufficient amounts for the payment of taxes and sent the remainder to North Carolina coastal towns in payment for goods as a means of dividing more "proportionately" the losses resulting from depreciation.[38] By the end of 1783 rumors of that depreciation had grown so alarming that one of the state's delegates in Congress requested that his salary be converted from paper into produce as quickly as possible lest depreciation take a further bite from his income.[39]

35. William Blount to John Gray Blount, August 31, 1783, Keith and Masterson, eds., *Blount*, I, 98.

36. *Ibid.*

37. Thomas Blount to John Gray Blount, June 11, 1783, *ibid.*, p. 62.

38. Adelaide L. Fries and others, eds., *Records of the Moravians in North Carolina* (10 vols.; Raleigh: State Department of Archives and History, 1922-66) IV, 1856, 1858; V, 2045-46.

39. Hugh Williamson to John Gray Blount, December 5, 1783, Keith and Masterson, eds., *Blount*, I, 137-38.

The year 1784 did not see the reputation or acceptability of the currency improve. A traveler passing through North Carolina reported that those persons who came into the possession of more paper than could be used for taxes often sought to rid themselves of it as quickly as possible; that residents of the "middle part" of the state, around Halifax and on the Roanoke River, declined to give the currency any value at all; and that the paper, when accepted, was taken "squeamishly and unwillingly" everywhere in the state.[40] From the start Virginia merchants with branch houses in North Carolina absolutely and categorically refused to touch the currency at any of the branches.[41] Even the Moravians could not claim that they were unanimously abiding by the Tender Act, for the Richmond County Court in February, 1785, found two brethren guilty of "depreciating the currency," as indeed other Salemites were also doing. Hoping to prevent such unpleasantries, the town authorities gradually perfected means of circumventing the currency. Although continuing to honor paper arriving from outside the community, the inhabitants circulated among themselves "tickets" which, the town authorities maintained, would attract little attention from outside and would discourage the impression that a surplus of money resided in the town.[42] Emphasizing that the tickets must always be honored promptly with cash if they were to remain creditable, the Moravians thus disassociated themselves as much as possible from fiat currency and created their own circulating medium based upon Salem's specie resources.

The foregoing account amply illustrates that public confidence in and acceptance of the 1783 currency was far from universal and that depreciation therefore occurred. With that depreciation the traditional and perfectly predictable conflict between debtors and creditors began. Prominent members of

40. Schoepf, *Travels*, II, 129-30.

41. "Bill to prevent the selling of Goods . . . for hard money only and to prevent the depreciation of the currency," in Legislative Papers, LXXII, December 19 folder.

42. Fries, ed., *Moravian Records*, V, 2074, 2099.

the latter group claimed to be suffering terribly.[43] One creditor, when handed the unwanted currency as payment of a specie contract, expressed "surprise" and "disappointment" and threatened not to accept such payment again.[44] Another individual, doubtless voicing the sentiment of others, flew into a towering rage and bellowed that "licenteous perfidy, fraud, pride and poverty . . . spring of rags and paper . . . [and] are perfectly epidemic with us. The [losses] I have experienced deprive me of all patience on this subject."[45] Resentment reached such a point that, as the Moravians observed, the payment of hard-money contracts in paper money by "evil-minded" persons led to several "broken heads."[46] The Moravians, like many other North Carolinians, believed that the use of fiat money to pay specie contracts was a dishonest if not illegal practice—but one which, at least the Moravians felt, could occasionally involve extenuating circumstances and an object lesson. When a resident of Salem paid an exhorbitant medical fee with paper, for example, the elders censured the patient for setting a bad precedent but also informed the physician that the excessive fee had caused the unfortunate episode.[47]

Not all debtors rushed to pay their specie debts with paper, perhaps in some instances because they themselves were also creditors. John Wright Stanly, prominent New Bern merchant, prescribed in his will that his debts should be paid "honestly," that is, in specie rather than paper where specie had been specified.[48] Another "honest" policy, if one had insufficient specie, was to pay in currency with adequate al-

43. For typical remarks concerning injury from depreciation, see Samuel Johnston to Alexander Elmsly, June 24, 1784, Hayes Collection (microfilm), reel number four, Southern Historical Collection.

44. William Littlejohn to Mrs. Pearson, May 15, 1784, *ibid.*

45. Walter Jones to Frederick Jones, December 20, 1784, Swann Papers, Southern Historical Collection.

46. Fries., ed., *Moravian Records*, V, 2045.

47. *Ibid.*, p. 2234.

48. A typed copy of the will, dated 1788, is in the Edmund Ruffin Beckwith Papers, Southern Historical Collection.

lowance for depreciation.[49] Some persons wrestled with their consciences before succumbing to the temptation or necessity of proffering the currency at nominal value, as one may see in the case of a debtor who, while paying his hard-money debt with legal tender currency, informed his creditor emphatically that the currency would serve all the purposes of specie and that all rumors to the contrary were groundless.[50] Undoubtedly many debtors would have preferred to honor their specie obligations but could find no means to do so and thus reluctantly used the paper. Their state of mind is exemplified by the gentleman who proclaimed that he felt honor-bound to pay a specie debt with hard money—unless absolute necessity demanded the use of currency.[51] Other debtors, of course, felt no qualms of conscience. Regardless of the debtor's mental attitude, creditors had to bear the burden of depreciation.

The outcry of creditors, together with the hesitancy or refusal of individuals to accept the currency, would seem to indicate a severe rate of depreciation. Because "severe" depreciation bears no absolute definition, the most appropriate comparison for passing judgment on the extent of that depreciation is the currency depreciation that the people had recently experienced, that is, the wartime emissions. When placed within that frame of reference and within the realities of eighteenth-century North Carolina finance, the 1783 currency enjoyed remarkable reputation and stability. In contrast to the steady, rapid, and complete depreciation of the war money, the postwar currency depreciated to an average of about 25 per cent off specie in the purchase of commodities and then stabilized at about 12.5 per cent to 15 per cent off nominal value when exchanged for hard money.[52] Most of

49. Thomas Blount to John Gray Blount, June 11, 1783, Keith and Masterson, eds., *Blount*, I, 62.

50. John Nelson to John Gray Blount, August 17, 1783, *ibid.*, p. 84.

51. Edward Rice to James Iredell, June 27, 1784, James Iredell Papers, Duke University.

52. William Blount to John Gray Blount, August 31, 1783, Keith and Masterson, eds., *Blount*, I, 98; James White to the President of New Hampshire, August 11, 1786, Edmund Cody Burnett, ed., *Letters*

this depreciation apparently occurred by late 1783, after which time the paper's value remained practically steady for two years. This relatively high degree of value may be attributed to factors covered earlier in the chapter. The various actions of the 1783 Assembly designed to bolster the currency contributed to the money's success; the fact that the currency could be used to pay the annual money tax on property increased the acceptability of the paper; the "extreme necessity" for mediums of exchange enhanced the currency's standing;[53] and, of critical importance, the merchant class generally supported the currency, which support was considerably induced —as with other segments of the population—by the fact that most of the money went to pay the Continental Line. Depreciation did occur and losses thus were sustained, but the burden, while painful to creditors, was not intolerable, and the chief purpose of the emission was served.

The forces that upheld the currency's value were sufficient to withstand the continued refusal of the Assembly to employ confiscated property exclusively as a fund to retire the 1783 emission. The 1783 Assembly, it will be recalled, had made such provision but had failed to pass enabling legislation.[54] As treated in the previous chapter, this failure is attributable to the fact that speculators and other persons as well preferred that the property be used to redeem elements of the certificate debt.[55] At the spring Assembly of 1784 the debate over redemption policies continued. Deadlock ensued. The Assembly, it will be remembered, turned back a bill that would have empowered certain individuals to sell confiscated property to retire the 1783 currency.[56] Advocates of a sinking tax, despite Governor Martin's backing,[57] found insufficient

of Members of the Continental Congress (8 vols.; Washington: Carnegie Institution, 1921-36), VIII, 420; John Huske to Governor Richard Caswell, September 28, 1785, Governors' Papers, XI, 102, State Department of Archives and History, Raleigh.

53. Schoepf, *Travels*, II, 129. The whole idea of fiat currency was, of course, that "extreme necessity" *would* give value to the currency.

54. Above, pp. 59, 60.

55. Above, pp. 35-37.

56. Above, p. 35.

57. Clark, ed., *State Records*, XIX, 498.

support to propose such a measure. As the Assembly session came to a close, the legislators were quite aware that the currency's reputation was in jeopardy because no redemption means had been established. Commenting on the Assembly's sensitivity concerning the paper money situation, James Iredell wrote privately and caustically that he dared not mention the term "sterling value" at the Assembly, for to do so implied a lack of confidence in the recent emission and would be considered disrespectful.[58]

At the fall Assembly of 1784, it will be recalled, a compromise was reached, after much debate and negotiation, between those who wished to retire certificates and those who wished to redeem the currency with the confiscated property.[59] The law specified that payment could be made in new currency or in certificates issued to the Continental Line. Evidence indicates that little if any currency was subsequently received,[60] and because the law did not make explicit that any such currency was to be destroyed, it is possible—for lack of any evidence of destruction—that money was received only to be quietly recirculated. Discreet recirculation, while ethically questionable, would cleverly serve the purposes of government because the amount of circulating mediums would not be reduced while the reputation of the currency would at the same time be aided—as long as the public remained unaware of the recirculation.

The fall Assembly of 1784, because of the government's need for revenue, took notice of the currency's depreciation. In a limited step reminiscent of the government's patchwork devaluation of the wartime currencies, the Assembly declared that in the collection of imposts the standard between the "monies" of North Carolina and sterling and the standard between the "monies" of North Carolina and the "monies"

58. James Iredell to Henry Eustace M'Culloch, June 15, 1784, Charles E. Johnson Collection, State Department of Archives and History, Raleigh.

59. Above, pp. 35-36.

60. The reports on the sale of confiscated property, above pp. 36-37, make no mention of currency received, and no other evidence has come to the attention of the author.

of foreign countries should be 77.66 per cent.[61] This cautious, limited step toward currency devaluation may have been part of the compromise between fiat elements and those who wished to retire certificates with the confiscated property. While the currency remained legal tender for all other purposes, the future of the currency remained a matter of debate and doubt.

An evaluation of the 1783 fiat emission clearly establishes that it was neither a smashing success nor a resounding failure. At no cost to itself the Assembly created a currency that did pay part of the arrears due the Line and retired some small part of the old wartime currencies. The complaints of creditors notwithstanding, the paper stabilized at a level not too far below par and greatly above that of the worthless wartime currencies. While enjoying these successes, however, the new money was attended by certain inescapable limitations and disadvantages. The very considerations that argued in favor of a modest emission precluded that a sufficient, viable medium of exchange could be created to meet the needs of the domestic economy. Also, the currency's appearance accelerated the tendency to hoard specie and, of course, did nothing to stem the exodus of specie from the state. As complaints arose that mediums of exchange—especially coins—were as scarce as before the emission or even more so,[62] the advocates of the emission did not deny the continuing or worsening shortage. John Gray Blount, for example, could offer only that the currency would increase in value as specie

61. Clark, ed., *State Records*, XXIV, 659.

62. These complaints and reports are numerous. See, for example, Schoepf, *Travels*, II, 129; James Read to Governor Richard Caswell, July 19, 1785, Clark, ed., *State Records*, XVII, 483; Thomas Polk to William Blount, July 5, 1783, and William Blount to John Gray Blount, September 4, 1783, Keith and Masterson, eds., *Blount*, I, 68, 101. See also the following in the Legislative Papers: petition of the inhabitants of Edenton, LX, December 19 folder; petition, LIX, December 14 folder; petition from Anson County, LX, undated folder. Also, P. G. Roulhac to his mother, March 1, 1786 (copy), Ruffin-Roulhac-Hamilton Papers, Southern Historical Collection.

grew scarcer,[63] the type of statement that gave absolutely no comfort to hard-money men. Undoubtedly reflecting the disgust of many other opponents of fiat policy, Archibald Maclaine of Wilmington observed bitterly that emission policy had resulted both in depreciation of the currency and a greater shortage of money.[64] If, then, the 1783 emission achieved its chief immediate purpose—payment to the Line—but failed to alleviate the tenacious shortage of money, the emission accomplished neither more nor less than most of its proponents asked of it. Advocates of fiat currency never considered the policy to be a panacea, for, in fact, there was no short-range solution to the state's economic and financial problems. The number and intensity of the government's financial responsibilities, moreover, continued to increase—and thus the battle lines began to form over the question of another emission of fiat currency.

The financial problems facing the government of North Carolina as of mid-1785 were generated by the state's internal needs and by its financial responsibilities to the government of the United States. Internally, money was most immediately needed to pay the civil list and to redeem, as a matter of justice and policy, certificates that had been issued by the state to the members of its Continental Line. As for the state's responsibilities to the United States, the public was well aware that North Carolina had made no contributions to the operating expenses of the national government, to the discharge of the foreign debt of the United States, or to the redemption of the domestic certificate debt of Congress. These urgent considerations, together with the continuing general shortage of money, caused the question of another emission to become a major issue during the election campaign for the 1785 Assembly.[65] Candidates opposing emission argued that the

63. John Gray Blount and Thomas Blount to Hugh Williamson, December 20, 1783, Keith and Masterson, eds., *Blount*, I, 142.

64. Archibald Maclaine to George Hooper, January 17, 1784, Clark, ed., *State Records*, XVII, 126.

65. William Richardson Davie to Spruce Macay, July 13, 1785, Macay-McNeeley Papers, Southern Historical Collection.

printing of more fiat currency would be unwise, self-defeating, and unconscionable; proponents—with attitudes ranging from enthusiasm to resignation—emphasized the many needs for money and the lack of alternatives to fiat emission. When the election results were tallied, it was clear that the forthcoming Assembly would be strongly disposed toward emission.

The prospect of more fiat currency appearing on the market created uncertainty and alarm among many creditors and merchants and thus served to undermine the reputation and market value of the 1783 money. Contemporary estimates vary somewhat, but it appears that in the purchase of commodities the currency's value slipped from about 25 per cent off nominal value to perhaps 35 per cent off par, while in exchange for specie the currency declined from about 15 per cent off par to about 25 per cent off nominal value.[66] Although the currency remained far from worthless, many persons had just reason to complain and to face the future with anxiety.

As the 1785 Assembly convened at New Bern on November 19, it was clear that mercantile support—so vital to the stabilization of the 1783 currency—would not be enjoyed by any further emission. A petition to the Assembly from the merchants and traders of New Bern opposed additional fiat currency on the grounds that they, as creditors, would be the chief victims of depreciation.[67] The inhabitants of Edenton, emphasizing that they had supported the 1783 money on the understanding that no further emissions would occur, argued that another emission would not solve the state's financial difficulties. The Edenton petition maintained that an additional fiat issue would further depreciate the existing currency and drive specie out of circulation through the hoarding

66. Petition from the town of Washington to the General Assembly, Legislative Papers, LX, December 19 folder; Hugh Williamson, *Letters from Sylvius* ("Historical Papers of Trinity College Historical Society," Series 11 [Durham: Trinity College Historical Society, 1915]), p. 8; Clark, ed., *State Records*, XX, 75.

67. Legislative Papers, LIX, December 14 folder.

process. A scarcity of currency works its own relief in time, continued the petition, by lowering the price of commodities and thereby attracting specie from abroad to purchase them; a new emission, to the contrary, would cause inflation and thus discourage foreign purchases of state produce. The true solution to North Carolina's problems, the petition concluded, was the honoring of contracts.[68] From the town of Washington came a petition opposing emission and stating that rumors of a new emission had already depreciated the 1783 currency.[69] With these petitions the merchants put the Assembly on notice that widespread mercantile support of new currency could not be expected.

Gathering the spectrum of traditional arguments against fiat currency, a trenchant minority of legislators struggled furiously to persuade the Assembly against emission. As at the 1783 Assembly, their essential problem was that their alternatives, while valid in theory, were long-range in nature and thus could do nothing to meet the exigencies of government. To talk of the development of industry, the creation of a favorable balance of trade, the virtues of a specie economy, and the wisdom of honoring contracts was to ignore the economic and financial realities of eighteenth-century North Carolina.[70] Their arguments, in short, were flawless but irrelevant. Thus not only agrarians and debtors at the Assembly advocated emission, but also others who saw no other course than to issue fiat currency. As the money depreciated, they argued, it would, in effect, serve as another tax to distribute the cost of government.[71] Opponents might grumble in reply that it

68. *Ibid.*, LX, December 19 folder.

69. *Ibid.*

70. The argument for the development of industry and all that would follow from that development was presented during the ratification struggle in North Carolina, and it is reasonable to assume that the same argument was made at the 1785 Assembly. Hard-money men at that Assembly could only have been embarrassed by a petition suggesting that the state mint gold and silver and place the specie in the treasury to support the currency. Where the state was to obtain the specie the petitioner did not explain. See Memorial of Henry Lutterloh, Legislative Papers, LVIII, November 27 folder.

71. Williamson, *Letters from Sylvius*, p. 11.

was a pernicious tax indeed that primarily harmed the honest and frugal man,[72] but their rebuttal was lost amid the eloquence of immediate necessity. Hard-money legislators held no illusions that their fight would be successful; one of them, Archibald Maclaine, acknowledged privately that "the great majority" in both houses favored emission.[73]

If the Assembly was determined upon a new emission, the legislators were well aware that upholding the new money's reputation was all the more an important and difficult task in view of merchant opposition and the existence of the 1783 currency. As a first step, the great majority of legislators favored limiting the amount to £100,000,[74] an amount which could sufficiently meet the immediate needs of government yet which had not led to drastic depreciation following the 1783 emission. A second move was to retain the pounds-value denominations so that the new money would be associated with the relatively successful 1783 currency rather than with the discredited war currencies. Also, as in 1783, the Assembly avoided the pretense that the 1785 currency would be redeemed with specie.

The primary consideration was, of course, what redemption pledge *would* be made, and, predictably enough, the advocates of tangible property and of fiat policy were once again joined in debate. As revealed in the previous chapter,[75] opposition to employing confiscated property exclusively to retire currency remained steadfast at the 1785 Assembly, and in fact the legislators broadened the use of the property so as to include the retirement of new currency (both 1783 and

72. *Ibid.* Another argument advanced by the advocates of emission was that Britain, France, and most other commercial nations circulated paper mediums in the form of bank notes and government securities. Critics easily retorted that those mediums proved useful because nobody was compelled to accept them and because the public was confident that specie lay behind the paper, all-important factors missing in the case of fiat legal tender. *Ibid.*, p. 8.

73. Archibald Maclaine to Samuel Johnston, December 24, 1785, Hayes Collection (microfilm), reel number four, Southern Historical Collection.

74. *Ibid.*

75. Above, p. 36.

1785), currency certificates at their legal values, and all types of certificates issued to the Continental Line.[76] This action, essentially a speculators' victory, was taken despite the new emission and could serve only to weaken the postwar money. Deeply concerned about the currency's future, four senators formally protested that the 1783 emission had been based entirely upon the pledge that confiscated property would be used exclusively to retire the money.[77]

Concern for the currency was, in fact, general throughout both houses. Aware of the money's jeopardy and content with their victory regarding certificates and confiscated property, speculators were prepared to join fiat men in the enactment of a sinking tax. The tax, which was a light one considered inadequate by some observers, was incorporated into the 1785 emission bill and was to be levied annually upon property until the "paper money in circulation" should be retired.[78] That some measure, even a fiat one, was taken to uphold the currency was some measure of cold comfort to recalcitrant hard-money men.[79] Also of comfort was the explicit provision that currency collected by the sinking tax should not be recirculated, a provision designed to reassure persons who suspected such governmental chicanery.[80] The currencies of 1783 and of 1785 would, then, be supported

76. Clark, ed., *State Records*, XX, 115.

77. *Ibid.* The protest argued additionally that some certificates had already been refused for the purchase of confiscated property.

78. *Ibid.*, XXIV, 725. The tax rates were six pence per one hundred acres of land, eighteen pence per poll, and eighteen pence per one hundred pounds value of town property. These rates were around one-sixth the rates levied by the certificate sinking tax. For comment that the currency sinking tax rates were too low to be effective, see James Madison to Thomas Jefferson, August 12, 1786, Julian P. Boyd and others, eds., *The Papers of Thomas Jefferson* (17 vols.; Princeton: Princeton University Press, 1950-65), X, 231.

79. Benjamin Hawkins to James Madison, June 3, 1789, Elizabeth Gregory McPherson, ed., "Unpublished Letters from North Carolinians to James Madison and James Monroe," *North Carolina Historical Review*, XIV, No. 2 (April, 1937), 165.

80. Recirculation of fiat money collected by regular taxes was itself a painful experience for hard-money advocates. See Williamson, *Letters from Sylvius*, p. 10.

by the existence of a sinking tax and the acceptability of the money in the purchase of confiscated property. If the Assembly had failed again to use confiscated property exclusively as a currency redemption fund, something of a compromise between fiat and hard-money legislators had been reached over the matter of currency retirement: each approach was to be employed.

As the emission bill made its way through the Assembly, its opponents did what they could. On the measure's second reading in the House, Representative John Gray Blount moved to lay the bill over until the next Assembly and, in the meantime, to have it published in the *North Carolina Gazette* "for the information of the public at large." Rather than indicating opposition to emission, Blount's action simply demonstrated a desire that the public—especially merchants and other creditors—have time to become accustomed to the prospect of more fiat currency, but in view of his family's sponsorship and advocacy of the 1783 emission, his caution is significant. By a vote of twenty-six to fifty-four Blount's motion and caution were rejected.[81] After the House passed the emission bill on second reading, opponents took another tack by proposing an amendment specifying that if the new emission depreciated the 1783 currency (a certainty which, as indicated, was already underway), jurors should take such depreciation into account when rendering debt judgments. This amendment, which had wartime precedent and which would have effected the abandonment of legal tender in private transactions, met defeat by a vote of twenty-two to fifty-five, and shortly thereafter the emission bill passed final reading in the House by a vote of fifty-two to twenty-one.[82] Support

81. Clark, ed., *State Records*, XVII, 364-65. The minority consisted of twenty eastern-county votes, three western votes, and the votes of Edenton, Wilmington, and Halifax. The majority consisted of strong support from east and west, in addition to the votes of New Bern and Hillsborough. Obviously support for a fiat emission could be found in the towns, as evidenced also by a fiat petition from the inhabitants (as opposed to the "merchants and traders") of New Bern. *Ibid.*, p. 349.

82. *Ibid.*, pp. 365-66, 405-6. The minority favoring the amendment consisted primarily of eastern votes together with the votes of several

for the measure had come from representatives of western and eastern counties and of several towns; the legislators who had sought to defeat, delay, or amend the bill represented eastern counties primarily, with support from several towns. While many merchants clearly opposed the measure and while some eastern counties with significant out-of-state commercial contacts were also against emission, the voting pattern establishes that emission had strong support in both east and west and within some towns. Despite the opponents' disposition to look upon the act as class legislation, the impelling needs of government and of the economy caused the issue to cut across sectional lines and, to a considerably lesser degree than in 1783, across class lines. Upon the bill's final passage in the House, eight of the measure's enemies—including, significantly enough, John Gray Blount—formally protested its enactment on the following grounds: that it would only further depreciate the existing legal tender; that the merchants, whose backing was necessary to support the credit of the currency, could no longer be depended upon to support a fiat emission; that creditors would be injured by having to accept depreciated money at nominal value; that inflation and specie hoarding would prevent the emission from relieving the shortage of money; and that the lack of confidence in the currency and in the government of the state would further decrease the flow of commerce into the ports of North Carolina.[83] Again, the arguments were completely sound but unfortunately irrelevant to the pressing needs of government and the conditions of the times. Thus, one may at the same time sympathize with those who favored emission and those who bitterly complained, as did another of the protest-signers, that the 1785 emission was passed because of the absence of sufficient knowledge, principle, and "gentlemen" at the Assembly.[84]

towns. On the bill's third reading in the House, the majority was comprised of strong support from east and west and the votes of New Bern and Hillsborough.

83. Clark, ed., *State Records*, XVII, 410-12.

84. Archibald Maclaine to James Iredell, March 6, 1786, McRee, ed., *Iredell*, II, 138.

In the Senate the emission bill breezed through its three readings by votes of thirty-six to seven, thirty-one to eight, and thirty-one to seven.[85] Realizing the hopelessness of their cause, its opponents attempted, upon second reading, to reduce the size of the emission, but by a vote of twelve to twenty-eight, even that concession was denied them.[86] Upon the bill's final passage in the Senate, a formal protest argued, among other things, that fiat emission was founded upon mistaken policy and was inaccurately justified on the basis of necessity; that paper money, as experience with the 1783 currency had shown, worked to the disadvantage of commerce because the paper served no purposes outside the state; that fiat currency worked to the advantage of the dishonest debtor and to the injury of the impartial creditor; that Virginia and South Carolina merchants, by refusing to accept North Carolina paper and insisting upon payment in specie or produce, had greatly benefited by North Carolina's fiat policy; and that in order to escape being paid in depreciated currency, citizens of North Carolina had been instituting suits against other North Carolina citizens in out-of-state courts, a practice by which North Carolina merchants especially had suffered.[87] This Senate protest, together with that of the House, served only to emphasize that a new emission had been enacted.

Justified by the "pressing circumstances of our foreign and domestic debt," the act of 1785 emitted the £100,000 specifically to discharge a portion of the foreign debt of the United States, to pay part of the current expenses of the United States, to make provision for the state's civil list, to redeem continental loan office certificates (part of the domestic debt of the United States), and to redeem final settlement certificates issued by the state to its Continental Line. As with the 1783 money, each pound of the 1785 currency was declared to be equal to 2.5 Spanish milled dollars; issued upon the

85. Clark, ed., *State Records*, XX, 68, 81, 102.

86. *Ibid.*, p. 82. Opponents sought to reduce the emission from £100,000 to £80,000.

87. *Ibid.*, pp. 111-12.

faith and credit of the state, the money was proclaimed legal tender in payment of all public and private contracts. Because the currency was worthless outside the state and thus could not be directly used to meet North Carolina's responsibilities to the United States, the emission act set aside £36,000 of the new emission for the purchase of tobacco, which would in turn be sold outside the state for specie or bills of exchange acceptable at the United States Treasury. The money going into the United States Treasury was to be credited to North Carolina in discharge of the state's portion of the foreign debt of the United States.[88]

If the emission act's sinking-tax provision somewhat aided the new currency's reputation, the act contained another feature that some legislators believed was undermining the money before it ever hit the market. In providing for commissioners to purchase the tobacco for the state, the act authorized them to pay up to fifty shillings per one hundred pounds weight of tobacco, a price well above the market price for tobacco. Critics maintained that the high maximum price authorized by the Assembly implied that the legislature itself did not consider the new currency to be truly a legal tender and thus was acting in bad faith in making it such; and, since the market price for tobacco was actually dropping everywhere at the time the Assembly was prescribing an artificially high price, the new emission would be doomed from the first to rapid depreciation.[89] There is reason to think that the legislators, many of whom grew tobacco, were indeed acting in bad faith. During debate on the emission bill the House had defeated by a vote of thirty-four to forty-eight an effort to establish the maximum purchase price at forty shil-

88. *Ibid.*, XXIV, 722-25. The intent of the act was to apply the revenue from the public tobacco program to the foreign debt of the United States, but the word "foreign" was unintentionally omitted from the act. The omission had great political significance and caused considerable uncertainty as to North Carolina's intent. See above, pp. 198, 200-1.

89. Williamson, *Letters from Sylvius*, p. 10; Archibald Maclaine to Samuel Johnston, December 24, 1785, Hayes Collection (microfilm), reel number four, Southern Historical Collection.

lings. In the Senate an attempt to provide a flexible procedure of paying the current, local market price for the tobacco had met defeat by a vote of seventeen to twenty-three.[90] One basis for the protest in the Senate to the passage of the bill was that the fifty-shilling price would be a "mischievous and ruinous policy." The protest reflected, perhaps intentionally, the impression that the commissioners were restricted to paying fifty shillings per hundred pounds weight, when in fact they were to pay no more than that amount. Whether honestly or dishonestly held, such a mistaken conviction could only harm the reputation and value of the new currency as it entered the market.

Within a few weeks the currency was suffering as if a mandatory fifty-shilling price had indeed been established by the Assembly, for the commissioners adopted the practice of paying the maximum authorized price.[91] Not only was the postwar money undermined, but, as growers rushed to sell their tobacco to the state at a price that individual purchasers could not or would not pay, private transactions ground to a halt.[92] The Moravians noted in November, 1786, that public tobacco policy had left tobacco rotting in the streets of Wilmington, a phenomenon probably caused in part by planter unwillingness to deal with private merchants.[93]

Although the public tobacco program harmed the market status of the currency, the forewarned hostility of most of the merchant class was a more ominous and detrimental factor militating against the money. Distaste for the paper was strong, and there was a significant disposition among North Carolina merchants to refuse the currency in defiance of the law. Merchants in the Fayetteville area, for example, took "uncommon pains" to deprecate the currency by pointedly

90. Clark, ed., *State Records*, XVII, 365; XX, 82-83.

91. See advertisement in the *North Carolina Gazette* (Hillsborough), February 16, 1786 (microfilm), North Carolina Collection, The University of North Carolina at Chapel Hill.

92. Archibald Maclaine to James Iredell, March 6, 1786, McRee, ed., *Iredell*, II, 139; James Madison to Thomas Jefferson, August 12, 1786, Boyd, ed., *Jefferson Papers*, X, 231.

93. Fries, ed., *Moravian Records*, V, 2145.

informing local planters that the merchants would not sell merchandise for currency that was no better than blank paper except for the payment of taxes.[94] Many tradesmen throughout the state, in fact, would sell goods only for specie, or for currency at "considerable discount."[95] Even western merchants, who generally had more use for fiat currency, were suspicious of the new emission.[96] The Salem community considered the currency "bad money," and so serious became the dislike for it that the town authorities declined to dictate a common policy toward accepting it; instead, each merchant was to be guided by the circumstances. While warning that Moravians could get into trouble by openly depreciating the currency, Salem authorities continued to advise local merchants to traffic in the paper as little as possible. Eventually, as currency continued to pour into Salem, Moravian respect for the law crumbled and the elders proclaimed that paper money would have to be accepted at its local real value rather than at its face value.[97] It is clear, in summary, that the support of the merchant class, so vital to the stabilization of the 1783 currency and of any fiat emission, was sadly lacking on behalf of the 1785 money. The merchants who had supported the previous emission out of a sense of justice to the Continental Line and upon the understanding that no further emission would be forthcoming felt betrayed by the 1785 Assembly. The purposes of the new emission made no appeal to sentiment and, to many persons, spoke only of the all-too-familiar many-headed monster. The experience of the 1783 emission indicated, moreover, that the new fiat emission would not alleviate the shortage of money. Also, in their role as creditors, the merchants stood to lose from the currency's depreciation. For many reasons, therefore, most merchants

94. Robert Rowan to Governor Richard Caswell, April 20, 1786, Clark, ed., *State Records*, XVIII, 597.

95. A bill designed to prevent such practices is in the Legislative Papers, LXXII, December 19 folder.

96. James Hogg to James Iredell, January 19, 1786, McRee, ed., *Iredell*, II, 132.

97. Fries, ed., *Moravian Records*, V, 2135, 2138, 2141, 2276, 2283.

were unprepared to support the 1785 fiat currency to the extent that they had backed the 1783 emission.

Suspicion of the currency again extended beyond commercial elements and into the ranks of the general population. Only with great difficulty, for example, could troops being sent to the frontier in 1786 employ the paper to purchase provisions from western residents.[98] It was later reported that in the western areas of the state the tender was uniformly rejected and that in private transactions specie alone could purchase land.[99] Open and flagrant violations of the law could also be found to the eastward, as exemplified by a public announcement that the Warrenton Academy would accept tuition payments in currency at its "real" (rather than its nominal) value.[100]

Understandably, creditors—whether merchants or otherwise—were especially alarmed and nervous at the prospect of being handed the new currency in payment of specie contracts. As debtors, some few with pangs of conscience, began to offer the paper, the rage and disgust of creditors knew no limits. Richard Dobbs Spaight, a leading citizen, stated bluntly that the 1785 Tender Act was "alarming and destructive" and had disgraced the character of the Assembly.[101] A New Bern creditor publicly labeled paper money a "cursed engine of fraud, oppression and vexation" and condemned every "dishonest" debtor "who with a bundle of ragged, depreciated paper in each hand is bidding defiance to his creditor."[102] Another sputtered that "Government has no Idea, that [paper] Money is an equivalent for Forgery or any Crime."[103] The irascible Archibald Maclaine commented bit-

98. Deposition concerning John Markland, Legislative Papers, XCII.

99. John Wilson to James Wilson, January 11, 1789, L. C. Glenn Papers, Southern Historical Collection.

100. *State Gazette of North Carolina* (Edenton), September 28, 1788 (microfilm), North Carolina Collection.

101. Richard Dobbs Spaight to James Iredell, August 12, 1787, McRee, ed., *Iredell*, II, 169.

102. *State Gazette of North Carolina* (New Bern), March 27, 1788 (microfilm), North Carolina Collection.

103. William Cumming to James Iredell, July 25, 1787, Charles E.

terly as the new money came into circulation, "I believe those who have sold their property for paper, will be good boys, and never do so again."[104]

The existence of fiat currency within North Carolina plagued out-of-state creditors. Advising one such creditor not to sue for recovery of a debt, James Iredell regretfully informed a Charleston firm in June, 1787, that judges would not allow the nominal value of the currency to be altered even with the consent of the debtor and creditor involved in the case.[105] When Iredell indicated that only a jury composed of merchants would be interested in seeing justice done, he oversimplified the situation. As indicated previously, North Carolina merchants were not always above defying their creditors and daring them to sue for recovery in the depreciated currency.[106] Indeed, it should be re-emphasized that no generalizations may be made regarding support for the money without the firm realization that exceptions existed. Thus, while most merchants were firmly opposed to the 1785 emission, some merchants and other prominent individuals continued to support the emission policy for lack of immediate alternative solutions to the state's financial difficulties;[107] and while, as we have seen, debtors used the currency to pay specie debts, popular suspicion of fiat currency—due in large part to wartime experience—could also be found.

The hue and cry over the 1785 money would indicate, once again, that depreciation was severe, and, again, the only valid basis for passing judgment is the previous experience

---

Johnson Collection, State Department of Archives and History, Raleigh.

104. Archibald Maclaine to James Iredell, March 6, 1787, McRee, ed., *Iredell*, II, 139.

105. James Iredell to William McLeod & Co., June 26, 1787, Charles E. Johnson Collection, State Department of Archives and History, Raleigh.

106. William Attmore to Governor Samuel Johnston, February 29, 1788, Governors' Papers, Series II, Box IV (Johnston); Memorial of William Attmore to the Assembly, November 4, 1788, Legislative Papers, LXXXIII.

107. Attmore, *Journal*, pp. 20-21; Archibald Maclaine to James Iredell, November 26, 1789, McRee, ed., *Iredell*, II, 274.

of the population. Compared with the wartime emissions the 1785 currency retained considerable value, but, as one might anticipate, the 1785 money did not fare as well as had the 1783 emission. Evidence indicates that the 1785 currency depreciated steadily during 1786 so that by the meeting of the Assembly late that year twelve shillings currency would bring eight shillings specie, a depreciation of 33.33 per cent.[108] This exchange rate depreciation was roughly 2.5 times as great as that suffered by the 1783 currency before the second emission; and, as predicted, the 1785 emission dragged the earlier currency down to the same lower value.[109] The greater depreciation resulted from the alienation of most merchants, from the fifty-shilling provision and practice of the public tobacco program, and from the very fact that another fiat emission had taken place and had raised fears of yet additional emissions. The considerable value that the currency retained was due to the absolute need for money, to the acceptability of the money in payment of taxes, and to the employment of confiscated property and the sinking tax as redemption modes. The new currency did enable the state to pay the civil list, to redeem certificates issued to the Line, and to provide a means, however faulty, of making payments upon the foreign debt of the United States.[110] While achieving these immediate goals, the 1785 currency failed to alleviate the general shortage of money and continued to drive specie from circulation. As one person described the latter process in January, 1786, specie grew scarcer every day in proportion to the amounts of the new money initially hitting

108. Richard Bennehan's business ledgers, Cameron Papers, Southern Historical Collection; William Cumming to Governor Richard Caswell, July 17, 1786, Clark, ed., *State Records*, XVIII, 689; Governor Richard Caswell to Benjamin Hawkins, September 29, 1787, *ibid.*, p. 751; *ibid.*, p. 309; James Madison to Thomas Jefferson, August 12, 1786, Boyd, ed., *Jefferson Papers*; X, 231; James Iredell to Mrs. James Iredell, October 17, 1786, Charles E. Johnson Collection, State Department of Archives and History, Raleigh.

109. Samuel Johnston to Nathaniel Dukinfield, January 11, 1786, Hayes Collection (microfilm), reel number four, Southern Historical Collection.

110. The public tobacco program is examined above, pp. 198-214.

the market, and, indeed, as even businessmen resorted to burying their gold and silver, specie virtually ceased to circulate for the remainder of the confederation period.[111] At the same time, the undeniable arguments in favor of restricting the size of fiat emissions meant that the amount of currency was insufficient to meet the economy's needs. Echoing an observation that had been made by Archibald Maclaine after the 1783 emission, James Iredell wrote, following the second emission, that paper money was genuinely scarce despite the fact that it was of so little value.[112]

The shortcomings of fiat policy, the absence of any feasible short-range alternative, and the continuing needs of government left the Assembly without options except to consider more emissions and to attempt to shore up the existing currency. Toward the latter goal the 1786 Assembly modified the public tobacco program so that the commissioners were to pay no more than the local market price.[113] How else to

111. See the following in Clark, ed., *State Records*: Charles Johnston to Governor Richard Caswell, January 14, 1786, XVIII, 503; Colonel Polk to Governor Richard Caswell, April 3, 1787, XX, 658; Governor Richard Caswell to Alexander Martin, April 11, 1787, XX, 666; General Shelby to Governor Richard Caswell, May 4, 1787, XX, 690. See also the following in Keith and Masterson, eds., *Blount*, I: John Skinner to John Gray Blount, May 21, 1788, p. 394; Thomas Blount to John Gray Blount, April 13, 1789, pp. 472-73; Hugh Williamson to John Gray Blount, June 2, 1789, p. 484. Also, Archibald Maclaine to James Iredell, December 22, 1789, McRee, ed., *Iredell*, II, 276. At the Southern Historical Collection: P. G. Roulhac to his mother, March 17, 1786 (copy), Ruffin-Roulhac-Hamilton Papers; John Nisbet's receipt for half the gold and silver that he and his business partner buried, dated August, 1789, John Nisbet Papers; Samuel Johnston to Nathaniel Dukinfield, January 11, 1786, Hayes Collection (microfilm), reel number four; Thomas Amis to Richard Bennehan, January 1, 1789, Cameron Family Papers. See Fries, ed., *Moravian Records*, V, 2237, 2243, 2282. See the following in the Legislative Papers: Memorial of Roger Jones to the General Assembly, LXXXIX; petition from Salisbury District to the General Assembly, LXXXV. See the following at Duke University: John Sampson to ——, March 16, 1786, William Ross Papers; William Johnston Dawson to Helen Blair, November 17, 1788, James Iredell Papers. Also, James Iredell to Mrs. Iredell, April 27, 1786, Charles E. Johnson Collection, State Department of Archives and History, Raleigh.

112. James Iredell to Mrs. James Iredell, May 27, 1788, Charles E. Johnson Collection, State Department of Archives and History, Raleigh.

113. Clark, ed., *State Records*, XXIV, 813.

uphold the currency's market value was a perplexing and self-defeating problem to the Assembly, for to acknowledge, even tacitly, that the legal tender had depreciated was not only to call into question the integrity of the Assembly but also to depreciate further the money's market value. With Virginia merchants particularly in mind, legislators at the 1786 Assembly introduced a bill that would have made it a misdemeanor to demand specie payment for merchandise, to refuse to accept paper money in payment, or to accept paper money at less than nominal value.[114] This affirmation of the Tender Acts implied the ineffectiveness of the Acts themselves, and thus, in the opinion of other legislators, promised to do more damage than good by undermining further the reputation of the currency. The bill narrowly passed the House on first reading by a vote of thirty-seven to thirty-two only to encounter a quick death in the Senate by a vote of seventeen to twenty.[115] Had the Assembly been willing at that point to set aside the remaining confiscated property exclusively as a fund to redeem the currency, the money's market value would have improved, but the Assembly chose to continue and confirm existing policy.[116] Thus the 1786 Assembly made no changes regarding currency other than to alter the public tobacco program.

During most of 1787 the currency remained at the exchange rate of twelve shillings currency for eight shillings specie, or about 33.33 per cent off nominal value.[117] As the meeting of the 1787 Assembly approached, rumors began to spread that a new emission would be forthcoming. Merchant apprehensions, reflected by petitions from the nervous inhabitants of Edenton and Halifax, drove the exchange value down to 40

114. Bill in Legislative Papers, LXXII, December 19 folder.

115. Clark, ed., *State Records*, XVIII, 155-56, 361-62.

116. *Ibid.*, XXIV, 803. Above, p. 36.

117. Governor Richard Caswell to John Gray Blount, April 24, 1787, Clark, ed., *State Records*, XX, 682-83; Joseph Hardy to John Gray Blount, March 22, 1787, Keith and Masterson, eds., *Blount*, I, 272; Samuel Johnston to Nathaniel Dukinfield, June 13, 1787, Hayes Collection (microfilm), reel number four, Southern Historical Collection; James Iredell to William McLeod & Co., June 26, 1787, Charles E. Johnson Collection, State Department of Archives and History, Raleigh.

per cent off nominal value by the meeting of the 1787 Assembly.[118]

At that Assembly no emission bill was introduced. So strong, in fact, were the opponents of legal tender that they dared sponsor a bill proposing to allow for depreciation in private transactions. Declaring that debtors purposefully villified and depreciated the currency in order to make the payment of debts easier, the measure provided that thereafter justices of the peace were to assess the "true value" of the currency at the time the debt became due and were to award "damages" to the creditor accordingly.[119] Advocated almost exclusively by eastern legislators, the bill met defeat in the House by a vote of twenty-eight to thirty-six; and, in the Senate, a similar bill died by a vote of sixteen to twenty-seven.[120] A measure to reduce the currency's legal value from eight to twelve shillings per dollar was contemplated but not introduced.[121] Having maintained the currency as legal tender, the Assembly ordered that statistics be published on the amounts of money retired by the sinking fund and because of the ragged condition of the bills. The first set of figures was designed to improve the status of the currency and the latter statistics were intended to allay suspicions that the government had intentionally issued the money on thin paper that would quickly wear out and thus pass from circulation without the necessity of redemption.[122]

During 1788, as the currency's exchange value declined to about 53 per cent of nominal value,[123] even some proponents of fiat policy began to believe that the degree of depreciation warranted the enactment of a scale of depreciation for the

118. Clark, ed., *State Records*, XX, 270. Memorial of William Blount to the General Assembly, Legislative Papers, LXXVI, December 12 folder.

119. Bill in Legislative Papers, LXXVI, December 10 folder.

120. Clark, ed., *State Records*, XX, 179-80, 347-48.

121. Fragment in Legislative Papers, LXXVIII, December 12 folder.

122. Clark, ed., *State Records*, XX, 282; Schoepf, *Travels*, II, 130.

123. Richard Blackledge to William Blount, July 23, 1788, Keith and Masterson, eds., *Blount*, I, 412; Memorial of William Attmore to General Assembly, Legislative Papers, LXXXIII; business transactions in Cameron Family Papers, XX, Southern Historical Collection.

postwar money.[124] Other persons, because of that depreciation and because of the considerations covered earlier in this chapter, began to urge yet another emission. The merchants, of course, were adamantly opposed to more fiat currency, and after the election of 1788 indicated there would be a struggle at the Assembly, a town meeting at Wilmington that reflected mercantile opposition unanimously called upon the town's representative to favor a law designed to retire the currency as soon as possible and to support a law that would abandon the legal tender by providing for payment of contracts according to the real value of the currency.[125] The fears of another emission contributed to the currency's decline in value during the year, a decline that further agitated creditors.

The 1788 Assembly did witness a struggle between opponents and proponents of fiat policy, but neither group was able to obtain its goals because a centrist faction remained unpersuaded that either element had a solution to the state's financial woes or indeed that there was any solution. In order to gain support, the advocates of a legal tender emission, who were thinking in terms of £70,000, were prepared to combine such an emission with a legal devaluation of the existing postwar currency.[126] This major concession was insufficient enticement, and for lack of any prospect of passage, no emission bill was introduced. At the same time, the legislators who favored devaluation without emission were unable to sesure a victory. As previously indicated, talk of a scale of depreciation could be heard among some fiat men as well as among hard-money men of Governor Samuel Johnston's ilk,[127]

124. Attmore, *Journal*, pp. 20-21; petition of Superior Court Judges to General Assembly, Legislative Papers, LXXXVI.

125. Archibald Maclaine to James Iredell, October 27, 1788, McRee, ed., *Iredell*, II, 243-44.

126. Archibald Maclaine to Edward Jones, November 14, 1788, Clark, ed., *State Records*, XXI, 504-5; Archibald Maclaine to James Iredell, November 15, 1788, James Iredell Papers, Duke University; Archibald Maclaine to James Iredell, November 17, 1788, McRee, ed., *Iredell*, II, 246.

127. Attmore, *Journal*, pp. 20-21; Governor Samuel Johnston to William Winder, May 5, 1788, Governors' Papers, XVI, 44. Johnston com-

but no such bill appeared at the 1788 Assembly. Perhaps either proposal, if introduced, would have failed, but either would probably have fared better than the bill that did appear; for that bill, proposing to abandon any specific value for the money in the private sector, proved too extreme for the centrist faction. Stressing that the emissions of 1783 and 1785 had "depretiated considerably," to the injury of creditors, the measure proposed that the currency be accepted in payment of specie debts at its real value rather than its nominal value. To adjust this local, real value "from time to time," the Superior Court jury of each district would declare at every term what the current value was within the district; all court decisions at that term within that particular district would be governed by the grand jury's evaluation.[128] Although the Senate passed the bill on first reading, the House quickly laid the measure over until the next Assembly. A second effort with a similar bill met defeat in the Senate by a vote of nineteen to twenty-five.[129] The inherent problems and dangers of the proposed valuation procedure contributed to the measures' demise. The 1788 Assembly thus remained on dead center, and the existing financial system remained intact for another year.

During that year, 1789, the currency's exchange value reached a low of 50 per cent nominal value.[130] Hard-money men desperately feared that the depreciation would only

plains that the Assembly has not yet recognized the currency's market depreciation, "which is a matter of publick noteriety."

128. Bill in Legislative Papers, LXXXIII.

129, Clark, ed., *State Records*, XX, 545-46; XXI, 61.

130. Fries, ed., *Moravian Records*, V, 2275, 2282; Archibald Maclaine to James Iredell, December 22, 1789, McRee, ed., *Iredell*, II, 276; Benjamin Hawkins to James Madison, June 3, 1789, McPherson, ed., "Unpublished Letters," p. 165; Abishai C. Thomas to John Gray Blount, May 22, 1789, Keith and Masterson, eds., *Blount*, I, 481; Michael Payne to Francis Child, April 3, 1789, Treasurers' and Comptrollers' Papers, Correspondence of the Comptroller, II, State Department of Archives and History, Raleigh; John Steele to Governor Samuel Johnston, April 19, 1789, Henry McGilbert Wagstaff, ed., *The Papers of John Steele* (2 vols.; Raleigh: North Carolina Historical Commission [State Department of Archives and History], 1924), I, 36.

lead the 1789 Assembly to emit more currency.[131] Fiat policy became a major issue of the election campaign, as reflected in the statement of a candidate from Edenton who said that he considered paper currency to be a form of public robbery and patently an unsound policy fatal to the interests of a commercial center.[132]

At the 1789 Assembly there appeared the bill, laid over by the previous session, to allow grand juries to set the real value of the currency. The justifications for the measure were that the money was held in greater esteem in some parts of the state than others; that in debt cases some juries had allowed for depreciation while others had not; that the depreciated legal tender discouraged outside trade and injured the honest man; and that the proposed system would stimulate external trade and do justice internally.[133] Unpersuaded, the Senate rejected the measure upon second reading. While legal tender was retained, the Assembly showed concern that some action be taken to improve the currency's reputation among the public. Toward that end the Assembly received and subsequently published a report on the effectiveness of the sinking tax inaugurated by the 1785 Assembly. The report, however, was discouraging; since its enactment the tax had retired only £21,847/19 out of £200,000 emitted.[134] This information was greeted with considerable dismay by persons who wished to see the currency retired as quickly as possible, that is, by hard-money men who were reconciled to fiat redemption as the only practicable way of eliminating the paper money. The desire to accelerate currency retirement played a role, although a minor one, in bringing about the introduction of the unsuccessful bill, mentioned in the previous chapter, to erect a separate state west of the "Great Iron and Stone Mountains" and to open a land office there

131. Archibald Maclaine to James Iredell, September 15, 1789, McRee, ed., *Iredell*, II, 266-67.
132. *State Gazette of North Carolina* (Edenton) August 13, 1789 (microfilm), North Carolina Collection.
133. Bill in Legislative Papers, XC.
134. Clark, ed., *State Records*, XXI, 373.

to redeem specie certificates and the "present Money" of North Carolina.[135] With most confiscated property already sold for certificates, the sinking tax remained the only mode of redemption. Several thousand additional pounds of worn currency lay temptingly within the government's possession, but in order to allay the suspicions of persons who had been accusing the government of issuing money designed to wear out quickly, the 1789 Assembly ordered that all ragged money in the treasury be included in the sinking-fund money to be destroyed.[136] As North Carolina joined the Union in late 1789 approximately seven-eights of the state's postwar money remained unredeemed.

In the state's protracted ratification debate, the paper money problem had played a major role.[137] Hard-money Federalists counted the escape from fiat currency as one of the chief benefits offered by the constitution.[138] One leading North Carolina Federalist, Hugh Williamson, had summarized, in 1787, the arguments against fiat money. In a series of public letters signed "Sylvius,"[139] Williamson attributed many of North Carolina's financial difficulties to its penchant for such paper. Arguing that it inevitably depreciated and thus was a dishonest tender, he emphasized that paper money drove specie out of circulation; raised prices and thus discouraged foreign trade; penalized the honest and frugal man in order to help the irresponsible and extravagant individual; destroyed domestic industry; and did nothing to solve the problem of the foreign debt. The ultimate cause for

135. *Ibid.*, p. 271. The bill is in Legislative Papers, LXXXVII. Above, p. 40.

136. Clark, ed., *State Records*, XXI, 331.

137. Louise Irby Trenholme, *The Ratification of the Federal Constitution in North Carolina* ("Studies in History, Economics and Public Law," No. 363 [New York: Columbia University Press, 1932]), pp. 142-43. This study makes numerous references to the part that the paper money issue played in the debate.

138. See, for example, Governor Samuel Johnston to James White, May 8, 1788, Clark, ed., *State Records*, XXI, 470.

139. The seven letters were originally published in the *American Museum*. The entire series is reprinted, as previously indicated, in Williamson, *Letters from Sylvius*, pp. 5-46.

the scarcity of specie, he argued, lay in excessive purchases abroad and the failure of American industry to develop. Williamson maintained that the only solution to the shortage of specie lay in the expansion of American manufacturing facilities which would attract foreign specie to the United States. Fiat emission was completely unsound and self-defeating, he wrote, for it discouraged the development of industry and drove specie out of circulation. Emission and depreciation, he continued, would lead inevitably to a rise in taxes, which in turn would lead to a scarcity of money, which would demand another emission. Thus fiat policy was futility itself. Answering the traditional argument that emission helped the poor, Williamson proposed the substitution of a luxury (escapable) tax for the land and poll (inescapable) taxes—a substitution that, said he, would truly benefit the poor. In his final "Sylvius" letter Williamson speculated that "if there were a state in this union, in which it was treason to attempt the making of paper, such a state would become the asylum of honesty, arts and industry."[140]

Williamson's arguments were the traditional ones, and they had generally been employed at the 1788 Hillsborough Convention.[141] While some Federalists there had been willing to acknowledge that fiat currency had given momentary relief and had assisted in financing the war, they had stressed that fiat policy's ultimate consequences were baneful because paper money drove specie out of circulation, injured commerce, depreciated property, and destroyed incentive. Advocates of ratification had exaggerated when they argued that the postwar currency had destroyed a developing specie economy and had depreciated 100 per cent,[142] but their other criticisms

140. *Ibid.*, p. 45.

141. Elliot, ed., *Debates*, III, 17-220, is the fullest coverage of the North Carolina Convention of 1788. See also, Clark, ed., *State Records*, XXII, 1-35. References for the convention coverage presented in the text are Elliot, ed., *Debates*, III, 33, 84, 87, 89, 155, 156, 160, 161, 162, 163, 164, 167.

142. The argument that specie was in adequate supply until paper money drove it out of circulation has been accepted by some authorities. See, for example, Bullock, *Monetary History*, p. 191. While there

were valid enough to cause fiat men to defend the currency somewhat apologetically upon the basis of necessity.

Another facet of the currency debate at the 1788 Convention had been whether or not ratification would destroy the state's paper money currently in circulation. Antifederalists had argued that the currency would be invalidated as the constitution went into effect in North Carolina. Federalists had replied that the constitution not only forbade ex post facto laws but also declared that the states "shall" emit no currency in the future: hence ratification would not affect existing state money. Antifederalists had suggested that even if the state currency were not constitutionally destroyed, it would, in effect, be invalidated because it would be worthless in the same market with United States money. Federalists had insisted that ratification would enhance the value of North Carolina currency.

The constitution's silence concerning existing state paper had made the currency's redemption another sensitive matter at the Hillsborough Convention. A constitutional amendment proposed at the convention stated, in part, that Congress should not interfere directly or indirectly with any of the states in the redemption of paper money already emitted and presently in circulation and that the states should have the exclusive right of making such laws and regulations for that purpose as the states should think proper.[143] Failing to ratify the constitution, the convention had unanimously recommended that the General Assembly take "effectual measures for the redemption of the paper currency, as speedily as may be, consistent with the situation and circumstances of the

---

was undoubtedly more specie in 1783 than in 1789, there was always a shortage, and the decline in amount may be attributed not only to the introduction of paper money but also to the end of wartime specie expenditures by foreign nations and to the excessive purchasing of goods abroad. The several statements at the convention that the currency had declined 100 per cent may have represented a misunderstanding that when currency circulated at two for one the depreciation was 50 per cent and not 100 per cent.

143. Clark, ed., *State Records*, XXII, 22-23.

people of this State."[144] As indicated by the recommendation's unanimous endorsement by an Onslow County meeting, that is, by a Wilmington meeting, creditors strongly favored such redemption.[145]

After the Hillsborough Convention had failed to ratify the constitution, Federalists, as they had intensified their efforts, had warned that non-ratification was a mandate for more fiat emissions.[146] Antifederalists had answered weakly that while many persons would probably be happy to pay their debts in depreciated paper, such debtors were individuals of no consequence.[147]

The Fayetteville Convention of November, 1789, which met during the Assembly session, was, as we have seen, clearly controlled by the Federalists. Antifederalists attempted to make the 1788 redemption amendment a condition for ratification, but this effort was defeated by a vote of 82 to 187. After the convention ratified the constitution, however, the delegates unanimously resolved that the state's congressmen should promote a constitutional amendment that would give the states the exclusive right to redeem their respective currencies already in circulation.

Although the proposed constitutional amendment never came about, the United States government did not interfere with existing state currencies. North Carolina proved in no hurry to retire the money. The 1789 Assembly, as we have seen, undertook no additional redemption policies. The 1790 Assembly, as part of the reaction against fiat financing, terminated the sinking tax on the postwar money and provided that specie and state currency would be received in purchase of public land.[148] By this method and by the gradual wearing

144. *Ibid.*, pp. 32-33.

145. Archibald Maclaine to James Iredell, October 27, 1788, McRee, ed., *Iredell*, II, 243-44.

146. Anonymous, "To the People of the District of Edenton," *A Plea for Federal Union*, ed. by Hugh Talmage Lefler (Charlottesville: The Tracy W. McGregor Library, 1947), pp. 65-66.

147. *State Gazette of North Carolina* (Edenton), November 3, 1788 (microfilm), North Carolina Collection.

148. Clark, ed., *State Records*, XXV, 77, 79.

out of the bills, the fiat currency slowly disappeared from the market. As it diminished in amount, it continued to circulate within the state at about 50 per cent of its nominal value, bearing, then, some usefulness until its ultimate demise.[149]

An evaluation of North Carolina's postwar fiat currency program must be mindful of E. James Ferguson's position that fiat money was a logical and inevitable answer to the financial conditions and problems of eighteenth-century America.[150] Beset by a number of pressing demands, the Assembly resorted to fiat currency and in so doing met, with some degree of success, the exigencies of government: the Line received pay; some certificates and old currency were retired; public salaries were paid; and, in a process that shall be described in a later chapter,[151] the state was able to make some payment toward discharging the foreign obligations of the United States.

While achieving these goals with varying degrees of success, fiat policy did indeed bring about the pernicious consequences that hard-money men predicted and bemoaned: specie was driven out of circulation; inflation occurred; no commercial purposes outside the state were served; foreign commerce was discouraged; creditors were injured; and, despite a measure of relief to particular individuals, a sufficient, viable medium of exchange was not and could not be created. The opponents of fiat policy were perfectly correct in saying that the only true solution to the state's financial difficulties lay in the development of domestic industry and the creation of a favorable balance of trade, but these solutions could come only with time and with the incorporation of North Carolina into an economic entity with more resources than the state possessed. Given the underdeveloped condition of North Carolina in the eighteenth century and given the eco-

149. Governor Alexander Martin's address to the General Assembly, November 2, 1790, Governors' Letter Books, X, 140, State Department of Archives and History, Raleigh.

150. E. James Ferguson, *The Power of the Purse: A History of American Public Finance, 1776-1790* (Chapel Hill: The University of North Carolina Press, 1961), pp. 1-24.

151. Above, pp. 198-214.

nomic independence of each state under the Articles of Confederation, there simply was no satisfactory, short-range solution to the state's economic and financial problems. Painfully aware of that fact, fiat men, who were neither more nor less public-spirited than their opponents, advocated emission because paper currency offered private and public advantages even though it entailed disadvantages and shortcomings. Assessed in light of North Carolina's previous fiat experience, the postwar program was conducted with restraint and with a considerable degree of success.

IV. *North Carolina's Foreign Debt: The Obligation to Martinique*

An ample illustration of North Carolina's fiscal difficulties and of the chaos attendant to eighteenth-century public finance is the record of the state's spasmodic, ill-informed, costly, and prolonged effort to discharge its one foreign obligation: a sum owed directly to the government of the French West Indies island of Martinique and thereby to the navy department of the government of France. During the Revolution, North Carolina had commissioned one Marquis de Bretigny as an agent to procure war supplies for the state. Upon Bretigny's application, the governor and the intendant of Martinique had withdrawn from the king's storehouse there French naval supplies valued at 5,487 Spanish milled dollars (almost £2,195 nominal value of postwar North Carolina currency).[1] In receipt for these war materials Bretigny had pledged himself that North Carolina would make effective payment. Thereafter North Carolina had placed in the agent's hands funds that were to be forwarded to Martinique in partial payment of the debt.[2] By the end of the war the exact details of the above transactions had somehow become lost to the government of North Carolina. The haphazard manner of keeping public records, the inherent problems of a nomadic capital, and the confusion and destruction associated with the war—one or more of these factors probably contrib-

1. M. de la Forest's statement of June 12, 1790, Governors' Letter Books, X, 69-74, State Department of Archives and History, Raleigh. For ease of reading, fractions of dollars will be omitted in the chapter.

2. Walter Clark, ed., *The State Records of North Carolina* (16 vols.; Winston, Goldsboro, and Raleigh: State of North Carolina, 1895-1906) [volumes numbered consecutive to William L. Saunders, ed., *The Colonial Records of North Carolina* (10 vols.; Raleigh: State of North Carolina, 1886-90)], XIX, 345, 646.

uted to the lack of complete and precise information concerning the Martinique debt. In any event the inability of North Carolina to determine the facts and to discharge the debt effectively were to prove embarrassments during the postwar period.

At war's end the government of North Carolina was under the impression that Bretigny had either personally paid for the goods and therefore deserved reimbursement or that he was going to be held accountable by Martinique and thus needed to be supplied with state funds to meet the demand. Governor Alexander Martin, who believed that reimbursement was in order,[3] called upon the 1783 Assembly to ascertain the facts of the Martinique obligation. The resulting committee report erroneously set the original value of the goods at £2,111/10 (instead of approximately £2,195), which together with the agent's expenses of £907/10 and a "protested Bill" totaled £3,099. Of that amount, continued the report, £734 had already been paid to Bretigny in tobacco, pork, and warrants upon the treasury, leaving a balance due him of £2,365 specie. Upon the committee's recommendation the Assembly resolved to turn over to Bretigny 1,670 pounds weight of public gunpowder at four shillings per pound and to have warrants issued to him for the remainder.[4]

Later during 1783 Governor Martin received a letter, with enclosures, from French Minister to the United States Chevalier de la Luzerne, urging prompt payment of the debt to Martinique and offering Luzerne's services in receiving remittance at Philadelphia on behalf of the island if such mode of payment should be more convenient to North Carolina. Governor Martin, who must have been surprised that Bretigny had not paid the debt, assured Luzerne that the next Assembly would be urged to make speedy payment to Martinique.[5]

When the Assembly convened in the spring of 1784, Martin

3. *Ibid.*, XIX, 253.

4. *Ibid.*, XIX, 224, 345, 360, 646; XXI, 147. The printed report mistakenly sets the total debt at £3,090.

5. Governor Alexander Martin to Chevalier de la Luzerne, December 8, 1783, *ibid.*, XVI, 879-80.

presented Luzerne's correspondence and accounts concerning the debt due Martinique. Upon the basis of the minister's information and other available data, a joint committee reported that Martinique had apparently furnished North Carolina, through Bretigny, arms, ammunition, and other items amounting in value to 6,000 Spanish milled dollars (£2,400 nominal value of North Carolina postwar currency). The committee recommended that the governor be empowered and required to take measures for paying the 6,000 Spanish milled dollars, with interest, out of the tax revenues for the year 1783 if any such monies remained unappropriated. The committee members, after examining papers relating to Bretigny's account with North Carolina, found "sufficient matter to induce them to believe" that part of the money due Martinique had been paid to the former agent in the settlement of his accounts with the state. The committee recommended, therefore, that all papers on the subject be referred to the comptroller and that he be required to take proper measures for final settlement with Bretigny. The comptroller was to recover from Bretigny all money that the state had intended should be paid to Martinique and that Bretigny had not subsequently remitted to the island. Both houses concurred with the report and recommendations.[6] Burdened by inconclusive and possibly contradictory information, the spring Assembly of 1784 had acted according to its best lights and had made some provision, however unpromising, toward discharging the debt. The fact that legislative action had been taken undoubtedly came as a relief to Hugh Williamson, North Carolina delegate in Congress, who was anxious that the state's reputation and character not be stained in the eyes of foreigners and that the governor of Martinique not suffer in his private fortune or incur the displeasure of the king for having trusted the state of North Carolina.[7]

If the desire to pay the debt existed, the resources did not.

6. *Ibid.*, XIX, 512, 646-47. The author has found no information upon efforts to settle accounts between North Carolina and Bretigny.

7. Hugh Williamson to Governor Alexander Martin, April 8, 1784, *ibid.*, XVII, 32.

In June, 1784, Governor Martin regretfully informed Luzerne that the revenue from 1783 taxes had already been expended for other purposes. Warning that it would take some time for 1784 tax revenues to reach the state treasury, Martin pledged that the earliest collection therefrom would be designated toward the Martinique debt. The governor explained that the principal collection would be in paper money and that the currency would have to be converted into North Carolina produce, which would subsequently be shipped to Philadelphia or Martinique as Luzerne preferred. Martin warned that the process would cause delay, and he requested the minister's patience. The settlement between Bretigny and North Carolina, wrote Martin, was a separate matter and would not impede payment to Martinique.[8]

Replying on behalf of the absent Luzerne, M. de Marbois, secretary of the French Legation and consul general, expressed satisfaction with the measures being taken by North Carolina to pay the debt to Martinique. Marbois suggested that he would be pleased to accept payment at Philadelphia if the state should find such a course more convenient than shipment to the island itself.[9] As months passed and North Carolina made no remittance, Marbois' confidence in and satisfaction with the state's intentions gradually dissipated. In December, 1784, he successfully entreated Congress to recommend to the states a speedy settlement of all war accounts with France.[10] During the same month Marbois wrote Governor Martin to express keen disappointment. Noting that North Carolina's delegates in Congress had led him and the government of France to believe that payment would be

8. Governor Alexander Martin to the Minister of France to Congress, June 4, 1784, *ibid.*, 76.

9. M. de Marbois to Governor Alexander Martin, July 13, 1784, *ibid.*, p. 87.

10. M. de Marbois to Congress, December 1, 1784, *ibid.*, p. 113; Resolution of Congress of December 16, 1784, *ibid.*, p. 114. Congress did not follow Marbois' specific suggestions about modes of settlement, but Congress did recommend that the states pass remedial legislation to facilitate settlement.

made in the summer of 1784, Marbois complained that he was under pressure from France to urge payment of North Carolina's debt to Martinique. The French consul stressed that it was essential that Martinique and the government of France be informed of a final settlement.[11]

Even as Marbois sought satisfaction by way of Congress, state revenues had become sufficient to enable Governor Martin to act. Late in 1784 he issued warrants totaling eleven hundred or twelve hundred pounds[12] to John Gray Blount and Thomas Blount, merchants of Washington, North Carolina, who were given the broad authority to spend the money as they deemed wise and to remit the purchased produce quickly to Marbois at Philadelphia.[13] The governor informed the Blounts that more warrants on the treasury would be forthcoming as soon as money could be obtained from the tax collectors.[14] On November 30, 1784, Martin wrote Mar-

11. M. de Marbois to Governor Alexander Martin, December 24, 1784, *ibid.*, p. 117.

12. The exact amount of the warrants sent by Martin remained a matter of uncertainty, as this chapter's text will make clear. John Gray Blount erroneously wrote in 1785 that Martin's warrants had totaled eleven hundred dollars. See John Gray Blount and Thomas Blount to Governor Richard Caswell, July 2, 1785, *ibid.*, p. 478. Caswell pointed out that the amount actually had been eleven hundred pounds. See Governor Richard Caswell to John Gray Blount, August 16, 1785, Alice Barnwell Keith and William Henry Masterson, eds., *The John Gray Blount Papers* (3 vols.; Raleigh: State Department of Archives and History, 1952-65), I, 207. The merchants responded that the amount had been twelve hundred pounds. See John Gray Blount and Thomas Blount to Governor Richard Caswell, August 18, 1785, Governors' Papers, XI, 79. Governor Martin's letter informing the Blounts of the warrants stated that the amount was twelve hundred pounds. See Governor Alexander Martin to John Gray Blount and Thomas Blount, December 3, 1784, Keith and Masterson, eds., *Blount*, I, 184. As the text will soon reveal, Governor Martin's letter of November 30, 1784, to Marbois made reference to a sum nominally equivalent to twelve hundred pounds North Carolina currency. The 1788 Assembly concluded that Martin's warrants totaled eleven hundred pounds. Above, p. 114. The author is inclined to set the amount at twelve hundred pounds.

13. Governor Alexander Martin to John Gray Blount and Thomas Blount, December 3, 1784, Keith and Masterson, eds., *Blount*, I, 184.

14. John Gray Blount and Thomas Blount to Governor Richard Caswell, July 2, 1785, Clark, ed., *State Records*, XVII, 478. The letter states that Martin intends to send the Blounts more warrants. Gov-

bois that three thousand dollars (North Carolina currency, equal to twelve hundred pounds North Carolina currency) had been sent to the Blounts for the purchase of produce.[15] Following Martin's advice that the Blounts be directly contacted, Marbois wrote the merchants on January 15, 1785, to request full information and prompt remittance.[16]

Apparently Marbois had insufficient understanding of the difficulties involved in converting currency to produce, shipping the produce, and converting the produce to specie. Also, he may possibly have thought that Martin had appropriated three thousand dollars specie or the market equivalent in currency. Thus initially expecting prompt and substantial reduction of the debt, Marbois became increasingly dismayed as no payment arrived. On April 16, 1785, he wrote North Carolina's new governor, Richard Caswell, that the state's entire debt to Martinique remained unpaid.[17] The next month Marbois asked Richard Dobbs Spaight, North Carolina delegate in Congress, to urge prompt discharge of the state's obligation.[18] More fully informed by Spaight or someone else of the difficulties of the remittance procedure, the French official dispatched to the Blounts a request that produce be quickly shipped. Marbois complained that his government had drawn drafts upon him for the amount of the debt and that his failure to receive North Carolina's payment

---

ernor Martin, however, did not send additional warrants during the remainder of his administration.

15. M. de Marbois to Richard Dobbs Spaight, May 18, 1785, *ibid.*, pp. 450-51. Marbois quotes a letter written to him by Martin and dated November 30, 1784.

16. M. de Marbois to John Gray Blount and Thomas Blount, January 15, 1785, Keith and Masterson, eds., *Blount*, I, 188. In what is likely an editor's error, the printed letter has Marbois stating that he understands the Blounts have received "7000. Dollars" from North Carolina. As previously indicated, Marbois understood the Blounts to have received three thousand dollars in warrants. See also, M. de Marbois to Governor Alexander Martin, January 15, 1785, Governors' Letter Books, V, 800.

17. M. de Marbois to Governor Richard Caswell, April 16, 1785, Clark., ed., *State Records*, XVII, 439.

18. M. de Marbois to Richard Dobbs Spaight, May 18, 1785, *ibid.*, pp. 450-51.

would result in his personal hardship and embarrassment.[19]

Marbois' letter of April 16 to Caswell completely surprised the governor, who had assumed that the debt had been paid.[20] Upon Caswell's inquiry, Marbois confirmed that nothing had been received in favor of Martinique, and he implored Caswell to give positive direction for payment.[21] The governor, who was at a loss concerning the entire matter, subsequently contacted former Governor Martin and the Blounts to find out exactly what had transpired. Upon learning from Martin that the warrants issued to the Blounts had been inadequate to pay the entire debt, Caswell assured Marbois that every effort would be made to pay the balance as speedily as possible. The governor was forced to confess, however, that the condition of the treasury was such that no further payments could be made at that time.[22] The Blounts, meanwhile, had replied to Caswell's inquiry. Erroneously stating that they had received warrants totaling eleven hundred dollars (rather than approximately that sum in pounds), the Blounts wrote that they were at that very time (July, 1785) loading a vessel at Wilmington with naval stores purchased with the warrants. They requested more warrants so that the vessel might be loaded to capacity.[23]

Also in July, 1785, Governor Caswell came under pressure from one M. Petry, a representative of the French vice-consul to North Carolina, South Carolina, and Georgia.[24] In re-

19. M. de Marbois to John Gray Blount and Thomas Blount, May 19, 1785, Keith and Masterson, eds., *Blount*, I, 198.

20. Governor Richard Caswell to M. de Marbois, January 4, 1785. This letter does not appear in the *State Records*, nor has it been located in the State Department of Archives and History. For reference to the letter, see M. de Marbois to Governor Richard Caswell, June 21, 1785, Clark, ed., *State Records*, XVII, 475.

21. M. de Marbois to Governor Richard Caswell, June 21, 1785, Clark, ed., *State Records*, XVII, 475-76.

22. Governor Richard Caswell to M. de Marbois, July 23, 1785, *ibid.*, p. 488. Caswell sent a copy of the letter to the Blounts. See Keith and Masterson, eds., *Blount*, I, 203.

23. John Gray Blount and Thomas Blount to Governor Richard Caswell, July 2, 1785, Governors' Papers, XI, 40, State Department of Archives and History, Raleigh.

24. M. Petry to Governor Richard Caswell, July 6, 1785, Clark, ed., *State Records*, XVII, 480.

sponse to Petry's request for prompt payment by way of Philadelphia, Caswell replied that the warrants sent to the Blounts had been inadequate and that more warrants would be sent as soon as the condition of the treasury permitted.[25] On August 8, 1785, Petry wrote Caswell in a state of excitement and urgency that the vessel loading produce for Philadelphia would not sail from Wilmington. The Blounts were detaining the craft because prices at Philadelphia had plunged and probably also because the merchants were hopefully awaiting additional warrants on the treasury, but Petry's impatience was unrestrained by these considerations. He urged Governor Caswell to execute full and immediate remittance because Marbois, in anticipation of full payment, had authorized the governor of Martinique to draw upon Marbois for the entire amount of the debt.[26] In view of North Carolina's past delays, one may suspect Marbois either of considerable naïveté or of using the draft to try to force the state into effective action.

Genuinely concerned about the ineffectiveness of North Carolina's efforts to that time, Governor Caswell brought the matter of the Martinique debt before the Council of State, which advised him to write the Blounts for an estimate of what the produce would bring so that warrants could be issued for the anticipated balance. On August 16 Caswell wrote the Blounts and, probably with the intent of spurring them generally, requested a prompt response so that warrants could be sent.[27] The Blounts replied on August 18 to review past transactions, comment upon the requested estimate, and explain the delay in shipment. The warrants from Governor Martin, they wrote, had totaled twelve hundred pounds, and the entire amount had been used to purchase naval stores. Subsequent to the purchases, however, the prices of naval

25. Governor Richard Caswell to M. Petry, August 4, 1785, *ibid.*, pp. 498-99.

26. M. Petry to Governor Richard Caswell, August 8, 1785, *ibid.*, p. 502.

27. Governor Richard Caswell to John Gray Blount, August 16, 1785, Keith and Masterson, eds., *Blount*, I, 207.

stores had dropped at Philadelphia. The lower prices, combined with freight charges and other expenses, would greatly reduce the amount of specie that could be remitted to Martinique. The Blounts informed Caswell that they had written Marbois to ask if he would accept the naval stores at the present price. If they did not hear from Marbois, continued the Blounts, they would ship the stores to Philadelphia in November or December, when prices were highest there.[28]

The Blounts were unwilling to estimate the balance due Martinique because they felt they had no way of anticipating what the produce would bring. In the absence of precise information Governor Caswell, following narrowly the council's advice, declined to send additional warrants to the merchants. Thus, when the vessel sailed, the only state produce aboard was that purchased with Martin's warrants. In March, 1786, the Blounts wrote Caswell that they had shipped naval stores to Philadelphia, but did not know what the goods would bring and thus could not yet know what would still be due Martinique. Noting that a seasonal shortage of produce would soon exist in the state, they requested that warrants on the treasury be sent immediately.[29] Caswell repeated that he would send the warrants whenever the merchants could let him know the balance due.[30] Again stating that they could not know the balance due, the Blounts intimated that the low prices in Philadelphia might cause a loss to the state. The letter concluded with the suggestion that the governor make his own estimate of what amount of warrants to send.[31] Apparently convinced that the situation demanded immediate action, Caswell sent warrants totaling thirteen

28. John Gray Blount and Thomas Blount to Governor Richard Caswell, August 18, 1785, Governors' Papers, XI, 79.

29. John Gray Blount and Thomas Blount to Governor Richard Caswell, March 14, 1786, Clark, ed., *State Records*, XVIII, 575. The naval stores shipped to and sold in Philadelphia comprised only part of the products purchased with Martin's warrants. As the text will reveal, the remaining naval stores were shipped to New York for sale.

30. Governor Richard Caswell to John Gray Blount and Thomas Blount, March 29, 1786, *ibid.*, p. 587.

31. John Gray Blount and Thomas Blount to Governor Richard Caswell, April 22, 1786, *ibid.*, pp. 598-99.

hundred pounds and promised to send more if the Blounts should find additional sums necessary to extinguish the debt.[32]

Confident that the Blounts would act promptly, Governor Caswell felt prepared to meet the continuing French pressure. When M. Petry, acting vice-consul to North Carolina, expressed hope that part of North Carolina's 1785 currency emission could be used to purchase state commodities, Caswell replied that he had sent warrants to the Blounts to the full amount of the balance due Martinique and that by that time produce had been shipped to Philadelphia.[33] The governor's statement was less than candid, for the warrants that he and Martin had sent expressed nominal value North Carolina currency, a medium painfully less valuable than the specie debt. Petry, having learned not to expect the best, acknowledged without comment receipt of Caswell's letter.[34] Caswell, indicating some exasperation with the prolonged delay in meeting the debt, informed the state's delegates in Congress of the warrants that he had sent to the Blounts.[35] Hopefully, the delegates might be better armed against the onslaught of official French criticism.

Caswell would have been more perplexed had he known that the Blounts were not using his warrants to discharge part of the Martinique debt. Alarmed by the low prices to the north and the resultant losses to the state, and perhaps desirous of using the public money temporarily for their own private transactions,[36] the Blounts had decided not to make

32. Governor Richard Caswell to John Gray Blount and Thomas Blount, April 24, 1786, *ibid.*, p. 600.

33. M. Petry to Governor Richard Caswell, July 17, 1786, and Governor Richard Caswell to M. Petry, September 18, 1786, *ibid.*, pp. 688-89, 741.

34. M. Petry to Governor Richard Caswell, October 26, 1786, *ibid.*, p. 771.

35. Governor Richard Caswell to Timothy Bloodworth, September 24, 1786, *ibid.*, p. 747.

36. The temporary use of public money for private purposes was a common, if increasingly unpopular, practice in the eighteenth century. The Blounts handled considerable public money, and it would not have been inconsistent with their characters or business practices to have employed public money in such fashion. See William Henry Master-

further remittances upon the debt.[37] Either through oversight or through their desire to employ public money for private purposes, the merchants did not inform Caswell of their decision to withhold further remittances. This failure, which later brought the Blounts trouble, left the governor under the impression that a total of at least £2,400 North Carolina currency (£1,100 and possibly £1,200 from Martin and £1,300 from himself) had been actively employed against the debt when, in fact, only Martin's warrants had been so used.

If the administration hoped that the French would be impressed with North Carolina's efforts, state officials were doomed to disappointment. On March 19, 1787, the French consul general to the United States, M. de la Forest, complained to North Carolina's delegates in Congress that the sale of state produce had brought only $661 specie while the total amount of the original debt stood at $5,487. The consul asked that his disappointment be conveyed to the governor and that additional warrants be issued. Though the mode of remittance might be disadvantageous to the state, he concluded, the justice of the claim would undoubtedly induce Governor Caswell to issue further warrants.[38]

Nothing, in fact, could induce Caswell to issue more warrants. His decision resulted in part from the condition of the treasury, but certainly the losses that he believed the state to have suffered would have prevented additional warrants had the treasury been brimming with money. Upon the logical but mistaken assumption that the Blounts had employed his warrants against the debt, the governor thought that the

son, *William Blount* (Baton Rouge: Louisiana State University Press, 1954).

37. In the spring of 1788 the Blounts first informed the North Carolina government of their decision not to use Caswell's warrants against the Martinique debt. The Blounts justified their decision upon low prices and the resulting losses to the state. The merchants' letters of the period all fail to mention what they had done with Caswell's warrants, and suspicions against them naturally arose.

38. M. de la Forest to William Blount and Benjamin Hawkins, March 19, 1787, Keith and Masterson, eds., *Blount*, I, 269. The printed letter mistakenly reads that the debt was $5,437.

legal equivalent of 6,000 Spanish milled dollars (that is, £2,400 North Carolina currency at 2.5 Spanish milled dollars per pound) had been converted by sale of produce into $661 specie. These figures, after expenses and commissions were taken into account, indicated that the state had realized no more than one-tenth its investment. Actually, because only Martin's warrants had been used, North Carolina had realized about one-fifth of its investment—still a severe loss. In view of Caswell's misconception, it is not surprising that during the remainder of his administration he turned a deaf ear to continued French pleas for remittance.[39]

Caswell's concern and chagrin perhaps help explain why Samuel Johnston, who became governor late in 1787, first learned of the Martinique debt upon receiving notice from the new French vice-consul to North Carolina, M. Ducher, that payment was long overdue.[40] Another probable reason that Johnston, like Caswell before him, assumed office ignorant of the whole affair was the traditionally disorganized fashion of handling public documents. In any event, Johnston was disturbed by his own lack of information and by the realization that the treasury could not at that time furnish money to meet the debt.[41] Determined to obtain all available information, Johnston immediately wrote former Governor Caswell for details.[42] Caswell replied that the whole business had begun during the administration of Governor Martin, who had issued warrants to the Blounts for about twelve hundred pounds and that he, Caswell, had issued additional warrants for thirteen hundred pounds, which he believed sufficient to discharge the balance.[43] Without men-

39. See M. de Marbois to Richard Dobbs Spaight, May 18, 1787, Governors' Papers, XIV, 38.

40. See Governor Samuel Johnston to M. Ducher, February 28, 1788, Clark, ed., *State Records*, XXI, 453.

41. Governor Samuel Johnston to Richard Caswell, February 28, 1788, and Governor Samuel Johnston to James White, May 8, 1788, *ibid.*, 453, 469-70.

42. Governor Samuel Johnston to Richard Caswell, February 28, 1788, *ibid.*, p. 453.

43. Richard Caswell to Governor Samuel Johnston, March 31, 1788, *ibid.*, p. 461.

tioning the subsequent sale of produce or the disappointing proceeds therefrom, Caswell suggested that Johnston write the Blounts, which Johnston did.[44] After some delay John Gray Blount replied that the warrants from Governor Martin had been spent to buy tar, which had been shipped to Philadelphia and New York for sale. The loss from the sale had been so great, Blount continued, that he and his brother had decided not to make remittance with the warrants sent by Governor Caswell. Making no statement as to how Caswell's warrants had been employed, Blount suggested that direct shipment to Martinique might result in a smaller loss to the state.[45]

Having yet to receive precise financial information, Governor Johnston sent a letter to John Gray Blount asking the merchant to provide specific details as to the amount of the original Martinique demand, the exact amount of all warrants issued to the Blounts, and the sums produced by the sale of the naval stores. Johnston approved the Blounts' decision not to remit further stores in view of the severe losses, and he asked John Gray Blount to suggest the most desirable form of remittance.[46] Vexed and embarrassed by the problem about which he knew all too little, Johnston called a meeting of the Council of State to advise him. On July 31, 1788, the council decided that it was unable to evaluate Blount's suggestion of direct shipment to Martinique since the merchant was unable to state the total amount of the debt or the exact amount of the remittances already made. The council advised the governor to write M. Ducher, the French vice-

44. Governor Samuel Johnston to John Gray Blount, April 12, 1788, *ibid.*, p. 462. The letter is also found in Keith and Masterson, eds., *Blount*, I, 388.

45. John Gray Blount to Governor Samuel Johnston, May 18, 1788, Clark, ed., *State Records*, XXI, 473. Obviously the date of this letter or that of Samuel Johnston to John Gray Blount, May 8, 1788, *ibid.*, pp. 470-71, is incorrect, for Johnston's letter is clearly in response to Blount's letter. Johnston's letter dated in *ibid.* as May 8 makes reference to Blount's letter of May 8, so it is probable that Blount's letter was written on May 8 and Johnston's on May 18.

46. Governor Samuel Johnston to John Gray Blount, May 8, 1788, *ibid.*, pp. 470-71. Again, the letter was probably written May 18.

consul, in order to ascertain the exact balance due by North Carolina and to whom it should be paid. The council advised also that Johnston press John Gray Blount for an exact statement of remittances northward.[47] The state's delegates in Congress, meanwhile, continued under pressure from French officials.[48]

Continuing his quest for enlightenment, Johnston, in the late summer of 1788, requested of Alexander Martin any information on the Martinique debt that the former governor might have. Again the chaotic nature of the whole affair becomes obvious, for Johnston expressed special interest in knowing the amount of the debt, the amount of the warrants that Martin had sent, and any mode of payment that the Assembly might have prescribed. Johnston complained that he possessed no documents that could shed light on these questions.[49] Following the council's advice, the hapless governor, in a letter to the vice-consul, pleaded for information and in so doing explicitly confessed his continued inability to determine the exact amount of the state's debt to Martinique.[50]

Ducher's letter of reply served as a basis of examination by the Assembly, which, after over four years of inactivity concerning the debt, reviewed in 1788 the entire history of the Martinique demand. A committee report[51] stated that Bretigny had drawn £2,365 from the treasury, an amount supposed to be adequate to discharge the Martinique demand. In May, 1784, continued the report, the Assembly had ordered the comptroller to collect from Bretigny the sum given the former agent to pay to Martinique.[52] The 1788 committee

47. Journal of the Council of State, July 31, 1788, Governors' Office Papers, CXXI, State Department of Archives and History, Raleigh.

48. James White to Governor Samuel Johnston, April 21, 1788, Clark, ed., *State Records*, XXI, 466-67.

49. Governor Samuel Johnston to Alexander Martin, August 3, 1788, *ibid.*, pp. 488-89.

50. Governor Samuel Johnston to M. Ducher, August 25, 1788, *ibid.*, pp. 492-93.

51. *Ibid.*, pp. 147-48.

52. The wording of the 1788 report, at one point, mistakenly indicates that the 1784 committee had reported that the comptroller had

stated that Governor Martin had sent warrants to the Blounts totaling £1,100 and that Caswell had sent an additional £1,300 making a grand total of £2,400. The vice-consul's report, continued the committee, indicated that the Blounts in April and July, 1786, had paid to the French agent at New York the sum of £170/17/8 specie and in May, 1787, to the agent at Philadelphia the sum of £93/7/9 specie. The total of £264/5/5, when converted into Spanish milled dollars ($661) and deducted from the original debt, left a balance of $4,826. The committee urged that the comptroller determine the amount of money paid to Bretigny which had been intended for Martinique and that the treasurer then immediately commence suit against Bretigny for recovery. The committee recommended that the Blounts make immediate settlement with the state and, if such settlement should not be made, that the treasurer sue for recovery.[53] The committee recommended also that the governor, with the advice and consent of the council, dispose of so much of the public tobacco for hard money or bills of exchange on Philadelphia, New York, or Martinique as to discharge the balance due Martinique.[54]

The investigation by the 1788 Assembly served several useful purposes: it established that the money issued to Bretigny

---

already collected the sum from Bretigny, but, as previously revealed, the 1784 committee had actually recommended that the comptroller should thereafter take action for such recovery. As the text shall shortly reveal, the 1788 committee realized that Bretigny had not been acted against, because the committee recommended that the sums in his possession should be recovered. The author has interpreted the 1788 report as it was meant to be presented.

53. William Blount, writing from Fayetteville, sent to John Gray Blount the Assembly's actions concerning the debt. William expressed the opinion that the Assembly would be happy to see the matter ruin Caswell, the Blounts, and their friends. See William Blount to John Gray Blount, December 4, 1788, Keith and Masterson, eds., *Blount*, I, 438-39. At the 1789 Assembly objection was made to the seating of John Gray Blount and Thomas Blount on the basis of their allegedly owing the state £2,400. The Blounts protested and the treasurer commenced suit to determine the facts. See Legislative Papers, LXXXIX, State Department of Archives and History, Raleigh.

54. The policy of purchasing public tobacco is treated above, pp. 198-214.

had not been recovered; it determined the payment made to Martinique and the balance due; it placed pressure on the Blounts to account for the funds that had been sent them;[55] and it made effective provision for payment of the debt. State officials were painfully aware, however, that while the sale of public tobacco could discharge the entire Martinique debt, the tobacco program had been instituted in order to meet North Carolina's portion of the interest on the foreign debt of the United States.[56] Thus to serve one purpose was to obstruct the other.

During early 1789 Governor Johnston received several mercantile inquiries about the purchase of the tobacco.[57] To evaluate these offers and to deal with the dilemma of having two purposes set for the tobacco, Johnston called a meeting of the council. On March 13, 1789, that body established minimum price guidelines for the tobacco and specified that payment should be in advance of delivery and should be in specie or bills of exchange upon Philadelphia or New York and acceptable to the United States Treasury.[58] Reference to the United States Treasury did not exclude the possibility of payment to Martinique, but the phrase probably indicates that the council gave priority to the state's obligation to the national government. Nevertheless, informing Ducher that the Assembly had authorized payment of $4,826, Johnston wrote that as soon as cash was obtained the money would be forwarded at Ducher's order.[59]

55. The author has located no information that the Blounts made settlement with the state during the period under consideration.

56. Above, p. 82. Again, the public tobacco program is covered in detail above, pp. 198-214.

57. See the following correspondence in Clark, ed., *State Records*, XXI: James Porterfield to Governor Samuel Johnston, January 10, 1789, pp. 516-17; George Hooper to Governor Samuel Johnston, January 14, 1789, p. 518; Governor Samuel Johnston to George Hooper, January 27, 1789, p. 520; George Hooper to Governor Samuel Johnston, February 27, 1789, p. 533.

58. Journal of the Council of State, March 13, 1789, Governors' Office Papers, CXXI.

59. Governor Samuel Johnston to M. Ducher, April 1, 1789, Governors' Papers, Series II, Box IV (Johnston). In a letter dated February 24, 1789, *ibid.*, Ducher had again inquired about remittance.

The test of priority between the state's two obligations never occurred, for the only definite and acceptable offer that Johnston received insisted upon purchase of all the tobacco and involved a mode of payment not authorized by the 1788 Assembly for discharge of the Martinique debt.[60] Fearful that the tobacco would spoil in storage and anxious to meet part of the state's obligation to the United States, Governor Johnston, with the advice of the council and the recommendation of Congress, successfully negotiated the firm's purchase of all North Carolina's public tobacco (at a price somewhat below the council's original guidelines), with payment to be made to the United States. Under the circumstances and the demands that the administration faced, the decision to sell was understandable and defensible; but the French could hardly be expected to sympathize with the state's action.

French displeasure was indeed pronounced, and after Ducher, in August, again complained about failure of remittance, the governor called another meeting of the council. Johnston was worried about legislative reaction to the sale of all the tobacco without payment to Martinique, and the council could only recommend that he explain to the 1789 Assembly that, under the previous Assembly's instructions, no prospect of a customer had come forward to make remittance to Martinique possible.[61] One week after the council adjourned, Johnston wrote Ducher to describe the turn of events, to explain his own actions, and to express confidence that the 1789 Assembly would make provision for effective payment. Johnston concluded with a statement that he was deeply troubled by the "great & unavoidable obstacles" that had so long delayed the

60. The firm, Royal Flint and Co. of New York, had obtained a credit with the United States Treasury and offered that credit to North Carolina. The transactions with Royal Flint are covered in detail above, pp. 209-10. Another merchant was discussing the purchase of a hundred hogsheads when Flint made the offer, and ultimately the hundred hogsheads were sold to the other merchant.

61. Journal of the Council of State, September 1, 1789, Governors' Office Papers, CXXI.

discharge of the debt to Martinque.[62] The governor's concern must have provided small comfort to the French official.

At the opening of the 1789 Assembly, the governor, in compliance with the council's recommendation, informed the legislators that the debt to Martinique had not been discharged because it had not been possible to sell the public tobacco for cash (or bills of exchange authorized by the Assembly).[63] Upon Johnston's request that the Assembly look into the problem, a subcommittee reported that the balance due as of October 15, 1788, had been $4,826, which with interest would presently total £2,151/14/4 (about $5,378). The report, endorsing Johnston's decision, stated that the public tobacco could not have been disposed of during the previous year in an authorized manner so as to discharge the debt. The subcommittee concluded by recommending that the Assembly adopt the most eligible method of extinguishing the debt.[64] The Assembly concurred with the report and resolved that any public tobacco rejected by the private firm be sold for cash to discharge part of the debt in such manner as the governor and council might decide.[65] The Assembly resolved also that money (about $1,625 specie plus interest) owed to the state by one Richard Blackledge, convicted of fraud against North Carolina, should be applied against the Martinique debt. The balance still due, if any, was to be withdrawn from the treasury by the governor, who, with the advice and consent of the council, was to use the money to discharge the obligation.[66]

Appropriately, the man whose responsibility it became to execute final payment of the debt as provided by the 1789

62. Governor Samuel Johnston to M. Ducher, September 10, 1789, Clark, ed., *State Records*, XXI, 564.

63. *Ibid.*, p. 206.

64. *Ibid.*, p. 421.

65. *Ibid.*, pp. 421-22, 722.

66. Governor Alexander Martin to M. Ducher, February 27, April 8, 1790, Governors' Letter Books, X, 10-11, 25-26. Blackledge, in whose warehouse public tobacco had been stored, had used part of that tobacco for his own purposes and had been unable to replace it before his actions were discovered.

Assembly was Alexander Martin, who became governor as Samuel Johnston resigned to become United States senator and under whose previous administrations efforts to pay the debt had originated. No sooner had Martin taken office than he came under pressure from M. Ducher, vice-consul to North Carolina, and M. de la Forest, consul general to the United States. The latter official was especially insistent because he had been instructed by the French marine minister to employ the anticipated money from North Carolina to provision French vessels due to arrive at United States ports in the fall of 1790. Governor Martin assured De la Forest, by way of the state's United States senators, that North Carolina was not unmindful of Martinique's long indulgence.[67] To Ducher, Martin wrote that the Assembly of 1789 had made definite provisions for payment.[68]

Actually, Martin considered the potential from the tobacco and Blackledge to be "very uncertain funds."[69] The former sum promised to be modest in amount, and Blackledge was enjoying a six-month stay of execution that would not be ended until early summer and whose termination might find Blackledge yet unable to pay. Convinced that a considerable sum, therefore, would have to be drawn from the treasury in compliance with the Assembly's instructions, Martin began to lay groundwork for exercising his authority to issue the warrants. His first move, taken during the spring of 1790, was to solicit offers from North Carolina merchants regarding the traditional practice of converting North Carolina currency (which, as we have seen, had not been destroyed by North Carolina's ratification of the constitution) into produce for shipment and sale for specie or bills of exchange.[70] Certainly with the Blounts in mind, the governor stressed that bond

67. Governor Alexander Martin to Samuel Johnston and Benjamin Hawkins, May 25, 1790, *ibid.*, p. 41.

68. Governor Alexander Martin to M. Ducher, February 27, April 8, 1790, *ibid.*, pp. 10-11, 25-26.

69. Governor Alexander Martin to Samuel Johnston and Benjamin Hawkins, May 25, 1790, *ibid.*, p. 39.

70. Governor Alexander Martin to M. Ducher, April 8, 1790, *ibid.*, pp. 25-26.

would have to be given for prompt payment to Martinique. After several offers had been received, Martin called a council meeting for June 24 to discuss the Martinique debt. While awaiting the council session, he assured Ducher that speedy and effectual measures were about to be taken.[71]

Also while awaiting June 24, the governor pursued the other two sums set aside by the Assembly. Lamenting the obligation "with which this State has so long been encumbered to its disgrace," Martin inquired of John Stewart, agent to sell the rejected tobacco, whether the tobacco had been sold and, if so, for how much. Stewart replied that the sales had not been completed and that a final report would be ready by the council's meeting.[72]

If the governor remained apprehensive about the tobacco, he received, upon pointed inquiry, a pleasant surprise from Richard Blackledge, who, in a letter dated June 10, informed Martin that he, Blackledge, had purchased a draft in New York for the amount of his obligation. The draft would undoubtedly be honored, wrote Blackledge assuringly, and would, in compliance with the Assembly's directions, be turned over to the French[73]

Governor Martin having carefully prepared the way, the council meeting of June 24 went smoothly. The council learned of Blackledge's draft and that the tobacco sales totaled a modest value in North Carolina currency.[74] In order to

71. Governor Alexander Martin to M. Ducher, May 25, 1790, *ibid.*, pp. 44-45.

72. Governor Alexander Martin to John Stewart, April 5, 1790, *ibid.*, p. 44; Governor Alexander Martin to John Stewart, May 24, 1790, *ibid.*, pp. 45-47; John Stewart to Governor Alexander Martin, May 31, 1790, *ibid.*, pp. 47-48.

73. Governor Alexander Martin to Richard Blackledge, May 25, 1790, *ibid.*, pp. 48-49; Richard Blackledge to Governor Alexander Martin, June 10, 1790, *ibid.*, pp. 56-57.

74. The exact amount of the tobacco sales does not appear in official correspondence. On March 13 Stewart had reported sales totaling £441/11/11 North Carolina currency. In May, Stewart reported some tobacco still unsold. The total amount was probably well less than one thousand pounds North Carolina currency. John Stewart to Governor Alexander Martin, March 13, May 31, 1790, *ibid.*, pp. 66, 47-48.

discharge the balance yet remaining the various mercantile offers were examined, after which the council advised Martin to supply Stewart and Muir, merchants of Halifax, with the tobacco money and with additional funds from the treasury. The merchants were to convert the currency into specie or bills of exchange and were then to deliver the sum to De la Forest at New York. They were also instructed to write that French official immediately.[75]

Undoubtedly feeling satisfied with the council's actions, Martin awaited information from M. de la Forest about a matter that, legitimately or not, had been troubling the administration for some time: whether the remittance should be delivered to De la Forest, Ducher, or to the administrator of the government of Martinique.[76] Martin's inquiry triggered De la Forest to vent the exasperation and frustration that French officials had increasingly felt as the years had passed. A statement by the consul general dated June 12, 1790, reviewed the origin and size of the debt and the repeated efforts to collect payment. De la Forest patronizingly explained that the so-called Martinique debt had always been due the navy department of the government of France, and he accused North Carolina of having pretended that the debt was owed to Martinique because to do so was less embarrassing than to owe money to the French government itself. Payment to the deputy treasurer of the navy department at Martinique or to the treasurer of France, he stated, would have sufficed at any time, but because "circumstances" had made it necessary to insist on payment in the United States, French officials in this country had repeatedly informed North Carolina that they would accept the money on behalf of Martinique, that is, the navy department of France. The letter expressed De la Forest's past embarrassment at being unable to supply the French fleet by use of North Carolina's payment, and he pleaded that remittance be made to the king's consul at Phil-

75. Governor Alexander Martin to Samuel Johnston and Benjamin Hawkins, June 29, 1790, *ibid.*, pp. 61-62.

76. See *ibid.*

adelphia or Boston before the French fleet arrived in the fall.[77]

While De la Forest's exasperation was understandable and justified and while French officials had indeed repeatedly offered to receive payment, one accusation was not altogether fair. As previously indicated, postwar administrations were hampered by a lack of precise information as to the origin and size of the debt, and it was the lack of knowledge rather than the desire for pretense that led North Carolina officials to assign the debt to Martinique rather than to the government of France. Genuinely believing that the money was owed to the island, the postwar administrations had received from French officials many letters that referred to the Martinique debt, and no information until that of June 12, 1790, had ever made clear the true nature of the debt. Certainly French officials had the right to assume that North Carolina was fully apprised of its own obligations, but earlier enlightenment by some French authority would have been a simple matter.

It was probably this element of unfairness in De la Forest's statement that led Martin to reply testily that he had no further apologies to make for the long duration of the debt, for a firm had been appointed agent to discharge the obligation. Unnecessarily Martin warned De la Forest that it would take some time to convert North Carolina currency into specie or bills of exchange.[78] After writing the consul general, the

77. M. de la Forest's statement of June 12, 1790, *ibid.*, pp. 69-74. M. de la Forest to Governor Alexander Martin, December 19, 1790, *ibid.*, p. 157, also cites the original debt and the state's payments against it. Illustrative of the confusion that frequently arose because of inadequate or inaccessible records is Martin's misunderstanding of the amount of the original debt. De la Forest set the original debt at $5,487, an amount which the governor interpreted to be a sudden increase of $661 over the amount of the original debt as reported by the 1788 Assembly. As we have seen, above, p. 114, that Assembly had agreed with the French debt statement and had stated the balance due after deducting the amount that the French had received from the Blounts. Martin misunderstood the balance due to be the original debt. See Governor Alexander Martin to Stewart and Muir, August 29, 1791, *ibid.*, p. 281.

78. Governor Alexander Martin to M. de la Forest, July 26, 1790, *ibid.*, pp. 74-75.

governor sent Stewart and Muir a warrant on the treasury and instructed them to write De la Forest immediately. The merchants and the consul general soon thereafter opened correspondence concerning shipment of produce.[79] By September, 1790, De la Forest, having established satisfactory arrangements with Stewart and Muir and having received $1,691 specie from Blackledge, was more favorably disposed toward North Carolina and conveyed his pleasure and appreciation to Governor Martin.[80] In addressing the Assembly on November 2 the governor stated that the Martinique debt which had long disgraced and burdened the state was well on the way to extinction.[81] In December, De la Forest announced that he had received $2,812 specie from Stewart and Muir, which amount, together with payments by the Blounts and Blackledge, left a balance of $322 due from North Carolina.[82] In the spring of 1791 the consul general received from Stewart and Muir the sum of $1,112 specie, which not only discharged the principal of the debt but also most of the interest.[83] Martin attempted prompt remittance of the remaining interest, but because all the state's information regarding the debt had been forwarded to North Carolina's agents for settling accounts with the United States, extinction was delayed until 1792.[84]

The papers connected with Martinique had been forwarded to North Carolina's agents because the United States had adopted the principle of general equity in settling war accounts with the states and therefore enabled North Carolina

79. Governor Alexander Martin to Stewart and Muir, July 26, 1790, *ibid.*, pp. 76-77.

80. See Governor Alexander Martin to Stewart and Muir, October 7, 1790, *ibid.*, pp. 118-19.

81. Governor Martin's address to the General Assembly, November 2, 1790, *ibid.*, p. 143.

82. M. de la Forest to Governor Alexander Martin, December 19, 1790, *ibid.*, p. 157.

83. M. de la Forest to Governor Alexander Martin, April 1, 1791, *ibid.*, p. 243.

84. Governor Alexander Martin to Francis Child, August 29, 1791, *ibid.*, p. 281; Francis Child to Governor Alexander Martin, August 31, 1791, *ibid.*, p. 284.

to claim part of the Martinique debt against the national government.[85] The state put forward the sum of $15,537 specie as the size of the Martinique claim, and in final settlement North Carolina was credited with the claim.[86]

The foregoing description of North Carolina's efforts to extinguish its foreign debt reveals a great lack of legislative and executive continuity combined with a deplorable deficiency of public records. The status of Bretigny's account with the state, the amount of the debt, the activities of the Blounts, the actions of previous Assemblies—these were among the fundamental matters about which the government, for years, knew all too little. Between 1784 and 1788 the Assembly failed to concern itself directly with the payment of the debt. Upon taking office neither Governor Caswell nor Governor Johnston could find any documents to reduce his ignorance of past transactions. The loose procedures of government contributed delay and confusion to what was inherently a difficult payment procedure.

North Carolina's struggle to discharge the Martinique debt clearly illustrates also the state's financial limitations, especially in meeting obligations outside its boundaries. The losses associated with converting currency into produce and produce into specie were significant, and it is understandable that men associated with the process entertained misgivings and uneasiness. As the Assembly, without cost to itself, created fiat currency and converted it to specie, the public shouldered the difference between the specie and the market value of the currency, that is, the currency's depreciation.[87] Fiscal

85. See Hugh Williamson to Governor Alexander Martin, August 2, 1790, *ibid.*, pp. 93-97. The settlement of accounts between North Carolina and the United States is treated above, pp. 132-68.

86. "General Abstract of the Claims of the State of North Carolina Against the United States," p. 6, Treasurers' and Comptrollers' Papers, Military Papers, LXVIII, State Department of Archives and History, Raleigh.

87. Forrest McDonald, *E. Pluribus Unum* (Boston: Houghton Mifflin Company, 1965), p. 83, evaluates the North Carolina tobacco program as an ingenius process by which the Assembly derived specie from paper. McDonald acknowledges that the currency depreciation spread losses among the population, but he does not take sufficiently into

conservatives, who maintained that an additional price was being exacted from the state's reputation, thus saw the Martinique affair as another pernicious example of fiat policy and financial impotence. Probably the Martinique episode alone converted no one to the Federalist persuasion, but it must have confirmed and intensified the conviction of North Carolina Federalists that the state was better off within the Union.

---

account the effect upon the state's reputation and the inherent limitations and disadvantages of the program.

PART II

STATE-FEDERAL FINANCIAL RELATIONS

V. *The Political Implications*

During the postwar years, relations between the United States and the individual states centered largely around two related financial issues. The first was that of the domestic Revolutionary debt contracted by the United States. The national domestic debt issue, in turn, consisted of two facets: the matter of the unliquidated debt, that is, the debt in the hands of individuals or owed to individuals; and the matter of settling the wartime accounts between the United States and the respective states for expenses incurred and services performed on each other's behalf. The second great financial issue consisted of the efforts to secure revenue for Congress, both through the requisition system established under the Articles of Confederation and through the establishment of independent revenue sources for the national government.[1] These financial issues had great political implications, for advocates of a stronger central government believed it essential to their purposes that Congress assume the unliquidated national debt, complete the settlement of accounts with the states, and acquire its own taxing powers.[2]

During the confederation period the national debt, with which Federalists hoped to bind its holders to the central

1. An enlightening and useful study of American public finance of this period is E. James Ferguson, *The Power of the Purse: A History of American Public Finance 1776-1790* (Chapel Hill: The University of North Carolina Press, 1961). The book comprehensively examines congressional finance and financial relations between Congress and the states.

2. The standard account of the political implications surrounding the Articles of Confederation and the questions of public finance is Merrill Jensen, *The Articles of Confederation* (Madison: The University of Wisconsin Press, 1940). Also valuable for its insight concerning politics and finance is Ferguson, *Power of the Purse.*

government, consisted of continental loan office certificates, certificates of future payment issued to individuals by continental authority, and final settlement certificates issued by the United States to members of the state Continental Lines. This debt, whose components shall shortly be described in more detail, had been contracted in the general defense of the United States, and according to the Articles of Confederation was therefore to be discharged out of a common treasury supplied by the individual states on the basis of their respective land values. In practice, however, it was uncertain—except for clear congressional control over continental loan certificates—whether Congress or the states were to discharge the national domestic debt.[3] Federalists violated the letter and the spirit of the articles by insisting that the debt was to be kept separate from the settlement of accounts between the United States and the individual states, that is, that the debt was not to be apportioned among the states but rather to be paid by Congress itself from congressional tax powers that did not actually exist but, the Federalists argued, were implied by the very existence of the debt. After 1783 Congress and the states, in fact, ignored the articles by acting as though the public debt was indeed to be kept separate from the settlement between the United States and the respective states, that is, as though the debt resided directly in Congress rather than among the thirteen states. Thus the Federalists won control of the debt, which was the key issue between the states and the United States during the immediate postwar period. In view of the great political importance of the debt, a brief examination of its components is necessary.

Issued through continental loan offices established in the states, loan certificates, unlike most other continental certificates, bore interest, and were therefore considered preferred securities.[4] Since loans were usually subscribed by

3. Ferguson, *Power of the Purse*, p. 179. The following summary rests upon Ferguson's study of public finance.

4. Interest rates on continental loan certificates were altered on several occasions. When first authorized in October, 1776, they bore 4 per cent annual interest; when that rate proved insufficient inducement,

well-to-do individuals, the certificates tended to remain in the hands of the original holders[5] Those loan certificates that did circulate fared comparatively well in the market because of the interest they bore. Although Congress' financial difficulties had eventually forced the suspension of interest payments and had compelled Congress to ask the states to assume the interest payments, the national government steadfastly refused to allow the states to redeem the certificates. Until 1782 the loan office certificates were the only debt that clearly belonged to Congress and that Congress clearly intended to discharge. In the postwar financial settlement the certificates were indeed assumed by the United States.

The second portion of the national debt, continental certificates issued to individuals in lieu of money, presented a much more difficult problem of settlement. Certificates had inundated the country during the Revolution, especially after the failure of continental currency had forced Congress to rely even more heavily upon impressments.[6] With its entire financial structure tottering, Congress, in 1780, had felt compelled to ask the states to accept continental certificates in the payment of state taxes. The states had received similar pressure from their own citizenry, who held vast quantities of the certificates and wished to use them in discharge of tax obligations. When Congress came under Federalist control during the 1781-83 period, the Federalists sought to have the central government assume the continental certificates that were still in the hands of individuals. The assumption process was to consist of an examination of privately-held continental

---

Congress raised the rate to 6 per cent paid in the equivalent of specie (February, 1777); after March 1, 1778, they drew interest only in paper. For a general discussion of continental loan certificates, see *ibid.*, pp. 35-40.

5. Not all persons who received loan certificates were voluntary recipients or well-to-do. Congress' desperate financial situation during the war had led to the practice of issuing the certificates to pay for goods and services. The practice, however, had not become generally enough known to destroy the relative esteem that the certificates enjoyed. *Ibid.*, pp. 53-55.

6. For treatment of congressional expropriation by certificates, see *ibid.*, pp. 57-69.

certificates and an issuing of final settlement certificates to replace validated certificates. Continental certificates that had been taken in by the states under congressional authorization were not considered part of the national debt but rather were to become a part of the general settlement of wartime accounts between the United States and the respective states.

The third part of the debt consisted of final settlement certificates issued by the United States to members of the Continental Lines. In 1780 Congress had been forced by its financial difficulties to ask the states to pay their respective Lines for services performed up to August 1, 1780. Moved by the plight of the continental troops, a number of states had paid their Lines for services performed beyond the date authorized by Congress. In 1783 the Federalists in Congress undertook to have the central government issue certificates to the Lines for whatever pay was still due the continental officers and troops.[7]

By the end of 1783, then, Congress had staked its claim to the continental loan certificates, the continental certificates still in the hands of or owed to civilians, and the arrears of pay due the Continental Lines as expressed through final settlement certificates. These categories of certificates comprised the domestic debt of the United States.

As previously indicated, the settlement of accounts between the United States and the individual states was considered distinct from the foregoing national debt. During the war the government of the United States had expended money and other resources on behalf of all the states, and the states, in turn, had contributed resources and performed services in the general defense of the United States. It was assumed that at the end of the war the account between the general government and each of the states would be settled; that all state expenses in the common cause would be determined and the states would be apportioned their shares of the national obligation according to the values of their respective

7. Settlement with the North Carolina Continental Line is treated separately, above, pp. 169-90.

lands; and that states which, according to the settlement, had actually contributed more than their quotas would be given a credit with the United States, while the states that had contributed less than their respective shares would make up the difference.[8] The key to the whole procedure lay in examining the claims that each state had against the United States. The original expectation was that the states could charge the following categories against the United States: state payments upon congressional requisitions; state retirement of continental money and continental certificates when such retirement had been requested by Congress; state expenses incurred in recruiting and equipping its own Continental Line; state expenses for militia called out in the service of the United States; back pay and depreciation notes given to the Continental Line for services before August 1, 1780; and state payments of money and certificates for supplies furnished to federal officers. The limitation upon all these categories was that all should have been incurred upon prior authorization by Congress.

For their own respective reasons Congress and the states proved anxious to commence settlement. Federalists were interested in having Congress assume any balance that the central government might owe a state, that is, in increasing the national debt and thereby the bonds of Union. The states, believing themselves to have expended more than their respective quotas, were eager to receive a credit with the United States.

8. The effort to change the mode of apportionment from land to population or the principle of equity is treated above, p. 138.

VI. *Settlement of State and Individual Revolutionary Accounts*

As previously revealed, North Carolina during the Revolution had been compelled to rely greatly upon its own resources and had undertaken sizable military activity and expense in its own defense and in the general defense of the United States.[1] Convinced early in the war that the state would be found a creditor to the national government,[2] the General Assembly in 1778 had rejected as premature a bill to establish a committee to prepare the state's claims,[3] but by 1780 the Assembly had concluded that North Carolina's mounting claims necessitated steps preparatory to settlement. The act of that year establishing a state board of auditors to examine claims against the state had provided that the board should also make a complete statement "from time to time" of North Carolina's account with the United States.[4] When the task of organizing state finances had proved beyond the board's capacity, the Assembly, it will be recalled, had supplemented the central board with district boards of auditors.[5] The act of 1781 creating the district boards had assigned them the task of examining claims against North Carolina,

1. Above, pp. 15-56, *passim*.

2. All the southern states believed they would be found to be creditor states. E. James Ferguson, *The Power of the Purse: A History of American Public Finance, 1776-1790* (Chapel Hill: The University of North Carolina Press, 1961), p. 212. As this chapter shall reveal, North Carolina had greater reason for optimism as the years passed.

3. Walter Clark, ed., *The State Records of North Carolina* (16 vols.; Winston, Goldsboro, and Raleigh: State of North Carolina, 1895-1906) [volumes numbered consecutive to William L. Saunders, ed., *The Colonial Records of North Carolina* (10 vols.; Raleigh: State of North Carolina, 1886-90)], XII, 619, 740, 741.

4. *Ibid.*, XXIV, 325. Above, pp. 27-28.

5. Clark, ed., *State Records*, XXIV, 373-75. Above, p. 28.

but, significantly, the legislation had given the boards no responsibilities regarding state-federal financial relations. This intentional silence had enabled the boards to make no distinction between claims against North Carolina and claims against the national government, and, not being legally prohibited from examining the latter category of claims, the boards had acepted large quantities of continental certificates and had issued in their stead certificates pledging redemption by the state.[6] Thus the continental debt within North Carolina largely passed from the hands of individuals into the possession of the state. The exchange of state certificates for continental securities significantly increased the state debt, all the more so because the boards were lax regarding supporting evidence and the stated monetary amount of individual claims.[7]

State absorption of the continental debt was a policy resulting from several considerations, not the least of which, as previously indicated, was the public's desire to be rid of such unpromising paper. North Carolinians had good reasons to think that their continental certificates had less prospect than state certificates for redemption—whether by payment of taxes or use of tangible property—because state government, with its redemption options and its susceptibility to pressure, would more heavily and directly feel a responsibility to retire state obligations. By opening opportunities for extensive and varied retirement of certificates, the exchange process afforded relief to taxpayers and hope to speculators.[8] A second, political motivation behind the exchange procedure was that it would discourage centralization proclivities. Finally, the exchange

6. Marion Gregory and Donald Lennon, "The North Carolina Revolutionary Debt" (unpublished manuscript at the State Department of Archives and History, Raleigh), p. 21. This manuscript, although limited in its scope, is not without merit.

7. As this chapter will reveal, the laxness of North Carolina's evidence became all the more apparent as final settlement proceeded. Ferguson, *Power of the Purse*, p. 208, indicates that in absorbing continental certificates the southern states were generally lax regarding evidence.

8. *Ibid.*, pp. 180-83.

—with the foregoing advantages—might only temporarily increase North Carolina's financial burden because the state's continental certificates could be presented against the United States in the final settlement of accounts.[9] Whether Congress would accept responsibility for certificates retired by the exchange process was uncertain; for although, as we have seen, Congress in 1780 had authorized and encouraged the states to retire by taxation certain categories of continental certificates, the wholesale retirement effected by the exchange exceeded congressional authorization. Thus in seeking to benefit the public (especially speculators) and stifle Federalism without permanently adding to the state debt, North Carolina was gambling that Congress could be persuaded to acquiesce regarding the exchange procedure. The gamble, which by war's end amounted to upwards of seven million dollars nominal value of continental certificates,[10] seemed all the more worth taking because other states were similarly engaged in absorbing the continental debt and would join North Carolina in pressuring Congress.

Far from being disposed to approve state absorption of the continental debt, Congress, coming under Federalist control in 1781, had been dismayed to see the national debt—the bond of union—significantly decreasing as it passed from individual hands into the possession of states. Indeed, North Carolina's policies of taxation and exchange—particularly the latter—were on the way toward eliminating the continental debt within the state.[11] Anxious for several political reasons[12]

9. Forrest McDonald, *E. Pluribus Unum* (Boston: Houghton Mifflin Company, 1965), p. 82, correctly points out that the states retired continental certificates in the expectation that the certificates could be charged against the United States. Although McDonald refers to retirement by taxation, the statement would apply also to retirement by the exchange process.

10. U.S. Congress, House. Speech of Representative Williamson. 1st Cong., 2nd sess., March 30, 1790, *Annals of Congress* (42 vols.; Washington: Gales and Seaton, 1834-56), II, 1487, 1489.

11. Above, p. 146. Statement in Treasurers' and Comptrollers' Papers, Military Papers, LXVII, State Department of Archives and History, Raleigh. Ferguson, *Power of the Purse*, p. 65, notes that it was politically impossible for states to refuse continental certificates in

to exert direct congressional control and responsibility over the remaining debt, Congress implemented its determination by a resolution of February 20, 1782.[13] The resolution called upon the superintendent of finance (Robert Morris) to nominate a commissioner to each state to liquidate and settle in specie value individual civilian claims against the United States, that is to examine continental certificates and to exchange such validated claims for new certificates obligating the national government. The resolution further authorized the commissioners to settle accounts between the respective states and the United States.[14] Shortly after Congress passed the resolution, Robert Morris nominated Thomas Montgomery of Delaware as commissioner to North Carolina and forwarded the name to Governor Alexander Martin, whose approval or that of the Assembly was required under the February 20 resolution.[15]

Morris' letter of nomination, dated March 7, 1782, almost certainly reached Governor Martin during the Assembly session that convened at Hillsborough on April 13, but Martin failed to present the correspondence—nor did he take it upon himself to approve Montgomery's appointment. Governor Martin's failure to act was motivated by the desire to have the state control the preparation of accounts against the United States. Such control, both for its financial and

---

payment of taxes. No North Carolina taxes were explicitly made payable in such certificates until 1782.

12. Above, pp. 127-31, *passim.*

13. *Journals of the Continental Congress, 1774-89* (34 vols.; Washington: Government Printing Office, 1904-37), XXII, 84-85.

14. Individual claims were to be settled according to the principles of equity and good conscience in all cases not provided for by the resolutions of Congress. Accounts between the states and the United States were to be estimated according to the table of depreciation framed by the Board of Treasury on July 29, 1780, except that supplies furnished under congressional requisitions were to be settled agreeable to the prices stated in the requisitions.

15. Robert Morris to Governor Alexander Martin, March 7, 1782, Clark, ed., *State Records*, XVI, 744-45. In the *State Records* the letter is dated March 7, 1783, but the context of the letter clearly establishes that the year was actually 1782. Morris stressed that no state would receive one of its own citizens as commissioner.

political importance, appeared imperative because the state's claims were in great disarray and were frequently unsupported or insufficiently supported by evidence. Sharing the governor's concern that order be brought to state finances and that North Carolina's claims be prepared under state direction, the 1782 Assembly created the office of comptroller with the broad authority "to check and controul all public accounts in every department."[16] Soon thereafter the comptroller, Richard Caswell, was busily engaged in preparing the state's claims against the central government.

After allowing a full six months for Caswell to get underway, Governor Martin wrote Robert Morris concerning North Carolina's failure to act upon Montgomery's nomination. Without explaining the inaction at the 1782 Assembly, Martin stated that an expected fall session of the 1782 Assembly had failed to materialize and that he had not approved the nomination because the council insisted upon legislative confirmation. The governor assured Morris that Montgomery's nomination would be presented to the 1783 Assembly and that in the meantime the state comptroller was constructively employed in collecting and preparing North Carolina's claims.[17] This information could hardly have pleased Morris, for if the delay suited North Carolina's purposes, Federalists were frustrated to see the state exert complete control over the preparation of accounts and continue to absorb the continental debt by means of the exchange process.

A few of those frustrated Federalists were at the 1783 Assembly, at which they charged that the comptroller was exceeding his authority by preparing the state's accounts against the United States. Controlled by a combination of persons who were worried about centralization tendencies and/or the state's disorderly finances, the Assembly responded to the Federalist challenge by explicitly authorizing the comp-

16. *Ibid.*, XXIV, 442.

17. Governor Alexander Martin to Robert Morris, January 21, 1783, *ibid.*, XVI, 731. Martin expressed his personal approval of Montgomery's nomination, but, as indicated, the council insisted on the Assembly's approval.

troller to settle with individuals who had drawn money from the continental treasury for the use of North Carolina; to settle with persons who had drawn money from the state treasury for the use of the United States; and to prepare North Carolina's claims against the United States.[18] Further to the dismay of Federalists, the Assembly directed the comptroller to settle individual claims against the United States and to do so on the basis of equity, that is, to issue state certificates for continental certificates for such amounts as the comptroller should deem just.[19] Thus the 1783 Assembly continued and confirmed the policies of absorbing the continental debt and controlling the preparation of accounts. The Assembly's failure to act upon Montgomery's nomination or upon any part of the February 20 resolution further attested significant opposition to the centralization implications of the debt question.

The Assembly did not convene again until the spring of 1784, by which time the comptroller had enjoyed two years' opportunity to pursue his assigned tasks. With the continental debt virtually extinguished within the state and with the state's records in somewhat better order, a number of legislators were prepared to consider the establishment of congressional authority so that the settlement process (which, it was believed, would undoubtedly find North Carolina a creditor) could begin. Federalist forces at the Assembly, stronger than at its predecessor,[20] argued for implementation of the congressional resolution of February 20, 1782, but what emerged from the Assembly was a compromise between the Federalists and those legislators who wished settlement to proceed but were worried about congressional incursions upon state sovereignty: a series of resolutions passed May 31, 1784, proposed that claims between North Carolina and the United States be jointly settled by the state comptroller (who in the meantime was to continue preparing the state's accounts) and

18. *Ibid.*, XXIV, 499-500.

19. *Ibid.*, XIX, 310.

20. For Federalist influence at the spring Assembly of 1784, see above, pp. 194-97.

a commissioner to be nominated by the superintendent of finance and confirmed by the state; if disagreements should arise between the two officials concerning the validity of claims, they were to appoint a third man to help weigh the claims in question, a majority decision being final; for commissioner North Carolina's delegates in Congress were authorized to approve any nominee from Delaware, Virginia, Maryland, South Carolina, or Georgia—latitude more apparent than real since the Assembly's coolness toward Montgomery served notice that North Carolina preferred someone from a neighboring state. Further to promote settlement, the Assembly directed the governor to present to the next Assembly an estimate of advances made by North Carolina on behalf of other states or the United States "as far as the same can respectively be known." To escape the impracticability of the Eighth Article of Confederation and the consequences of having opened the western land office the previous year, the Assembly provided that instead of being based on land values, each state's proportion of the war expenses of the United States could be determined by population or by the principle of equity. The Assembly's cession of western land, while motivated by other factors as well, served North Carolina's interests should the Eighth Article remain unchanged.[21]

21. Clark, ed., *State Records*, XIX, 663-65; XXIV, 561, 564-65. While anxiously awaiting the fate of the congressional impost, Congress had been forced to content itself with making the requisition system more workable and more acceptable to the states, particularly regarding the mode of determining the respective state quotas. The Eighth Article of Confederation provided that expenses for war, common defense, and general welfare were to be defrayed from a common treasury to be supplied by the states in proportion to each state's amount of granted or surveyed land together with the value of improvements thereupon. After this mode of proportionment had proved impractical under wartime conditions and after it became manifest that a state's suffering and sacrifice bore no relationship to its land area, Congress had recommended on February 20, 1782, that in the final settlement of the general expenses of the war up to January 1, 1782—except for the national domestic debt—Congress be allowed to adopt such principles and measures of apportionment as appeared to Congress to be just and equitable. The proposal had made little headway among the states, and on April 18, 1783, Congress had recommended that the Eighth Article be amended so as to base each state's proportion upon total

Any hopes that the central government would agree to North Carolina's settlement proposal were quickly dashed by Robert Morris' firm insistence that the congressional resolution of February 20 did not anticipate arbitration between the state and the congressional commissioner. It would, moreover, be a "remarkable circumstance," Morris commented, to have the state name one arbitrator (the comptroller) and possess the power of rejecting the other. Morris warned that Congress, having already settled a number of state accounts according to the February 20 resolution, would be most unlikely to yield to North Carolina's proposal, and he suggested that the Assembly's resolutions be brought into conformity with the congressional program.[22] The superintendent's intransigence against the state's participation in settling individual accounts or in settling its accounts against the United States could not have come as a surprise to anyone who even vaguely understood the political implications of state-federal financial rela-

white population and three-fifths of all other persons excluding Indians not paying taxes. North Carolina's delegation in Congress had voted for the April 18 proposal, and the spring Assembly of 1784 supported the measure because the state's proportion would be smaller if based upon population rather than land area. The decision was all the easier, as indicated above, because the opening of the land office in 1783 had greatly increased North Carolina's granted and surveyed land; and, as we have seen, above p. 38, it was the spring Assembly of 1784 that closed the land office. The cession of the state's western land is treated above, pp. 38, 195. See also Ferguson, *Power of the Purse*, p. 33; *Journals of Continental Congress*, XXII, 83-84, XXIV, 260-61; Clark, ed., *State Records*, XXIV, 561, 564-65. The spring Assembly of 1784 also instructed the governor to prepare an account of both taxable property and population so that whether the amendment succeeded or not North Carolina would not pay more than its proportion of the war expenses of the United States. Clark, ed., *State Records*, XIX, 663.

The Assembly was cool toward Montgomery because he was considered a northerner. Governor Alexander Martin to Hugh Williamson and Richard Dobbs Spaight, June 4, 1784, Clark, ed., *State Records*, XVII, 80.

22. Robert Morris to Governor Alexander Martin, August 4, 1784, *ibid.*, XVII, 165. Morris' letter pointed out also that the congressional resolution specified that individual claims be settled in specie whereas the Assembly resolution required that individual claims be settled by the continental scale of depreciation governing state claims against the United States.

tions, for his attitude clearly reflected Federalist desire to control the remaining debt.[23]

As Morris indicated, settlement between the United States and several states had indeed begun, and one aspect of that process both alarmed and intrigued North Carolina officials: several states were pressing claims for expenses that had not received prior authorization under congressional resolutions. The result largely of unauthorized military expeditions, these claims, if accepted by Congress, would greatly increase the national government's obligation and therefore North Carolina's portion of it (whether under the Articles of Confederation or by means of the congressional taxes that the Federalists hoped to establish). While this prospect naturally engendered concern, North Carolina's unauthorized military expeditions and other unauthorized expenses, if accepted by Congress, would greatly enhance the state's position at final settlement. Furthermore, congressional acceptance of unauthorized military expenditures would encourage congressional acceptance of continental certificates that North Carolina (and other states) had retired by the exchange process. Weighing the dangers and the potential advantages to North Carolina, state officials took the position that North Carolina would support the broad claims of other states if their delegates in Congress would reciprocate on North Carolina's behalf. That rational position would have been a more comfortable one had the amount of the state's unauthorized expenditures been known; until that total could somehow be determined and supported, no one could be certain that it was indeed to the state's interest to promote congressional acceptance of unauthorized claims.[24]

23. Ferguson, *Power of the Purse*, p. 184.

24. Hugh Williamson to Governor Alexander Martin, July 5, 1784, September 30, 1784, Clark, ed., *State Records*, XVII, 81-82, 94-98; Governor Alexander Martin to North Carolina's delegates in Congress, January 28, 1783, Governors' Letter Books, V, 72-73, State Department of Archives and History, Raleigh. The southern states had undertaken numerous military expeditions without prior congressional authorization and therefore generally supported the proposal that Congress accept responsibility for such expeditions. Ferguson, *Power of the Purse*, pp. 206-7.

Whether Congress would come to accept unauthorized expenditures was doubtful, for states without large amounts of such claims and states that had completed or nearly completed settlement would oppose the change in policy. In the meantime, North Carolina's immediate interest lay in collecting any material bearing on authorized or unauthorized claims. As the continuing search made the records' inadequacy all the more apparent, it became increasingly obvious that North Carolina had a large vested interest in promoting congressional relaxation of the rules of evidence. Thoughts that Congress might adopt the principle of equity regarding both unauthorized claims and supporting evidence were positively intoxicating, and North Carolina's position possessed considerable suasion in view of the fact that the state had approved employment of the principle of equity in determining the states' respective proportions of the war expenses of the United States.

Sharing the heady hopes for equity, believing the state to be a creditor in any event, having given the comptroller two years to collect material, and correctly concluding that the continental debt in private hands had been largely absorbed, the Assembly in the fall of 1784 decided that North Carolina's interests lay in prompt initiation of settlement. The Assembly therefore abandoned the arbitration concept and yielded completely, if not without lengthy debate, to the congressional resolution of February 20, 1782, by declaring it to be the law of the state.[25] At the same time serving notice that North Carolina intended to press broad claims against the United States, an act of that Assembly noted that other states were making claims for unauthorized services and expenditures; argued that the distance between North Carolina and Congress had combined with the imminence of danger to compel the state to undertake military activities in its own and the general defense without prior congressional authorization; required that the cost of all such expeditions be determined so that claims could be presented against the national govern-

25. Clark, ed., *State Records*, XIX, 470, 747.

ment; and provided for the collection of all pertinent information regarding claims.[26]

Even as the Assembly was clearing the way for settlement, the appointment of a commissioner was indefinitely delayed by the resignation of Robert Morris and the replacement of his office by a three-man Board of Treasury. These events reflected the fact that Congress had passed from Federalist control and was presently dominated by men who were opposed to a great strengthening of the central government.[27] No longer viewing the national debt as a blessing and anxious therefore to terminate its growth, Congress on March 17, 1785, modified the resolution of February 20, 1782, by setting a deadline for the presentation of individual civilian claims against the United States. Under the new stipulations, North Carolinians would have one year from the time the commissioner received his appointment and entered his duties to present their claims to him—a period that North Carolina's delegates in Congress considered too short and attempted unsuccessfully to expand.[28]

Under the modified settlement procedure and the restructured financial system of Congress, the man whom North Carolina approved as commissioner to examine private and public claims against the United States was James Hindman of Maryland, who officially informed Governor Caswell on October 20, 1785, of his arrival at New Bern to commence his duties. At Hindman's request, the governor began to solicit the assistance of accountants and the co-operation of persons possessing public accounts against the national government.[29] In addition Caswell issued a proclamation to expedite the submission of individual claims, and, when the Assembly

26. *Ibid.*, XXIV, 679-80.

27. Ferguson, *Power of the Purse*, pp. 171-76, *passim*.

28. *Journals of Continental Congress*, XXVIII, 167-68; Richard Dobbs Spaight and John Sitgreaves to Governor Richard Caswell, March 18, 1785, Clark, ed., *State Records*, XVII, 433.

29. James Hindman to Governor Richard Caswell, October 20, 1785, Clark, ed., *State Records*, XVII, 546; Governor Richard Caswell to Joseph Green, November 7, 1785, *ibid.*, p. 564; Governor Richard Caswell to James Hindman, November 7, 1785, *ibid.*, p. 564.

convened, he requested the enactment of all laws that the Assembly considered necessary to secure the settlement of claims.[30] Responding promptly, the Assembly empowered the commissioner to call witnesses and examine them under oath on matters touching upon claims against the United States.[31]

In addition to bestowing the aforementioned authority upon the commissioner, the 1785 Assembly displayed interest in the settlement question by directing the comptroller to report—in compliance with the instructions of the spring Assembly of 1784—upon the status of North Carolina's claims insofar as his office could determine. Stating that for the period up to November 1, 1780, the United States owed North Carolina a balance of £1,554,238/11/7 specie, the comptroller, Francis Child, explained that work had been slowed and time lost because his office had initially distinguished between militia (state) expenses and continental expenses, whereas the Assembly's resolution of May 31, 1784, had subsequently required that militia and continental charges be interspersed.[32] Actually, the resolution of May 31 had required no such interspersion but rather had stated that "in such matters of form as regard merely the stating of his accounts," the comptroller should "proceed agreeable to his own discretion."[33] The decision to blend state and continental charges had stemmed from the administration's conviction that the practice might help to secure credit for expenditures incurred without prior congressional authorization.

The comptroller's report indicated clearly that much time would be consumed in preparing, presenting, and examining the state's claims, a prospect all the more disturbing because the commissioner's arrival in October, 1785, had commenced the one-year period authorized by Congress and because

30. *Ibid.*, pp. 270, 289-90.

31. *Ibid.*, XXIV, 737-38. This legislation fulfilled a request made by the congressional resolution of February 20, 1782.

32. *Ibid.*, XVII, 279, 341-42; XX, 7. The comptroller, Francis Child, pointed out also that the Board of Treasury had instructed the commissioner to settle accounts in dollars rather than pounds, a conversion that would also cause delay.

33. *Ibid.*, XIX, 664.

James Hindman soon proved to be a somewhat difficult and dallying individual with whom to deal. Although a congressional resolution of June 3, 1784, had instructed the commissioner to proceed to the place designated by the state and although Governor Martin had requested that the commissioner repair to the comptroller's office at Kinston, Hindman steadfastly refused to leave New Bern. The personal factors are neither certain nor important, but apparently it was the commissioner's enjoyment of New Bern society that prompted him to insist that all pertinent materials be forwarded to that town from Kinston. The request seemed unreasonable and improper to Governor Caswell, who, upon the council's advice, wrote Hindman of the risks, difficulties, and expense that a transfer would involve and recommended that the commissioner establish himself at Kinston. Hindman remained unmoved and informed Caswell that, in any case, settlement could not begin until blank account books for that purpose arrived from Congress.[34] The commissioner might also have justified delay on the basis of congressional instructions to settle individual claims prior to state claims,[35] but his refusal to proceed to Kinston clearly violated his instructions to comply administratively with the governor and the Assembly. Understandably disturbed by Hindman's intractability, Caswell in the summer of 1786 successfully entreated the Board of Treasury to instruct the commissioner to move to Kinston. Stung by the Board's tone of reprimand, Hindman traveled northward late in the year to justify his delay, and, of course, his departure only further postponed the initiation of settlement. On November 18 Governor Caswell notified the Assembly of Hindman's absence and emphasized that the continued delay should not be attributed to the state of North Carolina.[36]

34. Governor Alexander Martin to Robert Morris, June 4, 1784, *ibid.*, XVII, 75. Governor Richard Caswell to James Hindman, February 2, 1786, *ibid.*, XVIII, 519-21; extract from the Journal of the Council of State, February 1, 1786, Treasurers' and Comptrollers' Papers, Military Papers, LXVIII.

35. Ferguson, *Power of the Purse*, p. 213.

36. Governor Richard Caswell to William Blount, June 7, 1786,

The behavior of Commissioner Hindman had, meanwhile, contributed to a growing conviction at the Board of Treasury that the decentralized system of commissioners was leading to laxness and lack of uniformity in the settlement of wartime accounts.[37] Sharing the Board's dissatisfaction, Congress, on October 13, 1786, passed an ordinance that centralized the settlement process and contained major concessions toward those states which, like North Carolina, had incurred heavy unauthorized expenditures and possessed inadequate records. The ordinance provided that after April 1, 1787, a central board of three men was to assume the authority of the commissioners in settling accounts between the states and the United States. For a period of one year from its initial meeting the board, furthermore, was to examine all claims—that is, to include those for expenses incurred without prior congressional authorization—and was to report its opinion on the claims to Congress, a procedure that did not guarantee acceptance of unauthorized expenditures but which did offer considerable hope. Significantly, the ordinance relaxed the rules of evidence by providing that if no written vouchers could be produced for claims founded upon congressional resolutions (that is, for authorized expenditures) and if the board received "satisfactory evidence that such Vouchers have been destroyed or unavoidably lost, or that from the circumstances of the case they have never been obtained," the board was to receive other evidence and judge its validity.[38] Congress had not gone so far as to adopt the principle of equity, but considering Hindman's performance, the state's many unauthorized claims, and its woefully incomplete public records, North Carolina had reason to be gratified and encouraged by the congressional ordinance of October 13, 1786.

Another welcome feature of the ordinance was that which

Clark, ed., *State Records*, XVIII, 646-47; Governor Richard Caswell to Timothy Bloodworth, September 24, 1786, *ibid.*, pp. 746-47; *ibid.*, p. 232; United States Board of Treasury to James Hindman, August 18, 1786, Legislative Papers, LXIX, undated folder, State Department of Archives and History, Raleigh.

37. Ferguson, *Power of the Purse*, p. 213.

38. *Journals of Continental Congress*, XXXI, 779-81.

empowered the Board of Treasury to extend until October 1, 1787, the authority of the commissioner to North Carolina to settle individual claims against the United States. This extension, a response to Hindman's delays and his absence from the state, was just and appropriate; but it was unnecessary from a practical standpoint because Hindman during his entire stay in North Carolina issued only twenty continental certificates for civilian claims totaling a meager $8,695.[39] When one realizes that the commissioners altogether issued over $3,723,000 in such certificates and that North Carolina had absorbed upwards of $7,000,000 in continental claims (wartime certificates), the extent to which the national debt had been extinguished among North Carolinians can be fully appreciated.[40]

Even as Hindman was completing what little business he had to conduct, Congress was coming to the conclusion that settlement with the states required a more explicit procedure and one that eased the burdens of the central board by distributing the massive task among other officials. The result of congressional deliberation was the ordinance of May 7, 1787.[41] The ordinance grouped the states administratively into five districts and provided that the Board of Treasury appoint a commissioner to each district. The commissioner was to receive from a state all vouchers and accounts connected with state payments to its Continental Line and state expenses for militia called out under the authority of the United States. The commissioner was not to judge the validity of such claims but was to give descriptive receipts for all such material and forward the claims immediately to the United States commissioner of army accounts, who was to examine the material, pass judgment upon which claims were

39. Statement in Treasurers' and Comptrollers' Papers, Military Papers, LXVII.

40. Ferguson, *Power of the Purse*, pp. 179, 182-83, 186. The South over-all held only 7 per cent of the national debt.

41. Clark, ed., *State Records*, XX, 694-97. This was the ordinance under which final settlement was concluded, and thus it is presented in detail. Congress continued to display interest in settling individual claims as quickly as possible.

authorized by resolves of Congress and were properly supported by evidence, and state all claims that were not clearly authorized or properly supported. The commissioner was to receive in like manner all accounts and vouchers connected with monies paid and supplies furnished on the congressional requisitions before October, 1781, and was to forward such vouchers and accounts to the Office of the Comptroller of the United States Treasury. The commissioner was to receive *and examine* all claims against the United States for advancements or disbursements made to the various continental departments—commissary, quartermaster, clothing, marine, and hospital—or any other type of claim whatsoever; to settle all of such claims as had been authorized by Congress and were supported by proper vouchers; and to make a statement of claims not so authorized or supported, which statement was to be forwarded to the central board. The ordinance provided that the states had six months from the commissioner's arrival to display authorized and unauthorized claims, after which deadline claims could only be applied against unpaid congressional requisitions or against money or articles advanced to the respective states during the Revolution. From the time he entered his duties each commissioner had one year to complete his duties within the district and to deliver all accounts to the comptroller of the United States Treasury. All claims validated by the commissioners were to be examined by the central board of commissioners so that uniformity could be assured, without bringing into question the judgment of the commissioners. The central board was also to receive from the comptroller of the United States Treasury and from the commissioner of army accounts all pertinent material deposited in their offices and to pass judgment upon all questionable claims and all claims definitely not authorized by Congress. In the last task, the board was to be guided by the principle of equity rather than by strict evidence or authorization. As previously indicated, the principle of equity promised to benefit North Carolina directly but also to increase the state's burden of an enlarged national obligation to the aggregate states.

The principle of equity regarding evidence and unauthorized expenditures lent importance to the deliberations of the 1787 Assembly. Anxious to call in all remaining claims against the United States or claims against the state that might be passed along to the United States, the Assembly provided one year (later extended) for the presentation of all outstanding claims.[42] The comptroller was to receive the claims and to present all claims that in his opinion could be charged against the United States—whether authorized or unauthorized, with proper evidence or without—to the congressional commissioner, who under a congressional resolution of July 23, 1787,[43] was authorized to receive them. Individual claims against the state that might be successfully applied against the United States would, of course, prevent the state's certificate debt from increasing by that amount. Incoming state claims against the national government would obviously improve North Carolina's position at final settlement with the United States.

Although the principle of equity ameliorated the problem of incomplete and confusing public records, the severity of the problem prompted the 1787 Assembly to take long-overdue remedial action. Pointing out that no systematic efforts had been made to preserve official dispatches that might bear on state claims against the United States, a resolution required that all official correspondence, journals, and books possessed by former governors or their representatives be lodged in the office of the secretary of state within twelve months; and that each Assembly should, upon adjournment, place all official

42. Clark, ed., *State Records*, XXIV, 896-97.

43. The resolution of July 23, 1787, gave claimants against the commissary, quartermaster, clothing, and marine departments eight months to present an abstract of their claims to the commissioner. All other types of claims against the United States were to be presented in abstract form within one year to the comptroller of the United States. *Ibid.*, p. 751. The resolution had no significance in North Carolina except as regards the Continental Line, a topic that is covered above, pp. 169-90.

dispatches in the same office.[44] Also, the 1787 Assembly required and received a report from the comptroller concerning the progress made by his office in preparing North Carolina's claims. The comptroller's news that little had been done since 1785 except to re-examine and adjust the state's claims through November, 1780, undoubtedly made the Assembly more anxious that the state's records be put in order.[45]

As the 1787 Assembly moved toward adjournment, William Winder, United States commissioner to the Virginia-North Carolina district, prepared to leave Richmond, Virginia, to assume his duties in North Carolina. From Halifax on February 11, 1788, he commenced the six-month settlement period, but, unfortunately, his examination of state claims did not begin until early March because his arrival found the comptroller's office in the process of being moved from Kinston to Hillsborough by order of the 1787 Assembly.[46] The unexpected delay disturbed Winder, but he soon became altogether perplexed by the condition of the public records. Not only were they incomplete, despite continuing efforts by the state to fill the gaps, but they lacked uniformity and were frequently confusing in form—the unfortunate result, in part, of the Assembly's failure to prescribe standards during the Revolution.[47] Faced with these problems, the commissioner

44. *Ibid.*, XX, 274.

45. Comptroller's Report in Legislative Papers, LXXIX, December 19 folder.

46. For details concerning Winder's arrival in the state and the delays associated with the transfer of the comptroller's office, see the following correspondence in Clark, ed., *State Records*: William Winder to Governor Samuel Johnston, December 31, 1787, XX, 792, January 16, 1788, XXI, 438-39; Governor Samuel Johnston to William Winder, January 22, 1788, XXI, 440; Governor Samuel Johnston to Francis Child, January 23, 1788, XXI, 440-41; William Winder to Governor Samuel Johnston, February 11, 1788, XXI, 445-46; Governor Samuel Johnston to William Winder, February 15, 1788, XXI, 447; William Winder to Governor Samuel Johnston, February 19, 1788, XXI, 450; Francis Child to Governor Samuel Johnston, February 19, 1788, XXI, 449-50; Governor Samuel Johnston to William Winder, February 23, 1788, XXI, 451; Francis Child to Governor Samuel Johnston, March 10, 1788, XXI, 455.

47. William Winder's remarks concerning the difficulties of settling North Carolina's claims are found in the Treasurers' and Comptrollers'

displayed great caution in the discharge of his office. He preferred, for example, that the comptroller decide the initial disposition of each claim under the various categories established by the congressional ordinance of May 7, 1787—a policy that relieved Winder of difficult and questionable decisions while it also paid deference to the state. Also, the commissioner insisted that the comptroller specify what descriptions and acknowledgments should be forwarded with unsettled claims, that is, claims touching the Continental Line, authorized militia expenses, and congressional requisitions, or claims unauthorized by Congress or insufficiently supported by evidence. The fact that many unsettled claims would be forwarded to the board was ensured not only by the condition of North Carolina's records but also by Winder's great concern that he settle only claims that clearly came within his jurisdiction. The commissioner's conservatism together with the bulk and status of the material made it quickly apparent to persons working at the comptroller's office that the task of preparing and examining the state's claims could not possibly be completed before the termination of Winder's authority in August, 1788.[48]

William Winder was not the only district commissioner encountering difficulties, and in response to their problems and the pleas of state officials, a congressional resolution of June 24, 1788, granted a three-month extension of the commis-

Papers, Military Papers, LXVII. Additional observations are in an extract from a letter by William Winder to Mr. Stokes, May 7, 1788, Governors' Papers, XVI, 45, State Department of Archives and History, Raleigh. Francis Child's comments on the subject are found in his undated letter to Governor Samuel Johnston, Governors' Letter Books, IX, 102-4. The comptroller's efforts to gather public records and the difficulties that he encountered are illustrated in Francis Child to Nicholas Long, October 12, 1788, and Nicholas Long to Francis Child, February 26, 1789, Treasurers' and Comptrollers' Papers, Correspondence of the Comptroller, II.

48. Francis Child to Governor Samuel Johnston, July 1, 1788, Clark, ed., *State Records*, XXI, 480-81. Winder had used excessive caution also in examining the accounts of Virginia. Ferguson, *Power of the Purse*, pp. 215-16.

sioners' authority, which extension gave Winder until November 24, 1788, to complete his task.[49]

The extension, while welcome, proved to be of no great importance to North Carolina, for as the summer and fall months passed, it became obvious that the remaining work would easily defeat the deadline. When North Carolina's requests for yet more time failed to move Congress,[50] state officials came to the conclusion that extraordinary steps would have to be taken to promote and preserve the state's interests.

Understandably, the official who proposed extraordinary measures was the man who knew most intimately how bad the situation was—the comptroller, Francis Child. To Governor Johnston and to the 1788 Assembly, convened at Fayetteville on November 3, Child suggested that the state appoint an agent to go northward in order to appear before the board of commissioners on North Carolina's behalf. Such representation, Child maintained, would help compensate for the vulnerable condition of many of the state's claims.[51] Persuaded by the situation at Hillsborough and the comptroller's argument, Governor Johnston labeled the settlement of accounts "a subject of the first importance" and called upon the Assem-

49. *Journals of Continental Congress*, XXXIV, 262. An accompanying resolution gave the states three additional months to submit additional vouchers or evidence to the other continental officials involved in the settlement process. William Winder, it will be recalled, had begun the six-month settlement period on February 11, which date would mean that his authority, after the three-month extension, would have expired on November 11. The ordinance of May 7, 1787, had provided, however, that the district commissioner should have one year to settle with the states of the district, and Winder, having spent less than six months in Virginia, was apparently prepared to give North Carolina the extra days, thus bringing his authority to a close on November 24. See Francis Child to Governor Samuel Johnston, July 1, 1788, Clark, ed., *State Records*, XXI, 480.

50. William Winder to Governor Samuel Johnston, November 15, 1788, Governors' Papers, XVII, 39. Winder wrote that the Board of Treasury had informed him that an extension of his authority was unlikely.

51. Francis Child to the General Assembly, October 31, 1788, Legislative Papers, LXXXIII; Francis Child to Governor Samuel Johnston, November 8, 1788, Treasurers' and Comptrollers' Papers, Correspondence of the Comptroller, II.

bly "to appoint a person of known integrity and approved abilities to attend the [Board of] Commissioners, in order to solicit and explain the just Claims of the State against the United States."[52] A legislative committee recommended that an agent be appointed to prevent the board's rejection of claims that, in the agent's opinion, were well founded but about which there might be doubt and to promote and support the equitable adjustment of legitimate claims. Subsequently deciding that two agents would be desirable, the Assembly selected Hugh Williamson and Abishai Thomas to represent the state before the board of commissioners.[53] Thomas' qualifications were derived primarily from his work at the comptroller's office in helping prepare the state's claims; Williamson's experience as a delegate in Congress would be valuable at New York, especially in view of the delicate situation created by North Carolina's failure to ratify the constitution. To facilitate their endeavors the Assembly gave the agents access to the various state offices for the purpose of locating and collecting vouchers and other pertinent materials. Furthermore, in each district of the state an individual was appointed to receive from citizens any vouchers or accounts bearing on North Carolina's claims against the United States.[54]

Another matter posed to the Assembly by the comptroller was the problem of protecting the examined and unexamined claims that were to be sent northward—a question of immediacy because William Winder was preparing to leave North Carolina. In response to Child's inquiry the Assembly resolved that no vouchers, examined or unexamined, should leave the comptroller's office until they had been registered at the office and specifically receipted by the commissioner in such manner as could serve to substantiate claims or accounts should the originals be lost. All registered and receipted vouchers were to be given to the commissioner; those not reg-

52. Clark, ed., *State Records*, XXI, 13.

53. *Ibid.*, XX, 486; XXI, 117, 128, 150.

54. *Ibid.*, XXI, 183; Subcommittee report on the letter from Benjamin Hawkins, Legislative Papers, LXXXII.

istered before his departure were to be sent under the supervision of Abishai Thomas.[55]

Agent Thomas arrived at Hillsborough in mid-December to find Winder and Child directing the registration of accounts that the commissioner had processed before the examination deadline. Complicating registration was the fact that many authorized and supported claims nonetheless contained ambiguous or contradictory information that had prevented Winder from ascertaining the correct amounts. The commissioner insisted that such uncertain claims be settled by the board of commissioners, and state officials could only agree with him that the claims would have to be a matter of negotiation between the board and the state's agents.[56] Added to those undetermined claims were the unauthorized and unsupported claims to be settled by the board and those to be examined by the United States comptroller and the commissioner of army accounts. Thus, when Winder left North Carolina early in January, 1789, with all registered claims,[57]

55. Clark, ed., *State Records*, XX, 501-2. The Assembly also asked Congress for an extension of the commissioner's authority. *Ibid.*, XXI, 90.

56. Francis Child to Governor Samuel Johnston, n.d., *ibid.*, XXI, 512-14; Governor Samuel Johnston to Francis Child, December 28, 1788, *ibid.*, p. 514; Abishai Thomas to Governor Samuel Johnston, December 15, 1788, Governors' Letter Books, IX, 106-11. By agreement, the materials taken by Winder were placed in chests, each chest having two locks. The key to one lock remained in Winder's possession, the other in Thomas'. See also, Journal of the Council of State, December 27, 1788, Governors' Office Papers, CXXI, State Department of Archives and History, Raleigh.

57. Winder did give a receipt totaling £3,274,394/8/6 "depreciated Money" and £131,225/14/6 in claims which he was to pass on for examination by the United States comptroller and the commissioner of army accounts. This receipt, which implied no acceptance of the claims by the United States, is found in the Governors' Papers, Series II, Box IV (Johnston). See also, Francis Child to Governor Samuel Johnston, April 23, 1789, Clark, ed., *State Records*, XXI, 549. At the comptroller's request, Winder estimated informally that the total of the claims that he had acted upon, that is, which he had examined and accepted for shipment northward—including unauthorized and unsupported claims, to be settled by the board—amounted to $8,185,986 "paper" and $328,064 specie. This estimate did not constitute a receipt, for in view of the uncertain and confusing claims that came within

North Carolina's status regarding final settlement was largely yet to be determined.

Following Winder's departure the comptroller's office continued the tedious business of registering state claims against the United States. For several reasons the seemingly interminable process created increasing frustration among North Carolina officials: first, of course, the very uncertainty regarding many claims caused anxiety; second, the board of commissioners, which had been ordered into session by one of the last actions of the Continental Congress, began to function in January, 1789, at which time North Carolina's claims were far from presentable; third, the aforementioned conviction that the state would be found a creditor—especially in view of the principle of equity—caused considerable fidgeting over delay in settlement; fourth, the anticipation that the new Congress, at Federalist urging, would promote early settlement caused considerable concern about the state's inadequate preparations; and, fifth, the uncertainty concerning what Congress' attitude would be toward settlement with a state outside the Union generated understandable uneasiness.[58]

If North Carolina officials had sufficient reason for a sense of impatience, caution persuaded the governor and council that only carefully registered vouchers should be committed northward. So formidable was the clerical task that the work

his jurisdiction he felt he could not give a formal receipt stating any total. Francis Child to Governor Samuel Johnston, n.d., Clark, ed., *State Records*, XXI, 512-14; Francis Child to William Winder, January 2, 1789, and William Winder to Francis Child, January 5, 1789, Treasurers' and Comptrollers' Papers, Correspondence of the Comptroller, II.

58. Hugh Williamson was especially concerned about the last factor and was prepared to petition the new Congress on North Carolina's behalf should the board refuse to accept the state's claims or should the state's position outside the Union jeopardize North Carolina's settlement with the United States. Hugh Williamson to Governor Samuel Johnston, March 2, 1789, Edmund Cody Burnett, ed., *Letters of Members of the Continental Congress* (8 vols.; Washington: Carnegie Institution, 1921-36), VIII, 824; Hugh Williamson to Governor Samuel Johnston, March 9, March 23, 1789, Clark, ed., *State Records*, XXI, 534, 538-39.

was not completed until late April.[59] As Thomas, to the relief of everyone, made preparations to leave with the registered material, the situation at New York changed as the Constitution of the United States brought the new national government into existence. After one member of the board of commissioners resigned to become a member of the new Congress, President Washington thought it improper to appoint a replacement until Congress should recognize the board by special act. On April 27 Hugh Williamson wrote Governor Johnston that it would therefore be several weeks before the board resumed activities.[60] For personal reasons and for the purpose of gathering additional materials Williamson returned to North Carolina, and during late May and June he and Thomas sought additional evidence connected with the state's claims.[61] The agents, together with a large mass of docu-

59. Francis Child to Governor Samuel Johnston, January 13, 1789, Clark, ed., *State Records*, XXI, 517-18; Governor Samuel Johnston to Hugh Williamson, February 19, 1789, *ibid.*, p. 526; Governor Samuel Johnston to Francis Child, February 19, 1789, *ibid.*, p. 526; Governor Samuel Johnston to Abishai Thomas, March 14, 1789, *ibid.*, pp. 537-38; Abishai Thomas to Governor Samuel Johnston, March 23, May 4, 1789, *ibid.*, pp. 539-40, 553-54; Journal of the Council of State, March 13, 15, May 5, 1789, Governors' Office Papers, CXXI; Governor Samuel Johnston to James Iredell, May 5, 1789, James Iredell Papers, Duke University; Abishai Thomas to John Gray Blount, May 22, 1789, Alice Barnwell Keith and William Henry Masterson, eds., *The John Gray Blount Papers* (3 vols.; Raleigh: State Department of Archives and History, 1952-65), I, 481. On April 23 Child wrote Johnston that Thomas had signed a receipt for vouchers and accounts totaling £11,-001,878/5 "depreciated Money" and £2,173,688/17/1 specie. Francis Child to Governor Samuel Johnston, April 23, 1789, Clark, ed., *State Records*, XXI, 549. Child reported to the 1789 Assembly that Thomas had receipted for £11,001,878/5 paper and £2,476,942/10/10 specie, excluding certain claims. Clark, ed., *State Records*, XXII, 1017-19; Francis Child to the General Assembly, November 5, 1789, Legislative Papers, LXXXV. Thomas' itemized receipts, dated April 23, 1789, and specifying the items in each chest, are found in Treasurers' and Comptrollers' Papers, Military Papers, LXVII.

60. Hugh Williamson to Governor Samuel Johnston, April 27, 1789, Clark, ed., *State Records*, XXI, 552; see also, Hugh Williamson and Abishai Thomas to Governor Samuel Johnston, October 17, 1789, Governors' Papers, XVII, 86-87.

61. Hugh Williamson to Governor Samuel Johnston, April 27, 1789, Clark, ed., *State Records*, XXI, 552; Hugh Williamson to James Iredell,

ments, arrived at New York before Congress, on August 5, empowered the president to nominate and appoint members of the board of commissioners to settle accounts between the states and the United States.[62]

The claims carried northward under the agents' supervision included over five million dollars nominal value of continental currency possessed by the state as the result of wartime policies designed to uphold the money's value. These policies, initiated during the Revolution by a Congress utterly unable to retire its currency, included the levying of state taxes in continental money. To encourage such tax policy Congress had authorized the states to use continental currency in partial payment of congressional requisitions.[63] Not until June, 1781, had the North Carolina Assembly responded—by requiring that one-fourth the annual property tax be paid in continental money for the sole purpose of discharging congressional requisitions upon the state.[64] The mandatory tax had encountered sharp public disapproval because many taxpayers experienced genuine difficulty in procuring sufficient continental currency and because they resented the tax at a

February 12, 1789, Charles E. Johnson Collection, State Department of Archives and History, Raleigh: Hugh Williamson to John Gray Blount, May 25, 1789, Keith and Masterson, eds., *Blount*, I, 482-83; Hugh Williamson and Abishai Thomas to Francis Child, June 20, 1789, Treasurers' and Comptrollers' Papers, Correspondence of the Comptroller, II. Before Williamson's arrival in North Carolina, Thomas had sought supporting evidence located at the secretary of state's office. Abishai Thomas to James Glasgow, April 14, 1789, Treasurers' and Comptroller's Papers, Military Papers, LXVIII; James Glasgow to Abishai Thomas, April 27, 1789, Abishai Thomas Papers, State Department of Archives and History, Raleigh.

62. *Annals of Congress*, II, 2295-96; Journal of the Council of State, July 29, 1789, Governors' Office Papers, CXXI.

63. For comprehensive coverage of congressional currency financing, see Ferguson, *Power of the Purse*, pp. 25-47. Congress had sought to uphold the currency also by asking the states to declare the money legal tender and by requesting that the states tax the money out of circulation and forward it to Congress to serve as the basis for a new currency. *Ibid.*, pp. 22, 32-33, 51-53. In 1777 North Carolina had declared continental currency to be legal tender. Clark, ed., *State Records*, XXIV, 34. Efforts to uphold the currency's value failed.

64. *Ibid.*, XVII, 829.

time when continental certificates were not officially accepted in payment of taxes.[65]

These resentments had helped bring about the previously-discussed state absorption of continental certificates and had caused the prompt substitution of an optional continental-currency tax for the mandatory one.[66] The relative scarcity of continental currency within North Carolina had prevented the optional tax from drawing in the full amounts authorized by the congressional requisitions, and, it will be recalled, North Carolina had made no payments of any sort upon those requisitions.[67] By war's end such continental money as taxation had retired lay scattered and uncounted among numerous tax and treasury officials. Preoccupied by its own financial problems, North Carolina was initially content to let the matter of the continental money—and of meeting congressional requisitions—remain in abeyance.

The continental currency question would not down, however, because several states—notably Massachusetts—in which continental currency was plentiful collected not only their respective quotas of the money but large amounts beyond those quotas. Even before the war ended these states were pressing Congress to accept all their continental currency at forty to one, a legal rate that Congress had set in 1780 but a rate that far exceeded the market value.[68] The threat to North Carolina was obvious: if at final settlement Congress

65. *Ibid.*, p. 437; Adelaide L. Fries, "North Carolina Certificates of the Revolutionary Period," *North Carolina Historical Review*, Vol. IX, No. 3 (July, 1932), p. 233; Ferguson, *Power of the Purse*, pp. 64, 65-66.

66. Clark, ed., *State Records*, XIX, 903; XXIV, 437. In February, 1782, Governor Thomas Burke, with the advice and consent of the council, had made the continental-currency tax optional until the Assembly should meet. The 1782 Assembly confirmed Burke's action.

67. In 1778 North Carolina had been credited with the ludicrously small amount of forty dollars nominal value of continental money. Up until final settlement North Carolina had received credit for $52,040 nominal value of continental money. See statement in Treasurers' and Comptrollers' Papers, Military Papers, LXVII.

68. Hugh Williamson and William Blount to Governor Alexander Martin, October 25, 1782, Clark, ed., *State Records*, XVI, 446-48; Hugh Williamson to Governor Alexander Martin, September 30, 1784, *ibid.*, XVII, 101-2; Ferguson, *Power of the Purse*, pp. 67, 205-6.

should credit the states' continental currency at forty to one and should accept the surpluses accumulated by certain states, North Carolina—which had not even determined the amount of its continental currency much less accumulated intentionally a surplus—would be called upon to pay its portion of a congressional sum that would benefit other states at North Carolina's expense. Keenly aware of the danger, state officials lamented the repeal of the mandatory tax; deplored the comparatively little continental currency in the state's possession; urged the collection of all it did have so that credit could be obtained against congressional requisitions; favored the greater use of tax power to pull in continental currency; and, of course, opposed the ambitions of the states having surpluses.[69] By late 1783, Governor Martin, after a year of effort, managed to estimate that the state possessed about 3,750,000 nominal value of continental dollars, but the money still lay in the hands of numerous officials and thus was not available for presentation to Congress.[70] The situation was all the more alarming because speculators could easily exchange their state currency for the continental currency held by revenue officials, and thus North Carolina could be deprived of its claim against the United States.[71]

The spring Assembly of 1784 took comprehensive measures to secure and promote North Carolina's interests regarding its continental currency. The comptroller was ordered to receive and collect the currency from tax officials; to preserve the money so that the state could receive a credit with the

69. Hugh Williamson and William Blount to Governor Alexander Martin, October 25, 1782, Clark, ed., *State Records*, XVI, 446-48; Benjamin Hawkins and Hugh Williamson to Governor Alexander Martin, September 26, 1783, *ibid.*, pp. 886-87; Richard Dobbs Spaight to Governor Alexander Martin, February 24, 1784, *ibid.*, XVII, 18; Hugh Williamson to Governor Alexander Martin, September 30, 1784, *ibid.*, pp. 101-2.

70. Governor Alexander Martin to the delegates in Congress, January 17, 1783, Governors' Letter Books, V, 74; Governor Alexander Martin to the delegates in Congress, December 8, 1783, Clark, ed., *State Records*, XVI, 919.

71. Hugh Williamson and William Blount to Governor Alexander Martin, October 25, 1782, Clark, ed., *State Records*, XVI, 447.

United States; and, for that purpose, to deliver the currency to the commissioner designated by the United States to settle accounts between North Carolina and the national government.[72] Furthermore, the Assembly returned to the policy—abandoned in 1783—of accepting continental money in partial payment of taxes.[73] In seeking thus to draw in additional currency that could be presented against the United States, the Assembly adopted two significant innovations designed to improve and protect North Carolina's position in final settlement: first, continental currency, which had been legal tender, was legally devalued to eight hundred to one, a rate that would draw in greater nominal amounts of currency and put the state in a better situation should Congress—despite North Carolina's opposition—accept the currency at forty to one; second, up to one-half the annual property tax could be paid in continental currency—a percentage twice that of any previous tax and intended to retire continental money rapidly. Tax policy remained unchanged until 1786, when the Assembly inaugurated the previously-discussed sinking tax on old state currency and state certificates and in so doing allowed the entire tax to be paid in continental currency at eight hundred to one.[74] These taxes between 1784 and completion of final settlement collected approximately 1,500,000 nominal value of continental dollars, giving the state as of that time slightly over 5,000,000 dollars nominal value.[75] After William Winder refused to accept the money because his authority to do so was not explicit, and after the United States

72. *Ibid.*, XIX, 503-4, 545. This policy was confirmed by the fall Assembly of 1784. *Ibid.*, p. 486. The commissioner to whom the Assembly referred was the one to be appointed under the congressional resolution of February 20, 1782.

73. *Ibid.*, XXIV, 477, 556.

74. *Ibid.*, pp. 658, 732, 802, 885, 952; XXV, 8.

75. As completion of final settlement neared, Abishai Thomas estimated that North Carolina had sent a total of $5,330,828 continental money to the United States Treasury. Abishai Thomas' estimate is in the Treasurers' and Comptrollers' Papers, Military Papers, LXVIII. Assuming Martin's 1783 estimate of $3,750,000 to be approximately correct, about $1,500,000 would have been collected in the postwar period.

Treasury insisted upon examining and counting the money, North Carolina forwarded the currency under the agents' supervision.[76] The United States Treasury indicated that the state would receive credit at forty to one,[77] but the attitude of the new Congress and of the board toward the continental currency was yet to be determined as Williamson and Thomas arrived in New York to do battle for the state.

As the agents waited for the board of commissioners to commence settlement with North Carolina, they and other state officials labored under several legitimate apprehensions. One of these concerns was eliminated when, upon North Carolina's inquiry, Secretary of the Treasury Hamilton assured the state that the board would receive the claims and the continental currency that continued to be collected in North Carolina.[78] A major uncertainty and fear regarding final settlement was terminated late in 1789 by North Carolina's entrance into the Union. If these two worries were quickly laid to rest, the greatest concern of all—the acceptability of North Carolina's claims—was a question that promised to linger indefinitely as the state sought to persuade the board. During the fall of 1789, while working with the commissioner of army accounts and awaiting the board's pleasure, the agents grew less confident of their own persuasive powers. Increasingly appreciative of the dismay that had afflicted William Winder,

76. After Winder refused to take the money, the continental commissioner of loans to North Carolina, William Skinner, agreed to receipt for the currency and count it prior to shipment northward. When the United States Treasury insisted upon counting the money, Skinner, at the council's instructions, turned the money over to Thomas. The alleged amount carried by Thomas was $5,066,861. Francis Child to Governor Samuel Johnston, March 10, 1788, Clark, ed., *State Records*, XXI, 455; XXII, 1019; William Skinner to Francis Child, November 18, 1788, Treasurers' and Comptrollers' Papers, Correspondence of the Comptroller, II; Journal of the Council of State, May 8, 1789, Governors' Office Papers, CXXI.

77. *American State Papers* (38 vols.; Washington: Gales and Seaton, 1833-34), IX, 59.

78. Francis Child to Hugh Williamson and Abishai Thomas, September 6, 1789, and Abishai Thomas to Francis Child, November 14, 1789, Treasurers' and Comptrollers' Papers, Correspondence of the Comptroller, II.

they were soon urging the state to remedy the "palpably deficient" muster rolls of the Continental Line and the large gaps in other areas of evidence and claims.[79] Responding to the pleas, the Assembly of 1789 provided for the collection of muster rolls in the possession of former officers of the Line; and for the ascertaining of wagons furnished and bounties paid on behalf of the United States. The 1789 Assembly ordered the comptroller to register all pertinent materials coming into his office and to forward them to the agents, a policy that remained in effect until completion of final settlement.[80]

It was during the session of the 1789 Assembly that the Fayetteville Convention ratified the constitution, and while entrance into the Union regularized the political framework surrounding final settlement, ratification made more immediate and significant the prospect of federal assumption of North Carolina's domestic debt. As we have seen,[81] there was a close relationship between the assumption issue and the matter of final settlement. With North Carolina's debt much smaller than the debts of certain other states, North Carolina would not benefit from assumption because the debt of which the state would be relieved would be less than her portion of the federal money necessary to discharge the aggregate debts of the other states. North Carolina's opposition to assumption was all the greater because it was feared and believed that once assumption passed, the benefiting states would block final settlement—for at final settlement the individual states were to be charged with their respective assumed debts. The possibility that settlement would not occur was doubly painful because, in the opinion of state officials, North Carolina at settlement would be found a creditor to the United States. Thus North Carolina considered it vitally important that settlement be promptly completed, after which the balances due from

79. Hugh Williamson and Abishai Thomas to Governor Samuel Johnston, October 17, 1789, Governors' Papers, XVII, 86-87.

80. Clark, ed., *State Records*, XXI, 313; XXV, 9-10. Itemized listings of materials sent to the agents until completion of final settlement are in the Treasurers' and Comptrollers' Papers, Military Papers, LXVII; Gregory and Lennon, "Revolutionary Debt," p. 56.

81. Above, pp. 53-55.

debtor states could be assumed by the United States and the possibility of assuming the domestic state debts—unpleasant though the prospect would remain to North Carolina—could at least be discussed on its own merits, without other implications and ramifications.

The individual who carried the burden of North Carolina's efforts to prevent assumption of state debts and to promote final settlement was Hugh Williamson, who continued to act as state agent while serving in the House of Representatives. While maintaining that "the General peace of Society seems to require that great dispatch should be made in settling the national accounts," Williamson opposed the 1790 assumption bill on two grounds: first, that the measure would lead to national taxes too large to be "conveniently paid"; second, that passage would deprive North Carolina of all her exertions in retiring certificates and currency because the state could not receive credit for them if final settlement were subsequently blocked.[82] These considerations, it will be recalled, had caused one North Carolina congressman to term the assumption bill "a bitter draught" and Governor Martin to label it an "iniquitous . . . measure . . . fraught . . . with ruin to this State."[83]

North Carolina's alarm and suspicions regarding assumption were exaggerated, for Congress generally agreed that the entire business of Revolutionary finances should be concluded. As part of what has been called the Compromise of 1790,[84]

82. U.S. Congress, House. Speeches of Representative Williamson. 1st Cong., 2nd sess., March 30, 31, 1790, *Annals of Congress*, II, 1489-90, 1493, 1496-97. See the following correspondence from Hugh Williamson to Governor Alexander Martin, Governors' Letter Books, X: March 6, 1790, pp. 27-28; March 20, 1790, pp. 31-32; April 24, 1790, pp. 29-30; May 13, 1790, pp. 53-56.

83. John Steele to Governor Alexander Martin, July 19, 1790, Governors' Letter Books, X, 112; Governor Alexander Martin to Hugh Williamson, June 29, 1790, *ibid.*, p. 63.

84. Ferguson, *Power of the Purse*, pp. 306-25, coins the phrase and examines the components of the compromise. He maintains that uninterrupted final settlement was an important part of the better-known arrangement involving assumption and the location of the nation's capital.

Congress enacted both the assumption of state debts and effective legislation to conclude final settlement. Hugh Williamson, although unsuccessful in his fight against assumption, took great comfort—and credit—in two related matters that, he stressed, had secured North Carolina's interests: first, the final settlement act had passed earlier than the assumption act, and only that sequence, Williamson asserted, had prevented the opponents of final settlement—that is, the beneficiaries of assumption—from blocking final settlement legislation; second, the final settlement act provided that the principle of general equity be applied in settlement regardless of whether an expense had been incurred in the general defense or that of a particular state.[85] If Williamson exaggerated the opposition to final settlement and therefore his role in the enactment of the final settlement act, he quite rightly took pride in his committee work that helped bring about the equity principle of the final settlement act. As Williamson knew as well as anyone, North Carolina in its settlement with the United States could benefit from that principle because of the state's poor records, unauthorized expenditures, and many wartime expenses in its own defense. Officials believed that since North Carolina had incurred a large domestic debt in defending the state and since a significant portion of that debt had been retired, the opportunity to present those retired state certificates on the basis of equity would greatly improve North Carolina's standing in final settlement.[86] As a pleased Governor Martin was wont to put it, the principle of equity would enable the state's claims to "wear a new dress."[87]

85. Hugh Williamson to Governor Alexander Martin, August 2, 1790, Governors' Letter Books, X, 93-97; Hugh Williamson and Abishai Thomas to Governor Alexander Martin, August 12, 1790, *ibid.*, pp. 127-29. This principle of equity enabled North Carolina to charge part of the Martinique debt against the United States. Above, pp. 122-23. The final settlement act is found in *Annals of Congress*, II, 2295-96.

86. See Abishai Thomas' replies to a series of questions regarding final settlement in Treasurers' and Comptrollers' Papers, Military Papers, LXVIII.

87. Governor Martin's address to the Assembly of 1790, Governors' Letter Books, X, 138-39.

Final settlement proceeded without congressional interference, indeed with congressional co-operation, but the formidable task of assessing the mass of material presented by North Carolina consumed more time than anyone had anticipated. The state's agents devoted month after month to receiving, arranging, presenting, and defending North Carolina's claims. Additional bundles arriving from the comptroller created additional problems as well as additional opportunities. Making a bad situation worse, the 1790 Assembly, apparently because of political factionalism, removed Hugh Williamson as state agent, thereby embittering Williamson and costing the state the benefit of his experience, knowledge, and ability. With later agents understandably unable to master the situation, the burden of the responsibility fell to Abishai Thomas, whose talents in preparing and justifying North Carolina's claims proved less than ample.[88] Fundamentally, however, it was simply impossible to bring order and system to the state's records, to find or replace many lost documents, to recreate destroyed ones, or to establish many claims even upon the principle of equity. As North Carolina's agents struggled bravely but often ineffectually to assert its claims, the board of commissioners remained unimpressed and became unsympathetic with the state's preparations and presentation.[89] Despite the many discouragements, state officials remained hopeful, even optimistic that the sheer magnitude of North Carolina's efforts and documents would overwhelm

88. *Ibid.*: Hugh Williamson to Governor Alexander Martin, August 2, 1790, pp. 93-97; January 16, 1791, pp. 174-75; January 29, 1791, pp. 182-85; Samuel Johnston and Benjamin Hawkins to Governor Alexander Martin, February 22, 1791, p. 196; Hugh Williamson to Governor Alexander Martin, February 7, 1791, pp. 198-99; Abishai Thomas to Governor Alexander Martin, February 22, 1791, pp. 201-2; Samuel Johnston to Governor Alexander Martin, March 9, 1791, pp. 206-7; Hugh Williamson to Governor Alexander Martin, March 4, 1791, pp. 226-28; Benjamin Hawkins to Governor Alexander Martin, March 6, 1791, pp. 229-30.

89. Samuel Johnston to Governor Alexander Martin, March 9, 1791, *ibid.*, pp. 206-7.

the board and result in the state's being declared a "respectable" creditor to the United States.[90]

The magnitude of claims ultimately put forth by North Carolina amounted to $65,809,428 nominal value of paper money and $9,275,688 in specie (exclusive of interest), whose "real value" Thomas estimated to be $11,179,109.[91] The hopes and expectations that the state would be found a creditor were dashed by the board's report, completed in the summer of 1793 and officially presented to Congress on December 5, 1793. The report set the value of North Carolina's claims against the United States at $10,427,586.13 and the state's obligation to the United States at $10,928,668.13, leaving North Carolina a debtor to the amount of $501,082.[92] The disappointingly small total of North Carolina's claims was caused by a number of factors. First, contrary to the state's expectations, the board evaluated the continental currency at the rate the money was retired—most of it at eight hundred to one—rather than at forty to one. A second factor was that continental certificates were credited to the state at their retirement rate or at the retirement rates for the state certificates issued in exchange for the continental certificates—in many instances, according to North Carolina's 1782 currency-certificate scale of depreciation. This certificate policy, while equitable and not unexpected, was nonetheless injurious to the state's ambitions and caused references to the "unfortunate" scale of 1782 and the painful fact that North Carolina would receive only several thousand pounds credit for the millions of pounds nominal value in the state's possession.[93] A third factor reducing North Carolina's claims was

90. Abishai Thomas to Governor Richard Dobbs Spaight, June 21, 1793, *ibid.*, XI, 66-67.

91. "General Abstract of Claims of the State of North Carolina Against the United States," Treasurers' and Comprollers' Papers, Military Papers, LXVIII.

92. "Certified Statement of the Account of the State of North Carolina as Settled by the Board of Commissionry," Treasurers' and Comptrollers' Papers, Military Papers, LXVIII; *American State Papers*, XXXVII, 69.

93. Benjamin Hawkins to the General Assembly, December 3, 1788, Legislative Papers, LXXXIV.

that the state boards of auditors had been too lax and uncritical in accepting continental certificates,[94] and thus the state had absorbed claims against the United States which the board of commissioners refused to accept altogether or to accept at stated value. Finally and most importantly, the poor condition of the state's public records prevented the establishment of many claims to the board's satisfaction, even within the principle of general equity.

If North Carolina's claims against the United States were greatly pared, the procedure established by the final settlement act for determining the national government's claims against the states also worked to North Carolina's disadvantage. That procedure—to which North Carolina had agreed in 1784—was that the aggregate of balances due by the United States to the creditor states should be distributed among all the states on the basis of their respective federal populations. As determined by the board of commissioners, North Carolina's portion of that aggregate amounted to the aforementioned $10,928,668.13[95]—far more than the actual wartime expenditures made by the United States on behalf of North Carolina.

The unhappy outcome of final settlement was, then, a bitter experience for those who had anticipated that North Carolina would be a creditor. In Congress, Hugh Williamson complained—as he had been doing for months—that the board had treated North Carolina ungenerously and had thereby deprived the state of legitimate claims totaling two million dollars.[96] Over the next several years North Carolina asserted that the board had been unfair both in eliminating legitimate claims by North Carolina and in accepting fraudulent or improper claims by other states. Had final settlement been justly

94. Ferguson, *Power of the Purse*, p. 208. Above, p. 133.

95. The board determined that the total of all state expenditures was $114,400,000 and the total of federal advances to the states was $36,700,000, leaving a balance of $77,700,000, which was distributed among the states on the basis of the census of 1790. *Ibid.*, pp. 332-33.

96. U.S. Congress, House. Speech of Representative Williamson. 2nd Cong., 2nd sess., January 10, 1793, *Annals of Congress*, III, 809.

conducted, it was charged, North Carolina would have been a creditor by perhaps two million dollars.[97]

North Carolina's accusations were the more bitter because the final settlement disappointment culminated a series of policies and developments that proved to the state's disadvantage. As we have seen, North Carolina, at the sacrifice of revenue, retired approximately half its domestic certificate debt. That policy placed North Carolina at a disadvantage when Congress assumed the state debts, and final settlement offered no relief or comfort when the state was declared a debtor. The principle of general equity, which seemed to hold such promise, worked to the advantage of states that could establish their claims to the board's satisfaction but to North Carolina's relative disadvantage, as the state could not establish many claims and was called upon to contribute money to discharge the sums due creditor states. The successful gamble that Congress would accept in principle the continental certificates absorbed by the exchange process was largely nullified by the inability of the state to establish the validity of many of those claims. Reflection upon this unfortunate sequence explains the rancor with which North Carolina leveled its recriminations and the indignation with which it refused to pay one cent of the money it owed to the United States. Faced with similar refusal by the other debtor states, Congress simply declared the debts "extinguished" in 1802.[98] Thus was terminated the matter of state-federal Revolutionary accounts.

One political consequence of state-federal relations remains to be stressed. North Carolina's absorption of virtually all continental certificates within the state undoubtedly diminished Federalist influence during the debate on the constitu-

97. U.S. Congress, House. Speeches of Representatives Holland, Macon, and Blount. 4th Cong., 2nd sess., December 30, 1796, and January 3, 4, 1797, *ibid.*, VI, 1758-59, 1777, 1787, 1802. The board treated Virginia, Maryland, and South Carolina generously but reduced the claims of North Carolina and Georgia. Ferguson, *Power of the Purse*, p. 324. Besides North Carolina the debtor states were New York, Pennsylvania, Delaware, Maryland, and Virginia.

98. *American State Papers*, IX, 734-35.

tion, or, again to quote Charles Beard, the inconsequential debt in North Carolina "must have had a very deadening effect on the spirit of the movement for ratification."[99] To those who had hoped that the absorption would check the Federalist movement, North Carolina's ratification of the constitution must have been the greatest disappointment of all.

99. Charles Austin Beard, *An Economic Interpretation of the Constitution of the United States* (New York: Macmillan Company, 1913), p. 287.

VII. *Payment of the Continental Line*

Among the public creditors whose allegiance Federalists hoped to obtain were the officers and men of the Continental Army. As in the case of public creditors generally, that allegiance would be directed, both Federalists and their opponents believed, toward that government which compensated them for their wartime contributions, and therefore the extent to which Congress or the individual states would assume responsibility for paying the Lines was far more than a matter of how simple justice to deserving patriots could most effectively be discharged. Thus, while Congress had been willing and desirous for the states to bear the expense of recruiting and equipping their respective Continental Lines, Congress had sought to retain sole responsibility for paying the army. That task had proved beyond the central government's capabilities, and, as we have seen, Congress in 1780 had felt compelled to ask the states to pay their respective Lines for arrearages of pay, current service, and depreciation of pay for the period before August 1, 1780. Pay for services performed from that date forward was to be discharged by Congress.[1]

During the early years of the war North Carolina had not only issued copious quantities of certificates and fiat currency to recruit and equip its Line—expenditures facilitated by the

1. E. James Ferguson, *The Power of the Purse: A History of American Public Finance, 1776-1790* (Chapel Hill: The University of North Carolina Press, 1961), pp. 50, 180. This congressional authorization meant that expenses incurred in paying the Line up to August 1, 1780, could be charged by a state against the United States in the final settlement of accounts. As revealed in the previous chapter, North Carolina encountered difficulty in gathering and presenting its claims for pay to the state's Line.

expectation that all such expenses would be successfully charged against the United States in the final settlement of war accounts—but had also issued to the Line, before the congressional authorization of 1780, pay amounting approximately to $575,000 nominal value of wartime North Carolina currency and $585,000 in specie certificates.[2] Subsequent to congressional authorization of state payments to August 1, 1780, North Carolina had not moved promptly to make additional payments to the Line, a delay probably caused by the many other demands and concerns facing the government; but in the spring of 1782 the Assembly turned its attention to discharging part of the arrearages due the Line.[3] With the intention of complying with the congressional authorization, the Assembly enacted that specie certificates be issued to compensate the Line, according to a congressional scale of depreciation, for depreciation of pay up to August 18, 1780. Another provision of the act, however, ignored the congressional limitation upon state payments and is attributable both to the plight of the Line and to the desire to counterbalance the Federalism currently dominating Congress: members of the Line were to receive specie certificates for arrearages of pay and subsistence—for an unspecified period of service potentially enabling state officials to move beyond the date August 1, 1780, and thereby to encroach upon the national debt. These specie certificates were, of course, promissory notes, but the discredited status of state currency and the depleted condition of the treasury precluded effective monetary payment. Keenly aware of the state's limited resources but con-

2. Walter Clark, ed., *The State Records of North Carolina* (16 vols.; Winston, Goldsboro, and Raleigh: State of North Carolina, 1895-1906) [volumes numbered consecutive to William L. Saunders, ed., *The Colonial Records of North Carolina* (10 vols.; Raleigh: State of North Carolina, 1886-90)], XXIV, 155, 184, 320-21, 337-38, 344-46, 347-48, 368, 371-72, 382; Ferguson, *Power of the Purse*, p. 204. Payments made by North Carolina to the Line prior to congressional authorization are found in "General Abstract of Claims of the State of North Carolina Against the United States," p. 19, Treasurers' and Comptrollers' Papers, LXVIII, State Department of Archives and History, Raleigh.

3. Clark, ed., *State Records*, XXIV, 419-22.

fronted with the dissatisfaction and hardship among the Line and the political importance of attaching the Line to the state, the Assembly believed it imperative that some amount of North Carolina's tangible assets be employed to compensate the Line. In order to meet that need and at the same time dispose of perishable confiscated commodities, the Assembly provided that each member of the Line should receive one arrearage certificate for twelve months' subsistence and pay, and that the certificate should be redeemable at nominal value in such perishable property; the other arrearage certificates received by an individual were to "be paid off by any treasurer of the State, as soon as the situation of the finances will permit."[4] Further to seek the gratitude and allegiance of the Line, the Assembly authorized the issuance of certificates for past clothing deficiencies and awarded the various ranks specified amounts of acreage from western land previously set aside as a bounty for the Line. The commission established to issue the arrearage certificates subsequently issued a total specie value of $35,840, and although the commission apparently did not move beyond the date authorized by Congress, the machinery for encroaching upon the national debt was readily available.[5]

Regretful that Congress in its weakness had ever called upon the states to make any payments to the Lines, Federalists were all the more concerned about unauthorized encroachments upon the national debt, that is, payments for the period beginning August 1, 1780. Reacting sharply to threatened incursions by North Carolina and threatened or actual incursions by other states, Congress on October 1, 1782, reminded the states that under the Articles of Confederation all expenses for war and other expenses for the common defense and general welfare were to be defrayed from a com-

4. *Ibid.*, p. 420. Above, p. 31.

5. The amount of land ultimately issued to members or their assignees totaled 2,912,198 acres, charged (as a bounty) against the United States at twenty-five dollars per acre. "General Abstract of the Claims of the State of North Carolina Against the United States," p. 16, Treasurers' and Comptrollers' Papers, Military Papers, LXVIII. For payments to the Line by the commission, see *ibid.*, pp. 1, 19.

mon treasury supplied by the states; and warned that if the states should undertake to disburse any of the monies required and appropriated for the army by congressional requisitions, the articles would be violated, Congress' uniform system of revenue would be subverted, more discord among the states would be created, murmurs from the Lines would increase, and final settlement of accounts between the states and the United States would be delayed. Pointing out also that Congress had discountenanced all partial payments by the states to their respective Lines (beyond July 31, 1780), Congress emphasized that state payments for the year 1782 would not be considered as advanced on behalf of the United States and would not be credited to the states in their respective settlements with the central government.[6] In a further effort to secure the remaining national debt due the army, Congress on January 25, 1783, recommended that the states promptly complete settlements due the Lines up to August 1, 1780, and that the superintendent of finance make such payments in such manner as to him seemed most proper—"as soon as the state of public finances will permit"—for the settlement of pay due the Continental Lines since August 1, 1780.[7] Within several weeks the superintendent, Robert Morris, directed the paymaster general of the United States, John Pierce, to serve as commissioner of army accounts to direct the settlement of all monies due the Lines from August 1, 1780, through the year 1782 and to determine what balances might still be due the Lines for services before August 1, 1780. In order that those balances could be determined, Morris dispatched a circular to the state executives requesting that the paymaster

6. *Journals of the Continental Congress*, 1774-89 (34 vols.; Washington: Government Printing Office, 1904-37), XXIII, 630-31. Clark, ed., *State Records*, XVI, 898-99, mistakenly dates the resolutions October 1, 1783. The resolutions were prompted by New Jersey's plan to pay the Line for 1782. Ultimately the August 1, 1780, deadline was exceeded by Massachusetts, Connecticut, New York, Rhode Island, New Jersey, Maryland, Virginia, South Carolina, and North Carolina. Ferguson, *Power of the Purse*, p. 50.

7. *Journals of Continental Congress*, XXIV, 93. The North Carolina delegation supported the date August 1, 1780, rather than a suggested alternative, December 31, 1780. *Ibid.*, p. 94.

general be furnished with an account of state payments or advances made to individuals serving in the "American Army." While indicating that such payments for the period before August 1, 1780, would be credited to each state in its settlement with the United States, Morris probably hoped and intended that any arrearages still due from that period could be discharged by the United States and the national debt thereby increased.[8]

The General Assembly that convened in April, 1783, faced not only the obvious intent of Congress to assume the debt due the North Carolina Line but also the presence of agents appointed by the Line to present a list of grievances. The agents reminded the legislators that except for the certificates issued by order of the previous Assembly, the Line had been without pay for almost four years; they informed the Assembly that most members of the Line had not used their twelve-month certificates because the men preferred not to acquire perishable confiscated property; the agents emphasized that officers and men were in genuine distress and that some were in danger of imprisonment for wartime debts; and they urged that the Line be paid its arrearages and be issued its individual titles to land set aside by act of Assembly.[9]

Moved by the plight of the Line, the desire to attach the Line to the state, and the need for a circulating medium, the 1783 Assembly, as we have seen, emitted £100,000 fiat currency, of which £72,000 ($180,000) was turned over to a commission at Halifax for the purpose of paying arrearages due the Line.[10] Each member of the Line was to receive the new currency for one-fourth of his arrearage and for the three-

8. Robert Morris to the Paymaster General, March 15, 1783, Clark, ed., *State Records*, XVI, 745-47; Robert Morris to Governor Alexander Martin, April 30, 1783, *ibid.*, p. 782.

9. Commissioners on behalf of the North Carolina Continental Line to the General Assembly, Legislative Papers, XLVII, mixed and undated folder, State Department of Archives and History, Raleigh. The officers of the Line had met at Hillsborough on August 30, 1782, to appoint the agents and prepare the list of grievances. When a fall session of the 1782 Assembly failed to materialize, the grievances had to await the 1783 Assembly.

10. Clark, ed., *State Records*, XXIV, 475-78. Above, p. 61.

fourths balance a final settlement specie certificate bearing 6 per cent annual interest until the condition of the treasury should allow redemption with specie. The emission act made no mention of the date August 1, 1780, probably an intentional omission designed to ignore the deadline and yet mislead individuals—as it did Governor Martin[11]—into believing that North Carolina was complying with congressional authorization. In truth, another act of the same Assembly instructed the commissioners to liquidate arrearages up to January 1, 1782,[12] and thereby North Carolina set about reducing the national debt that Robert Morris and other Federalists valued so highly as cement for the Union. The Assembly probably chose to go as far as January 1, 1782, and no farther because the congressional resolution of October 1, 1782, declaring that no state would receive credit for payments made to its Line for 1782 could be interpreted to mean—despite Congress' obvious intent otherwise—that state payments up to January 1, 1782, *would* be credited to the state in the final settlement of its account with the United States.

After ordering the currency emission, the 1783 Assembly resolved that the Line's agents inform the Line that the Assembly had adopted such modes of payment as the necessities of the state and the "deranged" condition of the treasury would permit; that the government was sensible that the Line's claims had complete merit; and that North Carolina intended to fulfill its obligation to the Line as soon as finances would permit. The Line's agents, mollified by the emission and also by the enactment of a stay law and the establishment of procedures for obtaining the Line's western land grants, thanked the Assembly for responding to the Line's plea for immediate relief.[13] Despite the agents' expression of appreciation and the previously-discussed efforts by the Assembly

11. Governor Alexander Martin to Governor Elias Boudinot of New Jersey, September 1, 1783, Clark, ed., *State Records*, XVI, 878.

12. *Ibid.*, XXIV, 484.

13. *Ibid.*, XIX, 222, 358, 366; XXIV, 480, 482-85. The act opening the western land office carefully prohibited private purchasers from obtaining original land titles in the area reserved for the Line. The stay law is treated above, pp. 62-63.

to lend reputation and support to the forthcoming currency,[14] the members of the Line were dissatisfied with the mode of payment and understandably suspicious of the money offered them by the commission. Believing that the government had used thin paper so that the bills could be retired quickly on the basis of raggedness, some members of the Line refused to accept their one-fourth arrearages in currency that was torn or damaged; one general, when faced with such refusal while distributing the currency among the veterans, resorted to tearing and cutting all the bills in his possession while warning the men that they would receive the torn money or nothing.[15]

If the currency emission failed to elicit the Line's heartfelt gratitude, the 1783 Assembly's failure to make final settlement certificates acceptable at the western land office or in the purchase of all categories of confiscated property added to the sense of disappointment. The absence of property redemption modes attests, among other things, to the limited resources of the state and the several demands upon those resources,[16] but suggests also that the issuing of final settlement certificates was motivated by political considerations at least as much as by concern for the Line. Aware that the United States was offering no redemption of continental final settlement certificates, the Assembly was able to slice into the national debt without having to provide for property redemption of its own final settlement certificates. The state certificates' specie value, 6 per cent interest feature, acceptability at nominal value in partial payment of the property tax, and non-liability to a sinking tax all made them preferred securities, but the lack of property redemption agencies and the vague promise of specie redemption when the condition of the treasury would permit—a distant day indeed—reduced the

14. Above, pp. 58-63.

15. Johann David Schoepf, *Travels in the Confederation*, ed. and trans. by Alfred James Morrison (2 vols.; Philadelphia: William J. Campbell and Company, 1911), II, 130.

16. The other demands being made upon confiscated property are discussed above, pp. 35-37, 59, 71-72.

certificates' value in the market. Frequently having to sell their hard-earned certificates to meet debts incurred during the war, members of the Line were embittered as speculators procured the securities at a small fraction of nominal value.[17] With both the central government and the Assembly unwilling to provide additional relief, the Line's frustration and despair deepened.

The central government's unwillingness to commit its limited resources to payment of the army during the latter stages of the war was Robert Morris' decision, a decision within the discretion given him by Congress and consistent with his policy of assigning the army low priority among the government's obligations.[18] When the war ended and Congress, as we have seen, came under the control of men who were opposed to significant centralization, a large national debt was no longer looked upon as a national blessing—and thus adamant congressional objections to state inroads beyond July 31, 1780, ceased. Congress, nevertheless, was obligated to discharge such arrearages of pay as the states chose not to extinguish, and Congress therefore resolved on November 3, 1783, that the paymaster general should convey continental final settlement certificates to regimental agents who were to deliver them to individual members of the Line or to deposit them for the recipients' benefit as the chief executives of the respective states should direct.[19]

The change in Congress' attitude toward the debt did not go unnoticed at the spring Assembly of 1784, which instructed the state commissioners to keep careful receipts for disbursements to the Line so that North Carolina could obtain full credit with the United States. Strong Federalist influence at that Assembly prevented further encroachments upon the debt due the Line, but the realities of state finances permitted the Federalists to only make the gesture that North Carolina would provide Congress with funds to pay the army "as soon

17. Petition from Orange County residents to the General Assembly, Legislative Papers, LXVI, November 28 folder.

18. Ferguson, *Power of the Purse*, pp. 134, 169, 181.

19. *Journals of Continental Congress*, XXV, 801.

as it may be deemed consistent with the circumstances of the State."[20] On the other hand, Federalist lack of enthusiasm contributed to the defeat of a proposed tax to pay the interest on state certificates issued to the Line, and the Assembly did not react overgenerously when the commissioners reported that most of the £72,000 had been issued to the Line and that the balance would be distinctly inadequate to discharge all remaining one-fourth arrearages. In allocating £10,000 ($25,000) of 1783 tax revenue for such purpose, the Assembly provided that any one-fourth arrearage claims presented after that sum had been expended should be met with a special certificate redeemable out of tax revenue for 1784.[21]

As Federalism reached a peak within the Assembly, it further diminished at Congress. Prepared to yield completely to state absorption of the national debt, Congress resolved on June 1, 1784, that in their respective accounts with the United States the states should be credited with the specie value of all sums paid to the Lines and due from the United States, provided that all such payments should be brought to the attention of the commissioner of army accounts and charged by him to the officers and men of the army in their individual accounts with the United States.[22] Having left payment of the Line entirely to each state's discretion, Congress proceeded to establish the machinery with which to discharge such obligations as the states saw fit not to extinguish. An agent to each Line, appointed under the congressional resolution of November 3, 1783, was instructed to scrutinize muster rolls, financial records, and other documents in order to determine the extent to which the state had paid its Line; and for the purpose of issuing continental final settlement certificates, offices of army

20. Clark, ed., *State Records*, XIX, 630-31; XXIV, 567-68.

21. *Ibid.*, XIX, 547, 575, 685-87; XXIV, 567-68. The commissioners reported that £70,693 had been issued to the Line, leaving, after expenses, a balance of £180 on hand. The defeat of the proposed tax was the result also of general economic conditions, resistance to new taxes, and other considerations.

22. *Journals of Continental Congress*, XXVII, 506.

accounts were established in the states, North Carolina's being assigned to New Bern.[23]

Despite the opportunity afforded by the congressional resolution of June 1, 1784, several considerations deterred the fall Assembly of 1784 (and later Assemblies) from seeking absorption of the entire debt due the Line—that part for services beyond December 31, 1781. First, the treasury's limitations and the arguments against a new currency emission precluded that the commissioners could be supplied with sufficient money to discharge one-fourth of each claim. Second, if the state moved into the period beyond December 31, 1781, large quantities of one-fourth arrearage certificates would have to be issued on the same basis as previous ones; they would have to be applied against the next year's badly-needed tax revenue. Third, the state could circumvent these problems and still probably absorb a good portion of the 1782 and 1783 debt by the previously discussed process of having the boards of auditors issue state certificates in exchange for the continental final settlement certificates. The exchange alternative involved some risk to the state because direct absorption of the debt due the Line had received congressional authorization whereas at that time the exchange process had not, but because of the state's financial limitations and other aforementioned considerations, the risk seemed worth taking.[24]

While deciding against direct and immediate absorption of the 1782-83 debt, the fall Assembly of 1784 proved anxious to complete assumption through December 31, 1781, before congressional machinery could be established to give the veterans an alternate source of relief. Thus, in order to pressure the Line into presenting its claims, the Assembly ordered that the state commissioners continue to act until February 1, 1785, after which their offices were to be dissolved and entirely annihilated. To convince the Line that North Carolina offered a better prospect for payment than did the United States, the

23. Robert Fenner to Governor Richard Caswell, July 27, 1785, Clark, ed., *State Records*, XVII, 490-91; Ferguson, *Power of the Purse*, p. 186.

24. Above, pp. 133-34.

Assembly ordered that the treasurer pay the commissioners the amount still deficient from the ten thousand pounds assigned by the previous Assembly and that the treasurer pay the holders of state final settlement certificates one year's interest in November or December, 1786, and each year thereafter. For the same purpose, and to profit speculators, the Assembly resolved that state final settlement certificates (or state currency) would be accepted at nominal value in the purchase of all categories of confiscated property.[25] The actions of the Assembly may well have convinced veterans with unsettled claims for the period before January 1, 1782, that the state offered better hope for justice, but the payment of interest and the use of all categories of confiscated property as a redemption agent could only have antagonized the many men who, as we have seen, had been compelled to relinquish their certificates to creditors or, worse, to sell the certificates to speculators at a small fraction of nominal value. Indeed, as previously indicated, the influence of speculators at the Assembly probably helped significantly to bring about the broad employment of confiscated property, and of approximately $711,000 in final settlement certificates retired between 1784 and 1790 by confiscated property, speculators and creditors benefited far more than did the Line.[26] Thus, in seeking to promote assumption of most of the debt due the Line, and to benefit speculators, the Assembly further forfeited the goodwill of men who felt, with considerable justification, that their wartime sacrifices had not been sufficiently appreciated or rewarded.

During 1785 it became apparent that North Carolina's efforts to absorb the debt due the Line for the period before January 1, 1782, were enjoying considerable success. Before the state commission's dissolution on January 31, 1785, it awarded approximately $200,000 nominal value of North Car-

25. Clark, ed., *State Records*, XIX, 455-56, 457; XXIV, 662, 686. A special property tax to pay the interest on the certificates was defeated. Bills in Legislative Papers, LIII, October 26 folder, and LVII, November 2 folder.

26. Above, pp. 35-37.

olina currency and slightly over $1,000,000 in specie certificates.[27] By no means had all claims been settled by the date the commission ceased to function, and that fact was disturbing to some individuals because the Office of Army Accounts was continuing to examine claims and issue continental final settlement certificates—exclusively for services performed during 1782-83 but potentially for the period through 1781. When in June, 1785—more than four months after North Carolina had ceased to issue final settlement certificates—the Office of Army Accounts at New Bern announced that it had issued 2,513 continental final settlement certificates for the total amount of $386,900 and that more claims remained to be settled,[28] the opponents of centralization became increasingly alarmed that North Carolina had ceased to accept the claims of the Line.

This political concern, and secondarily a sense of justice to the Line, led the 1785 Assembly to adopt several measures designed to attract the unsettled claims and the loyalties of the North Carolina Line. Most significantly, a commission to issue final settlement certificates was re-established for a limited time at Warrenton, for the purpose of receiving claims for services before January 1, 1782.[29] Further to appeal to the

27. The total sum of £82,000 ($205,000) had been set aside to discharge one-fourth of each arrearage claim, which sum minus expenses may be set at $200,000. The three-fourths certificates for that sum of currency would, of course, have amounted to $600,000. In 1791 Abishai Thomas, agent to present North Carolina's claims against the United States, set the total amount of certificates issued by the Halifax Commission at $1,011,638. This latter sum, minus the previously mentioned $600,000, would mean that the commission issued approximately $100,000 in one-fourth arrearage certificates and the remaining $300,000 in the usual three-fourths arrearage certificates. "General Abstract of the Claims of the State of North Carolina Against the United States," pp. 19, 21, Treasurers' and Comptrollers' Papers, Military Papers, LXVIII.

28. Eben Jackson to Governor Richard Caswell, June 14, 1785, Clark, ed., *State Records*, XVII, 470-71.

29. *Ibid.*, XXIV, 734-35. The Warrenton commission was to meet during the first ten days of April, May, and June, 1786; after June 10, 1786, unliquidated claims were to be of no effect. The original bill had allocated $72,500 for payment of arrearages, but the final act continued the policy of issuing a certificate for three-fourths the arrearage and

Line, and to benefit creditors and speculators, the Assembly enacted that all types of state certificates issued in payment to the Line—not just final settlement certificates—would be accepted at nominal value in the purchase of all categories of confiscated property. For the same purposes and also for the purpose of reducing the national debt within the state, the Line's continental final settlement certificates were likewise made acceptable in the purchase of confiscated property. Also, one of the stated purposes of the currency emission of 1785 was the redemption of the one-fourth arrearage certificates issued by the state commission.[30] Finally, the Assembly provided pensions to men disabled in the service of the United States and to widows and orphans of men killed in the service of the United States—pensions that would elicit gratitude toward the state, yet which were authorized by congressional resolutions and were chargeable against the central government in North Carolina's settlement with the United States.[31]

Another politically significant matter examined by the 1785 Assembly was the state's relationship with Robert Fenner, the Line's agent appointed pursuant to the congressional resolution of November 3, 1783, which, it will be recalled, had instructed the agent to deliver continental final settlement certificates to individual members of the Line or to deposit them as the chief executive of the state should direct. In compliance with the resolution, the Office of Army Accounts at New Bern in 1785 had conveyed such certificates to Fenner with instructions "immediately to deliver all the Certificates to the respective Individuals or lodge them where the Supreme Executive of the State of North Carolina shall direct."[32] After

a special one-fourth arrearage certificate redeemable from tax revenue. Legislative Papers, unnumbered box.

30. Clark, ed., *State Records*, XXI, 114; XXIV, 722. Above, pp. 36, 81.

31. *Ibid.*, pp. 735-37, 744. Pensions for widows and orphans were requested and authorized by a congressional resolution passed by Congress in 1780 when Congress had been most desperate financially. Pensions to disabled veterans were authorized by a congressional resolution of June 7, 1785, after Congress had passed from Federalist control.

32. Eben Jackson to Governor Richard Caswell, June 14, 1785, *ibid.*, XVII, 470-71.

Fenner, to the Line's dissatisfaction, had ensconced himself at Halifax in improper defiance of Governor Caswell's instructions to deliver appropriate certificates to the state's districts and "principal towns," the 1785 Assembly ordered the agent to convey all certificates currently in his possession to the state treasurer, who, in turn, was to transmit them to their recipients.[33] While state delivery of the continental certificates was not a displeasing prospect, the Assembly's resolution was motivated by a sense of justice—and was based upon a misinterpretation, intentional or not, of the congressional resolution of November 3, 1783, and of a congressional resolution of May 27, 1785, which had instructed the agent to deliver to the state executive all certificates that went unclaimed or proved undeliverable.[34] Officials of the United States—Robert Fenner, officers at the Office of Army Accounts at New Bern, Paymaster General Pierce—responded to the Assembly's resolution by arguing, correctly, that the agent

33. Governor Richard Caswell to Robert Fenner, June 14, 1785, *ibid.*, p. 468; Robert Fenner to Governor Richard Caswell, July 27, 1785, *ibid.*, pp. 490-91; advertisement announcing Fenner's presence at Halifax, dated July 15, 1785, Governors' Papers, XI, 45, State Department of Archives and History, Raleigh; Archibald Lytle to Governor Richard Caswell, August 14, 1786, Governors' Papers, XI, 73; Clark, ed., *State Records*, XVII, 371-72. Caswell instructed Fenner to deliver the certificates to the towns and to appoint a person in each district to deliver the certificates to appropriate individuals. Fenner justified his residence at Halifax by pointing out, correctly, that he had no appointment authority; he also argued that he did not know where the recipients resided and that he had not been supplied by Congress with pay or traveling expenses. These arguments were good, but Fenner's refusal to seek some satisfactory compliance with the governor's instructions violated the letter and the spirit of the congressional resolution of November 3, 1783. Members of the Line complained to Caswell that it was unreasonable to expect them to travel to Halifax to pick up their certificates.

34. *Journals of Continental Congress*, XXVIII, 399. The resolution of May 27, 1785, required that at the completion of their duties the agents were to deliver all certificates "that may remain in their hands"—that is, unclaimed and undeliverable certificates—to the state executives. A congressional resolution of October 11, 1785, required the agents to return all "Certificates which remain undelivered" to the commissioner of army accounts, who was to turn them over to the respective state executives. *Ibid.*, XXIX, 821. There is no indication that the October 11 resolution was taken into account by the 1785 Assembly.

was amenable to the state executive rather than to the legislature; that the executive's authority was limited to instructions regarding the physical location and distribution of the certificates (instructions that, as we have seen, Fenner had defied); that Fenner had not yet had sufficient time or opportunity to make the certificates available to recipients; and that Congress had intended that only those certificates that remained unclaimed or undeliverable should be turned over to the executive.[35] Implicit in all these protests against North Carolina's efforts "to meddle" with the continental certificates was the conviction that the state intended thereby to encroach upon the sovereignty of the United States. Indeed, Robert Fenner's subsequent refusal to deliver the certificates to the state treasurer—despite the demands of the Assembly, the council, and the governor—was encouraged and supported by "many members" of the Line who were apparently of Federalist persuasion and feared that the state would keep the continental certificates and issue state certificates in lieu thereof.[36]

Another illustration of the political overtones involved in payment of the Line concerned activities by William Blount, North Carolina delegate in Congress whose ability to combine public service and personal profit was well developed even by the demanding standards of the eighteenth century. Using his influence at the national government, Blount circumvented the Office of Army Accounts at New Bern by procuring drafts from the United States Treasury for $13,367 in arrearages of pay due from Congress to officers of the North Carolina Continental Line. The drafts were sent by Paymaster General Pierce directly to Robert Fenner for delivery and were to be honored by William Skinner, commissioner of continental loans in North Carolina. Anticipating correctly that Skinner

35. Memecun Hunt to Governor Richard Caswell, March 11, 1786, Clark, ed., *State Records*, XVIII, 568-69; Governor Richard Caswell to Robert Fenner, July 17, 1786, *ibid.*, p. 691; Robert Fenner to Governor Richard Caswell and the Council, August 1, 1786, *ibid.*, pp. 701-2.

36. Robert Fenner to Governor Richard Caswell and the Council, August 1, 1786, *ibid.*, p. 701.

would be unable to redeem the drafts, Blount quickly offered the Line's officers his own services and influence—for a 5 per cent commission—in persuading the United States Treasury to honor its own drafts.[37] As Blount had feared, if not expected, North Carolina intervened in these maneuverings. Because Congress had expressed readiness to credit any state with payments made its Line, because the drafts were not subject to regulations regarding certificates from the Office of Army Accounts, because Skinner could not honor the drafts, because a number of the intended recipients expressed a willingness to exchange their drafts for warrants on the North Carolina treasury, and because the August 1, 1786, deadline for presenting claims to the New Bern office had passed, Robert Fenner informed the 1786 Assembly that any of the drafts honored by the state would be credited to North Carolina against the United States at final settlement. Motivated by a sense of justice to the Line but primarily by the desire to absorb, for political reasons, the national debt represented by the drafts, the Assembly resolved that upon application of the individual officers the governor should receive the drafts and issue in exchange warrants payable out of the state contingency fund, with North Carolina to receive a credit with the national government.[38] Existing records establish that twenty officers received such warrants for a total amount of $3,127,[39] which statistics, if complete, would indicate that many other officers had even less confidence in the state than in the

37. For the account of Blount's activities, see the circular letter dated July 7, 1786, from William Blount to the officers of the North Carolina Continental Line, William Lytle Papers, Southern Historical Collection, The University of North Carolina at Chapel Hill. Also, John Pierce to Robert Fenner, June 15, 1786, Clark, ed., *State Records*, XVIII, 653.

38. Clark, ed., *State Records*, XVIII, 380-81. The August 1, 1786, deadline for presenting claims to the Office of Army Accounts was set by a congressional resolution of November 2, 1785. *Journals of Continental Congress*, XXIX, 866.

39. Memorandum in Treasurers' and Comptrollers' Papers, Military Papers, LXVII. The governor informed the 1787 Assembly that some but not all of the drafts had been presented to him and honored by warrants on the state treasury. Clark, ed., *State Records*, XX, 144-45.

United States. The entire episode clearly reveals the political implications of the debt and the dilemma of the Line in seeking effective payment.

A further matter at the 1786 Assembly was an examination of Robert Fenner's controversial relationship with the state. Although the Senate could not bring itself to accept a committee report endorsing the agent's position that he had not been amenable to the 1785 Assembly, the Assembly effectively accepted Fenner's view by resolving that he had settled his accounts "with the utmost accuracy and precision."[40] Because the certificates in Fenner's possession had long been available to claimants and because the deadline for presenting claims to the Office of Army Accounts had passed, the Assembly resolved that Fenner deliver all unclaimed certificates—amounting to $82,677 out of a total of $388,271 that had come into his possession—to the state treasurer. After the governor issued the same instructions, the unclaimed certificates passed into the possession of the state, and North Carolina took up the task of trying to locate the intended recipients. Although a number of individuals never claimed their certificates, probably because of death or removal from the state, a sizable portion of the certificates were claimed, and the state disposed of the remainder in order to receive a credit with the United States.[41]

The 1786 Assembly entertained also the unhappy news that the treasury had received and honored palpably fraudulent

40. *Ibid.*, XVIII, 381; committee report in Legislative Papers, LXVIII, December 15 folder. Fenner, incensed at the calumny directed toward him, was anxious to refute accusations by any "malicious detractor," and he had requested an investigation by the 1786 Assembly. Robert Fenner to Governor Richard Caswell, August 1, 1786, Clark, ed., *State Records*, XVIII, 700; Robert Fenner to the General Assembly, December 9, 1786, Legislative Papers, LXVII, December 9 folder.

41. Clark, ed., *State Records*, XVIII, 182, 189, 381, 415; XXI, 102, 413-14. Also, John Haywood to the General Assembly, Legislative Papers, LXXXVII. The undelivered certificates in Fenner's possession, totaling $82,677, consisted of the following: $20,677 belonging to commissioned officers; "about" $11,000 belonging to 55 "War Soldiers"; $17,000 belonging to 250 eight-month "drafts"; and $34,000 belonging to 850 twelve-month "drafts."

and counterfeit certificates among the $154,620 in Warrenton arrearage certificates redeemed by the state. Convinced that a thorough investigation was in order (and that revenue was limited), the Assembly terminated the annual interest payment upon the three-fourth arrearage certificates "until the just amount of that debt is ascertained." Probably as a gesture toward the innocent victims of the cancellation, the Assembly granted additional time for military land grants to be located, surveyed, and registered.[42]

Finally, the 1786 Assembly, which inaugurated the previously discussed certificate sinking tax, made the certificates issued to the Line before January 1, 1786, acceptable at nominal value in payment of the tax. The considerations leading to the tax were, as we have seen, broader than the matter of North Carolina's relationship to the Line, but one may suspect that the Line's certificates would not have been made liable to the fiat tax had the United States still been issuing its own payment certificates.[43]

The fraud investigation continued for a number of years and resulted ultimately in the dismissal of the state treasurer, the discrediting of the commissioners, and the conviction of a number of former continental officers and other individuals. The presence of fraud, moreover, greatly complicated the presentation of the state's claims against the United States. Eventually a commission was established at Hillsborough to examine such certificates of the Warrenton commission's $475,000 in specie certificates as were presented, and of the $211,745 examined through June, 1791, $156,250 had been rejected as fraudulent.[44] The Assembly had little choice, therefore, but

42. Clark, ed., *State Records*, XVIII, 162, 184, 282, 384; XXIV, 812.

43. Above, pp. 41-42. Because of the fraud involved in the issuing of the final settlement certificates of 1786, those issued by the Warrenton commissioners were not accepted in payment of the certificate tax or, as the text shortly reveals, in discharge of any other public obligation or purpose.

44. "General Abstract of the Claims of the State of North Carolina Against the United States," pp. 18, 19, 21, Treasurers' and Comptrollers' Papers, Military Papers, LXVIII. By order of the 1790 Assembly, the agents gave a complete description of all money and certificates issued by the Warrenton commissioners to the Line. "Reg-

to disqualify and disavow completely the unexamined Warrenton certificates, a legitimate and inescapable policy that nevertheless served at least as an inconvenience to honest veterans who had to present the certificates for examination at Hillsborough, and at worst as a loss to secondary holders who in good faith had accepted or purchased fraudulent certificates.

The disqualification of the Warrenton certificates was the latest in a series of disappointments that, as we have seen, plagued and disillusioned the Line throughout the 1780's. After years without pay, the men of the Line in 1782 had received partial pay in certificates redeemable only in perishable confiscated property or at an indefinite date; in 1783 they had received paper currency that they mistrusted and certificates that, again, were redeemable at an indefinite date; their certificates had not been made acceptable at the western land office, and all categories of confiscated property had not been employed as a redemption agent until after many of the veterans had been forced to yield their certificates—at a loss—to creditors or speculators; and in 1786 their certificates had lost their preferred status when made liable to the certificate sinking tax. The cumulative discontent engendered by this series of disappointments is evident in a veterans' petition that asked the 1789 Assembly if the country had forgotten their services; explained bitterly that Congress' former weakness had induced them to accept certificates of pay from the state; argued that North Carolina's resources, if properly managed, could discharge the unpaid and neglected Halifax certificates and all other purposes of government; and warned that Congress under the constitution would pay them if the state would not.[45] With the constitution's ratification by nine states and especially with North Carolina's ratification of it during the 1789 Assembly, state certificates held by the Line ceased to have political significance and thus were exclusively a burden

ister of the Settlement of Army Accounts of the North Carolina Line, made by Commissioners of that State at Warrenton in the Year 1786," bound volume in Treasurers' and Comptrollers' Papers.

45. Petition in Legislative Papers, XCI.

upon the government. The Assembly, therefore, ignored the petition's plea and failed to take any steps to aid the Line. Indeed, the Assembly refused to issue certificates for legitimate claims recently presented by members of the Line; continued the certificate sinking tax; and, for reasons previously discussed, devalued the entire certificate debt despite the protest that such devaluation would injure the Line.[46] When in 1790 the United States assumed the state debt, individual members of the Line benefited from whatever state final settlement certificates they had managed to retain, but by that year most of those certificates lay in the hands of men who had never served in the Continental Line of North Carolina.

The Line's experience with continental final settlement certificates proved a frequently unfortunate one also, for by the time that the certificates were made acceptable in the purchase of confiscated property, most of that property had already been sold; and by the time that certificates attained more value as speculation began to increase with the prospects of ratification and funding,[47] hardship had long since led many veterans to sell their continental certificates at the low market price that Congress' earlier weakness had established. To these individuals the appreciating value of continental securities was a source of bitterness, and especially disturbed must have been those persons who, for a lack of confidence in Congress' future, had exchanged their continen-

46. Clark, ed., *State Records*, XXI, 396, 662; above, pp. 45-47, 48. As treated above, p. 45, some monetary redemption was provided, but repudiation by devaluation was the chief feature.

47. Mindful of the speculation and the resulting appreciation of the value of continental certificates, Treasurer John Haywood urged the 1789 Assembly to retain the final settlement certificates that the state had received from Robert Fenner and to pay off any claimants with state currency instead. In that manner, Haywood suggested, North Carolina could sell the certificates and profit therefrom. John Haywood to the General Assembly, Legislative Papers, LXXXVII. The Assembly subsequently ordered that the continental certificates be held until July 1, 1790, after which date the governor was to sell the certificates or send them to the state's agents in New York in order to obtain a credit for North Carolina against congressional requisitions (in final settlement). Clark, ed., *State Records*, XXI, 413-14. Above, p. 185.

tal certificates for warrants on the state treasury or for state certificates issued by the boards of auditors.[48]

While individuals might stand to lose or gain significantly by ratification of the constitution and funding of the continental final settlement certificates, the general stakes in North Carolina were small when compared with the size of that portion of the national debt residing among the citizens of other states; for if North Carolina's policies regarding its own certificates did little to merit the loyalty of the Line, the state had achieved its purpose of slicing deeply into the national debt due its Line. Having paid the Line $575,000 in wartime state currency, approximately $200,000 in postwar state currency, and in the vicinity of $1,750,000 in legitimate final settlement certificates,[49] North Carolina had left the United States to issue only $388,271 in final settlement certificates, or about 15 per cent of the entire debt owed to the Line. When one realizes that the continental certificates issued to the

48. The exchange of drafts upon the United States Treasury for warrants on the state treasury has been treated above, pp. 183-85, in connection with William Blount's hopes of obtaining a commission. In 1791 Abishai Thomas listed $18,878 against the United States in warrants issued by North Carolina in exchange for drafts upon the United States Treasury. That amount exceeds the total of the drafts obtained by Blount's activity; the basis for Thomas' figure, therefore, is not clear. "General Abstract of Claims of the State of North Carolina Against the United States," p. 20, Treasurers' and Comptrollers' Papers, Military Papers, LXVIII. As another example of the Line's lack of confidence in continental final settlement certificates, an officer with nearly ten thousand dollars in such certificates asked the 1785 Assembly to honor the certificates with the 1785 state currency and to present the certificates subsequently as a claim against the United States. Memorial of Robert Howe to the General Assembly, Legislative Papers, LX, December 28 folder.

49. That is, $575,000 in wartime currency and $585,000 in specie certificates issued during the war by various officials, above, p. 170; $35,840 in certificates issued by the commission established in 1780, above, p. 171; approximately $200,000 in postwar state currency and slightly over $1,000,000 in specie certificates issued by the Halifax Commission established in 1783, above, pp. 173-74, 177, 179-80; and, based upon the ratio of legitimate Warrenton certificates examined at Hillsborough, about $100,000 in legitimate certificates of the $475,000 issued by the Warrenton Commission, above, p. 186. These certificates issued to the Line were not included in the 1789 report of the comptroller on the certificate debt, above, p. 48.

North Carolina Line constituted only about 3.5 per cent of the $11,000,000 in such certificates issued to the Army of the United States,[50] and when one contemplates further that some of the certificates to the state's Line went unclaimed, others were absorbed by the state, and yet others were procured by out-of-state speculators, the insignificance of that portion of the national debt within North Carolina becomes apparent and assumes significant political importance regarding the ratification debate. The absence of a large, influential, dynamic, self-interested group of continental certificate holders—the number of continental loan certificates within the state was small and, as we have seen, North Carolinians possessed only $8,695 out of $3,723,000 in certificates issued to civilians by the United States commissioners[51]—does much, as previously indicated, to explain North Carolina's slowness to ratify the constitution. In short, the continental debt within the state was largely extinguished, but once the constitution went into effect elsewhere the forces and considerations militating in favor of North Carolina's participation in the Union overrode the well-executed plan of the Antifederalists. In the struggle for control of the national debt owed to the Line, not the least casualty was the hapless Line itself.

50. Ferguson, *Power of the Purse*, p. 180.

51. Above, p. 146. Ferguson, *Power of the Purse*, pp. 69n., 183, reveals that only 10 per cent of the continental loan certificates were originally issued in the states from Maryland through Georgia and that three states alone—Massachusetts, Connecticut, and Pennsylvania—contained 66 per cent of all loan certificates at original issue.

VIII. Congressional Revenue

As the three immediately preceding chapters have disclosed, the settlement of individual civilian and military claims against the United States—the national domestic debt—and the settlement of wartime accounts between the United States and the respective states possessed political as well as financial significance and together composed one of the two issues upon which state-federal relations centered. The second and related issue was, as previously indicated, the matter of securing revenue for the United States government, either through the requisition system employed under the Articles of Confederation or through direct tax powers secured for Congress by amendment of the articles. These revenue options contained primary political importance, for the requisition system maintained Congress' dependence upon the states whereas the establishment of congressional taxes would significantly strengthen the central government at the financial and political expense of the states. Federalists thus deplored the requisition system, but they had little choice except to employ it as an expedient until such time as their efforts to secure congressional tax powers should meet with success.[1] The implementation of the requisition system and the struggle over the establishment of congressional taxes were, therefore, matters that proceeded simultaneously during the immediate postwar period.

The requisition system had been formally initiated in November, 1777, but, as previously revealed, North Carolina's own desperate financial needs—reinforced by disappointment

1. E. James Ferguson, *The Power of the Purse: A History of American Public Finance, 1776-1790* (Chapel Hill: The University of North Carolina Press, 1961), pp. 116, 140.

in Congress' limited assistance to the state—had led North Carolina not to make any payments against its requisition quotas.[2] The general failure of the requisition system had argued that the central government needed its own tax powers, and in 1781, the year that Federalists had gained control of Congress, the first congressional effort to secure a federal tax had come. The original proposal that Congress be given a permanent 5 per cent ad valorem duty upon foreign imports in order to discharge the foreign debt of the United States had been altered, moreover, so as to recommend to the states that the revenue be used to discharge all war debts contracted by the United States[3]—an alteration engineered by the Federalists in an effort to attract the holders of the national domestic debt and to strengthen the central government generally. In 1781 North Carolina had responded generously by enacting the congressional impost subject to similar action by all the other states,[4] a condition important to North Carolina's interests and necessitated by the obvious fact that the congressional impost constituted an amendment of the Articles of Confederation. Significantly, the Assembly had bestowed upon the United States the appointment and control of collection officials and had granted those officials broad enforcement powers—matters that Congress had not requested but which Federalists had believed vital if the impost were to be an effective source of revenue.[5] Finally, the Assembly had specified that the act was to remain in force "until the principal and interest of the debts . . . of the United States, for supporting the war, be fully and finally discharged, and no longer," a provision authorizing the tax for an indefinite period and enabling Congress to use the revenue toward funding the domestic as well as the foreign debt of the United

2. *Ibid.*, p. 33. Above, pp. 74, 157.

3. Ferguson, *Power of the Purse*, p. 117.

4. Walter Clark, ed., *The State Records of North Carolina* (16 vols.; Winston, Goldsboro, and Raleigh: State of North Carolina, 1895-1906 [volumes numbered consecutive to William L. Saunders, ed., *The Colonial Records of North Carolina* (10 vols.; Raleigh: State of North Carolina, 1886-90)], XXIV, 405-6.

5. Ferguson, *Power of the Purse*, p. 117.

States. The Assembly's prompt and enthusiastic approval of the congressional impost had been in no small part the result of the fact that North Carolina, a state that procured most of its foreign products by way of other states, preferred a uniform tariff system it could help shape in Congress to the various, fluctuating, and sometimes high rates of individual states upon which North Carolina could exert no direct influence. The discretion given Congress to apply the money against the national domestic debt had, moreover, not been clearly contrary to the state's interests because as of 1781 North Carolina's absorption of the continental debt in its citizens' hands had not begun on a comprehensive, systematic basis.

Although North Carolina's interests stood to be served by the establishment of the congressional impost, other states had refused to authorize the tariff because of its political implications and/or because it would be detrimental to their economic and financial welfare. After it had become clear during 1782 that the impost was in trouble, Congress, on April 18, 1783, sought to remove specific objections by recommending that the states rather than Congress appoint the collection officials (who were, nevertheless, to be amenable to and removable by the United States) and that the impost be established for twenty-five years rather than permanently.[6] These Federalist concessions were further prompted by the conviction that the coming of peace would soon erode support for a stronger central government. Indeed, Federalist fears regarding the impact of peace were soon realized by the North Carolina Assembly of 1783, which, to Governor Martin's surprise and the dismay of the state's delegates in Congress, and as a result of general economic optimism and the relaxation of interest in a stronger government, repealed the act of 1781 granting the congressional impost.[7]

6. *Journals of the Continental Congress,* 1774-89 (34 vols.; Washington: Government Printing Office, 1904-37), XXIV, 258-59.

7. Governor Alexander Martin to Benjamin Hawkins, Hugh Williamson, and Richard Dobbs Spaight, January 21, 1783, Clark, ed., *State Records*, XVI, 729-30; Benjamin Hawkins and Hugh Williamson to

If the 1783 Assembly disappointed the proponents of congressional tax powers, the spring Assembly of 1784 proved to be in that respect—and others—a Federalist delight. By that time postwar economic optimism was beginning to fade and awareness of North Carolina's vulnerability to the tariff whims of other states had reasserted itself, both of which developments had broadly shifted public opinion in favor of the Assembly's re-enactment of the congressional impost. This shift, encouraged, of course, by Federalists and supported strongly by mercantile elements and Governor Alexander Martin's administration, produced general legislative support at the Federalist-oriented Assembly and easy passage of the impost bill.[8] The 5 per cent ad valorem impost was to go into effect within the state only upon enactment of similar measures by all the other states; it was to be collected by men appointed by the state but amenable to and removable by Congress; and it was to be in effect for a maximum of twenty-five years in

Governor Alexander Martin, September 26, 1783, *ibid.*, p. 886; *ibid.*, XXIV, 510. The stated reason for the repeal was that other states had failed to grant similar powers and that the grant therefore had no probability of going into effect.

8. Mercantile-Federalist support for re-enactment of the congressional impost is illustrated by a resolution adopted at an Edenton town meeting of August 1, 1783, which resolution called upon the assemblymen from Chowan County and Edenton to vote for the impost, "a most wise and judicious measure" that would enlarge the authority of Congress. (The meeting called also for the establishment of a fund to discharge the foreign debt of the United States.) Griffith John McRee, ed., *Life and Correspondence of James Iredell* (2 vols.; New York: D. Appleton and Company, 1867-68), II, 60-61, 62-63. It was understood outside the state that North Carolina strongly favored the impost. Thomas Jefferson to James Madison, May 8, 1784, Julian P. Boyd and others, eds., *The Papers of Thomas Jefferson* (17 vols.; Princeton: Princeton University Press, 1950-65), XVII, 232. Governor Martin's support for the impost is revealed in Governor Alexander Martin to Hugh Williamson and Richard Dobbs Spaight, April 24, 1784, Clark, ed., *State Records*, XVII, 49, and XVII, 37. For the support given the impost by the state's delegates in Congress, see Benjamin Hawkins and Hugh Williamson to Governor Alexander Martin, September 26, 1783, *ibid.*, XVI, 885-86. For evidence of strong support of the impost bill at the Assembly, see Archibald Maclaine to George Hooper, April 23, 1784, and Governor Alexander Martin to High Williamson and Richard Dobbs Spaight, April 24, 1784, *ibid.*, XVII, 135, 49.

order to "discharge . . . the principal and interest of the debt contracted on the faith of the United States for supporting the war."[9] The last provision, as previously indicated, contained great political significance, for it placed within Congress' discretion the application of tariff revenue to attract and redeem the national domestic debt certificates; and the provision was clearly contrary to the interests of most North Carolinians, for, as we have seen, the state by 1784 had long been engaged in extinguishing the continental debt within the state. With ever-decreasing quantities of continental certificates in private hands, the spring Assembly of 1784 was acting to benefit the central government rather than large numbers of its own citizens.

Also, to strengthen the central government and to secure "ample justice to the public creditors . . . of the United States" (as well as for other purposes previously mentioned), the spring Assembly of 1784 ceded the state's western territory to the United States.[10]

An even more pronounced evidence of Federalist sentiment at the spring Assembly of 1784 was an act that, subject to similar action by all the other states, granted Congress the power to collect for a maximum of twenty-five years a property tax within North Carolina for the purpose of raising the state's proportion ($109,006) of $1,500,000 to be used toward discharging the principal and interest of the debts of the United States.[11] This startling manifestation of Federalism was an overresponse and probably an intentional misconstruction of another congressional resolution of April 18, 1783, which had recommended that, in addition to the congressional impost, the states establish substantial and effective revenues for

9. Clark, ed., *State Records*, XXIV, 547-49. Other restrictions imposed by the act were that it was not to cause any citizen of North Carolina to be carried out of the state; it was not to compel him to answer any action outside the state; and it was not to deprive him of trial according to the laws and Constitution of North Carolina. Certain procedural restrictions were also included in the act.

10. *Ibid.*, pp. 561-63. Above, pp. 38, 138.

11. *Ibid.*, XXIV, 557-59. The act was subject to procedural restrictions and the limitations listed in footnote nine.

twenty-five years to pay their respective quotas of $1,500,000 annually for the purpose of discharging the principal and interest of the wartime debts of the United States.[12] The resolution's reference to the impost and to the twenty-five year period may have conveyed to some individuals the impression that Congress was seeking taxation powers in addition to the impost, but the resolution's intention had clearly been to encourage the states to levy their own internal taxes for the purpose of meeting their respective quotas of the $1,500,000 annual requisition. Thus, in establishing the "continental tax" for Congress, the Assembly exceeded the fondest hopes and expectations of Federalists at Congress; and, if the Assembly's act authorized the total collection of $109,006 over a maximum of twenty-five years rather than that amount annually, the reduction was because of North Carolina's limited resources and tax base rather than lack of commitment to Federalism; indeed, most Federalists undoubtedly considered the enactment of the tax to be more important than the sum of money that might be subsequently raised. Also of supreme importance was the fact that the revenue from the continental tax could be applied against the domestic debt of the United States.[13] Because of the significant political implications of the tax, the bill met the most resistance of any Federalist proposal at that Assembly and passed only by means of a maximum effort by the advocates of a stronger central government.[14]

Displaying this impressive array of achievements designed to strengthen the central government, the spring Assembly of 1784 marked the zenith of North Carolina Federalism before the state's ratification of the constitution late in 1789. With

12. *Journals of Continental Congress*, XXIV, 258.

13. Governor Martin believed mistakenly that the tax was limited to discharging the foreign debt of the United States. Governor Alexander Martin to the President of Congress, December 4, 1784, Clark, ed., *State Records*, XVII, 111.

14. William Richardson Davie to General Nathaniel Greene, June 27, 1784, William Richardson Davie Papers, Southern Historical Collection, The University of North Carolina at Chapel Hill.

justifiable satisfaction Governor Martin wrote Robert Morris that the Assembly had complied with a number of congressional recommendations touching upon finance, and one ardent North Carolina Federalist commented happily that "we have done every thing consistent with the interest of the State to strengthen the Hand of Congress."[15]

The actions of the Assembly naturally pleased and encouraged Federalists in other states,[16] but the drift of sentiment and events in North Carolina and elsewhere was generally opposed to Federalist ambitions. The impost, the "continental tax," and all other efforts on the state and national level to achieve congressional taxation by amendment of the articles subsequently failed. With Federalism no longer dominating Congress and with that political viewpoint far less significant at subsequent Assemblies, North Carolina, without repealing the acts authorizing congressional taxation,[17] thereafter turned its attention to the task of supplying money to Congress within the framework of the requisition system. Decline of interest in congressional tax powers can be attributed in part to the failure of other states to approve such powers, but the lessening commitment to congressional taxes was undoubtedly related to the fact that North Carolina, as we have seen, was effectively absorbing the great bulk of the continental debt within North Carolina. Because relatively few North Carolinians would benefit from redemption of the national debt by congressional tax powers, the state was the more inclined to stress the requisition system that maintained Congress' dependence and left North Car-

15. *Ibid.*; Governor Alexander Martin to Robert Morris, June 4, 1784, Clark, ed., *State Records*, XVII, 75.

16. See Francis Dana to Elbridge Gerry, June [July], 1784, Edmund Cody Burnett, ed., *Letters of Members of the Continental Congress* (8 vols.; Washington: Carnegie Institution, 1921-36), VIII, 849.

17. The spring Assembly of 1784 had appointed a "continental tax" collector for each county. The fall Assembly of 1784 provided that the regular tax collectors were to collect the continental tax. The tax was collected for several years, but, as shall soon be revealed, the money was diverted to state use. Clark, ed., *State Records*, XIX, 705-7, 708; XXIV, 661.

olina's contribution to the Congress entirely within the state's discretion.

The diminishing interest in Federalist measures became apparent at the fall Assembly of 1784, which channeled the continental-tax revenue to state use on the basis of other states' failure to pass similar acts[18]—a failure hardly surprising since North Carolina had authorized the tax only a few months earlier and in so doing had exceeded congressional recommendations. In addition, the Assembly employed the failure of other states to cede western lands and grant the congressional impost to justify the repeal of the cession act of the previous Assembly, a repeal that, as we have seen, was largely the result of Franklinite pretensions[19] but represented also a reaction to the significant Federalism of the previous Assembly.

By the convening of the 1785 Assembly, the state's commitment to the requisition system, together with North Carolina's past failure to contribute toward its quotas plus Congress' severe financial difficulties, placed a heavy obligation upon the state to make effective payment to the national government. This sense of obligation, as we have seen, was one of the factors that led the Assembly to emit £100,000 of fiat currency,[20] of which £36,000 was allocated for state purchase of tobacco to be shipped to Europe, the West Indies, or elsewhere at the advice of the United States Board of Treasury for sale in order to discharge North Carolina's portion of "the debt due from the United States"—a purpose giving Congress the discretion of applying the money against the domestic debt of the United States, a discretion that the Assembly undoubtedly did not intend to convey in view of the North Carolina government's virtually complete absorption of continental certificates within the state.

Because the public tobacco program was intimately associated with the controversial matter of fiat currency and be-

18. *Ibid.*, XXIV, 650-51, 661, 678-79.
19. Above, p. 39.
20. Clark, ed., *State Records*, XXIV, 722, 724. Above, pp. 74, 81.

cause the program extensively involved the government in the private sector of the economy, state purchase of tobacco inevitably aroused doubts and opposition. In addition to the general questions raised, the initial implementation of the program created two specific problems. First, the wording of the act establishing the program did not make clear whether the Board of Treasury was to arrange and execute the sale as well as control the shipment of the tobacco. Second, the commissioners appointed by the act to purchase the tobacco resorted, as we have seen, to offering the maximum authorized price of fifty shillings per one hundred pounds weight, a price well above the market price and which therefore stalled private transactions in tobacco, served to undermine the new fiat currency, and faced the government with considerable losses in trying to sell the tobacco in the glutted world markets.[21]

During 1786, as Governor Richard Caswell arranged for collection and storage of the tobacco and corresponded with the Board of Treasury, these problems became increasingly apparent. While storage fees mounted and rumors spread that the commissioners had purchased poor quality tobacco and had allowed the purchases to be damaged by exposure to weather,[22] the state executive and the Board of Treasury attempted unsuccessfully to persuade each other to interpret the intent of the 1785 Assembly regarding arrangement and execution of the sale.[23] As discouraging as the delays were

21. Above, p. 83.

22. Governor Richard Caswell to John Haywood, July 9, September 1, 1786, Clark, ed., *State Records*, XVIII, 678, 723; Governor Richard Caswell to John Whitaker, September 20, 1786, *ibid.*, p. 744; depositions by Robert Mitchell and Austin Creat, Legislative Papers, LXXIV, January 3 folder, State Department of Archives and History, Raleigh; Adelaide L. Fries and others, eds., *Records of the Moravians in North Carolina* (10 vols.; Raleigh: North Carolina Historical Commission [State Department of Archives and History], 1922-66), V, 2145. A fire that destroyed warehouse facilities in Wilmington was at least partially responsible for tobacco's being exposed in the streets.

23. Governor Richard Caswell to John Haywood, March 26, 1786, Clark, ed., *State Records*, XVIII, 585-87; Governor Richard Caswell to the Board of Treasury, April 3, 1786, *ibid.*, pp. 592-93; Board of Treasury to Governor Richard Caswell, May 29, 1786, *ibid.*, pp. 634-36; Governor Richard Caswell to the Board of Treasury, June 21, 1786,

the extremely cautious inquiries and the unexciting offers made by prospective purchasers of the tobacco, the results both of market conditions and of North Carolina's notoriously poor system of inspection that gave the state's tobacco a tarnished reputation everywhere.[24] Thus toward the end of the year the conviction prevailed that the 1786 Assembly should thoroughly review the entire structure and concept of the tobacco program.

That review, which did not include an investigation of the tobacco commissioners for mismanagement, led the Assembly to reject all offers made for the tobacco; to specify that the delegates in Congress should arrange and execute the sale at the highest possible price; to restrict the commissioners to paying the local, market price for the tobacco; to allocate for additional purchases of public tobacco all revenue arising from state imposts, fees upon foreign tonnage, and the property tax upon land; and, significantly, to restrict the state's payments to Congress to the discharge of the foreign debt of the United States.[25] The latter provision was a corrective to the careless wording of the 1785 act which had inadvertently left the money to Congress' discretion. Federalists within and outside North Carolina quite properly interpreted the restriction as deliberate Antifederalism,[26] and—as in other instances—it was Antifederalism with a sound financial basis, because, as we have seen, the government of North Carolina had almost

ibid., p. 657; Governor Richard Caswell to the Board of Treasury, July 9, 1786, *ibid.*, pp. 679-80; Board of Treasury to Governor Richard Caswell, October 11, 1786, *ibid.*, p. 761. Caswell considered the arrangement of having the Board of Treasury direct shipment of the tobacco to be a "round about way of doing business."

24. Governor Richard Caswell to John Haywood, March 14, 1786, *ibid.*, p. 576; Board of Treasury to Robert Morris, May 12, 1786, *ibid.*, pp. 606-7; Robert Morris to the Board of Treasury, May 18, May 30, 1786, *ibid.*, pp. 620, 637; Nicholas Romayne to the Board of Treasury, June 1, 1786, *ibid.*, pp. 638-39. William McDaniel (Washington, North Carolina) to Governor Richard Caswell, March 14, 1786, Governors' Papers, XII, 49, State Department of Archives and History, Raleigh.

25. Clark, ed., *State Records*, XVIII, 64-65; XXIV, 797, 812, 813.

26. See William Blount to Governor Richard Caswell, January 28, 1787, Burnett, ed., *Letters of Congress*, VIII, 532-33.

extinguished the national domestic debt within the state and thus North Carolinians would benefit little from the money's application against that domestic debt.

If Federalists were greatly displeased with the termination of Congress' discretionary authority over the proceeds from North Carolina's tobacco, certain of the other actions taken by the 1786 Assembly failed to satisfy a number of state officials. A group of legislators who had studied the storage problems and fees associated with the program believed that the tobacco, which at that time amounted to 1,323,921 pounds weight, should have been immediately shipped abroad for sale. State Treasurer John Haywood and the delegates in Congress were convinced that assigning the latter the responsibility for selling the tobacco was an awkward and time-consuming arrangement because the delegates could not keep abreast of the quantity, quality, location, and other necessary details of the tobacco.[27] Despite the continuing misgivings about the details of the program, the application of significant revenues to it established that North Carolina was still very much committed to the purchase of tobacco for the discharge of the state's portion of the foreign debt of the United States.

Hampered indeed by a lack of precise information about the tobacco—information that they sought through official and unofficial channels—the state's delegates in Congress, Benjamin Hawkins and William Blount, conferred with the Board of Treasury and with prospective buyers about North Carolina's public tobacco. Although the 1786 Assembly had explicitly instructed that the tobacco be sold for the highest price offered, the general economic depression and resultant bankruptcies among American firms persuaded the delegates that good credit and unequivocal guarantees of payment should take priority over price.[28] Upon this conviction, and

27. Clark, ed., *State Records*, XVIII, 64-65; William Blount to Governor Richard Caswell, February 10, 1787, *ibid.*, XX, 613; John Haywood to John Gray Blount, March 16, 1787, Alice Barnwell Keith and William Henry Masterson, eds., *The John Gray Blount Papers* (3 vols.; Raleigh: State Department of Archives and History, 1952-65), I, 266.

28. William Blount to Governor Richard Caswell, February 10, 1787, Clark, ed., *State Records*, XX, 613; William Blount to Edward Dowse,

thus in violation of the Assembly's directions, Hawkins and Blount, in mid-March, 1787, contracted with the New York house of Constable, Rucker and Company for purchase of the public tobacco upon the following terms: 3.33 Spanish milled dollars (legally equivalent to 26*s.* 8*d.* North Carolina currency) per one hundred pounds weight tobacco, payable to the Board of Treasury in bills of exchange upon Amsterdam; payments dated (in the contract) so as to enable payment from North Carolina against the interest due (June 1, 1787) from the United States upon the principal of the Dutch loan; and re-inspection at state expense in the presence of the firm's agent.[29]

Having negotiated the sale at a price less than the maximum one received and thereby having acted contrary to the Assembly's instructions, the delegates quickly dispatched an explanatory letter justifying their decision on the following bases: Constable, Rucker and Company offered sound credit and guaranteed payment at a time when such advantages were not easily obtained; the delegates' lack of authority to control shipment of the tobacco had made sale to an American firm the only feasible course of action; and the sale to Constable, Rucker and Company assured payment of the interest on the Dutch loan to the United States.[30] The first and

February 28, 1787, *ibid.*, p. 625; Edward Dowse to William Blount, February 28, 1787, *ibid.*, pp. 625-26; William Blount and Benjamin Hawkins to the Board of Treasury, February 24, 1787, *ibid.*, pp. 620-21; Board of Treasury to Benjamin Hawkins and William Blount, February 28, 1787, *ibid.*, pp. 624-25; William Blount and Benjamin Hawkins to the Board of Treasury, March 1, 1787, *ibid.*, pp. 626-27; William Blount and Benjamin Hawkins to Governor Richard Caswell, March 19, 1787, *ibid.*, pp. 644-46. William Blount to John Gray Blount, March 8, 1787, Keith and Masterson, eds., *Blount*, I, 257-58.

29. For correspondence dealing with Constable, Rucker and Company, see Board of Treasury to Benjamin Hawkins and William Blount, March 14, 1787, Clark, ed., *State Records*, XX, 635; William Blount to Governor Richard Caswell, March 14, 1787, *ibid.*, p. 636; William Blount to John Gray Blount, March 8, 1787, Keith and Masterson, eds., *Blount*, I, 257-58. The contract, dated March 16, 1787, is found in Clark, ed., *State Records*, XX, 639-41.

30. William Blount and Benjamin Hawkins to Governor Richard Caswell, March 19, 1787, Clark, ed., *State Records*, XX, 644-46.

last justifications were weighty, but because the delegates could easily have consulted with the Board of Treasury, which by act of Assembly did have control of shipment, the delegates' statement that they would have preferred to ship the tobacco abroad for sale but could not for lack of authority seems questionable. Indeed, a major reason that the tobacco was sold to Constable, Rucker and Company rather than shipped abroad was a secret agreement between the firm and William Blount that, at the price the company paid North Carolina, Blount could purchase from the company one hundred hogsheads of the best-quality public tobacco—an agreement that Blount had apparently been demanding of all prospective purchasers and that climaxed months of clandestine efforts to use his position to benefit himself and his family from the state's tobacco sale.[31]

On the basis of the delegates' stated reasons for concluding the transaction with Constable, Rucker and Company, Governor Caswell gave his personal approval of their decision, but, commenting upon the delegates' hope that their actions

31. During 1786 John Gray Blount and Thomas Blount had been quietly negotiating through William Blount for purchase of part or all of North Carolina's public tobacco, but negotiations with the Board of Treasury had been promptly terminated after Thomas Blount had revealed the information to a "Babbling" acquaintance, who, intentionally or not, had broadcast the news. In March, 1787, William Blount informed John Gray Blount that the latter could undoubtedly purchase one hundred hogheads of the public tobacco from whoever purchased the tobacco from North Carolina and at the same price, a statement of such confidence that it clearly indicates that William Blount was secretly making such an opportunity a condition for purchase from the state. William Blount was even convinced that John Gray Blount could purchase the entire crop from the original buyer at terms favorable to the Blounts. Determined to remain at Congress until after the transaction had been concluded, William thereafter secretly purchased from Constable, Rucker and Company one hundred hogsheads of the public tobacco stored at a warehouse belonging to John Gray Blount and Thomas Blount. For details of these negotiations, see the following in Keith and Masterson, eds., *Blount*, I: Thomas Blount to John Gray Blount, February 3, 1787, p. 245; Thomas Blount to William Blount, March 7, 1787, pp. 255-56; Thomas Blount to John Gray Blount and Thomas Blount, March 10, 1787, p. 258; William Blount to John Gray Blount, April 5, 1787, p. 276; John Gray Blount to Thomas Blount, April 8, 1787, pp. 278-79.

would meet with official and popular satisfaction, Caswell warned that while "Judicious" men would react favorably, some persons would complain that the tobacco should have been parceled out for the highest price. Caswell's prediction of complaints was soon fulfilled as private individuals argued that the tobacco had been sold too cheaply and as the tobacco commissioners objected to the expense, difficulty, and inconvenience of the re-inspection.[32]

Complaints and objections aside, the transaction had been negotiated and it remained to be implemented. During the spring and summer of 1787 the company's agent, Robert Stewart, witnessed the re-inspection and supervised the loading of 1,106,606 pounds of acceptable tobacco at the ports of Washington, Edenton, and Wilmington.[33] While this process was underway, state officials became dismayed by reports that Constable, Rucker and Company was in financial difficulty,[34] reports that proved to be false but aroused anx-

32. Governor Richard Caswell to Benjamin Hawkins and William Blount, April 23, 1787, Clark, ed., *State Records*, XX, 680-81; John Haywood to Governor Richard Caswell, March 22, 1787, *ibid.*, p. 650; John Whitaker to Governor Richard Caswell, April 3, 1787, *ibid.*, pp. 658-59; Robert Rowan to Governor Richard Caswell, April 10, 1787, *ibid.*, p. 660.

33. John Whitaker to Governor Richard Caswell, April 3, 1787, *ibid.*, p. 658; Governor Richard Caswell to Robert Rowan, April 30, 1787, *ibid.*, p. 686; John Whitaker to Colonel Whitehead, June 16, 1787, *ibid.*, pp. 724-25; receipt in Governors' Papers, XIV, 83. A complete account of the sales is in the Governors' Papers, Series II, Box IV (Johnston). A statement of the ultimate poundage sold to Constable and Rucker is found in "General Abstract of the Claims of the State of North Carolina Against the United States," p. 13, Treasurers' and Comptrollers' Papers, Military Papers, LXVIII, State Department of Archives and History, Raleigh.

34. Thomas Blount to John Gray Blount, July 7, 1787, Keith and Masterson, eds., *Blount*, I, 316-17; John Cowper to John Gray Blount, July 15, 1787, *ibid.*, pp. 320-21; William Blount to William Constable, July 10, 1787, Clark, ed., *State Records*, XX, 734; William Constable to William Blount, July 11, 1787, plus enclosure, *ibid.*, pp. 738-39; Governor Richard Caswell to John Whitaker, July 17, 1787, *ibid.*, p. 749; William Blount to Governor Richard Caswell, July 12, 1787, *ibid.*, pp. 739-40. The rumors of financial difficulty originated after a Paris bank had refused to honor the firm's drafts until such time as Atlantic storms had abated sufficiently to allow more of the company's tobacco to reach France. Alarmed by this turn of events, John Rucker had

ieties that were laid to rest only when the Board of Treasury announced on November 1, 1787, that it had received the company's receipts for the tobacco and was crediting North Carolina with $28,487 specie, a figure later adjusted at the treasury to $36,887 specie.[35] A second and well-founded cause for alarm, one that touched off an investigation and prosecution lasting several years, was the discovery that a warehouse owner, Richard Blackledge, had used public tobacco stored at his establishment for his own private purposes.[36] Also of legitimate concern as the 1787 Assembly convened at Tarborough in mid-November were the terms of the sale to Constable, Rucker and Company and substantiated reports that the tobacco commissioners had purchased inferior quality tobacco and had allowed the purchases to suffer from exposure to the weather.

Quickly establishing that it was not composed of "Judicious" men, the Assembly manifested its sharp displeasure with the delegates' handling of the sale to Constable, Rucker and Company. The legislators protested "the heavy losses and expense" involved in the terms of the contract and in

---

hurriedly left France for the United States to arrange prompt tobacco shipments (one reason for the firm's interest in North Carolina's public tobacco). Unfortunately, Rucker's sudden departure left his business matters deranged and prevented additional drafts from being honored—giving rise to false rumors of general financial difficulty.

35. Treasury of the United States to the State of North Carolina, November 1, 1787, Legislative Papers, LXXVI, undated folder. The figure of $28,487 represented tobacco totaling 854,606 pounds weight. As stated in the text, the total ultimately received by Constable, Rucker and Company was 1,106,606 pounds. While working on the state's claims against the United States, Abishai Thomas discovered that the treasury had not credited the state with the proceeds of the additional tobacco. The treasury subsequently re-examined Thomas' contention and, agreeing with the agent's observation, credited North Carolina with an additional $8,400. See "General Abstract of the Claims of the State of North Carolina Against the United States," p. 13, Treasurers' and Comptrollers' Papers, Military Papers, LXVIII.

36. As revealed above, pp. 117, 118, 119, Blackledge was sued by the state and he ultimately reimbursed North Carolina, the money being applied against North Carolina's obligation to Martinique. Many unpublished documents pertaining to the Blackledge incident are in the Governors' Papers and the Legislative Papers.

the time-consuming mode of having the delegates execute the sale; transferred that responsibility from the delegates to the governor and Council of State; and required that the tobacco be parceled out if necessary to obtain the highest price. The tobacco commissioners were instructed to purchase only first and second quality tobacco under the state inspection system. Finally, and most significantly, the Assembly specified that the tobacco program would continue for one additional year, a step establishing that a dissatisfied Assembly intended a reappraisal of the entire program at the end of that year and was no longer willing to pledge its indefinite continuation until North Carolina's portion of the foreign debt of the United States was discharged.[37]

As the tobacco commissioners drew money from the treasury for purchase from the 1788 tobacco crop, the council designated warehouses and other storage places (a reaction to Blackledge's indiscretion and to past damage to the public tobacco from faulty storage); advised Governor Samuel Johnston to advertise the tobacco in the newspapers of several states; and advised that the tobacco be sold for specie or bills of exchange acceptable to the Board of Treasury, and at a price no less than two shillings below the Petersburg market price.[38] Because of the risks involved in delayed payment, Johnston was determined, moreover, to accept only immediate payment; and, acting on the basis of the Petersburg price, he soon came to set twenty-eight shillings ($3.5) per hundredweight without re-inspection as the absolute minimum terms for sale. These terms, despite numerous inquiries and negotiations during 1788, proved too stringent because North Carolina's inspection system did not enjoy the excellent reputation held by Petersburg inspection, and at year's end the state possessed 430,325 pounds of tobacco that had been purchased at an average price of about fifty-one shillings North

37. Clark, ed., *State Records*, XXIV, 451, 892-93.

38. Journal of the Council of State, March 18, July 26, 1788, Governors' Office Papers, CXXI, State Department of Archives and History, Raleigh.

Carolina currency per hundredweight.[39] As storage fees mounted, Governor Johnston held to the minimum terms and became increasingly disenchanted with the public tobacco program.

Convening at Fayetteville on November 3, the 1788 Assembly received a discouraging report from the governor and, as the previous Assembly had intended, undertook a critical review of the concept and execution of the public tobacco program. Certainly the purpose of the program had been served with only limited success to that point, as revealed by a committee report that the payment of $28,487 to the Board of Treasury left North Carolina in arrears of congressional requisitions to the amount of $435,419 specie as the state's quota of the principal and interest of the foreign debt of the United States.[40] In light of this information, which clearly established that the tobacco program could never enable the state to meet its quota, and in light of the losses and problems associated with the program, the Assembly instructed its revenue committee to consider the propriety of continuing the purchases. Within the committee it was originally proposed that the law allocating the revenue from the state imposts and other taxes be repealed; that the money already collected from those taxes be deposited in the treasury rather than with the tobacco commissioners; and that the commissioners expend only the money presently in their hands

39. For mercantile inquiries and unsuccessful negotiations between merchants and Governor Johnston, see the following: A. MacNaughton & Co. to Governor Samuel Johnston, July 30, 1788, Governors' Papers, Series II, Box IV (Johnston); A. MacNaughton & Co. to Governor Johnston, September 11, 1788, *ibid.*; Governor Samuel Johnston to A. MacNaughton & Co., August 30, 1788, Treasurers' and Comptrollers' Papers, Correspondence of the Treasurer, I; see also the following correspondence in Governors' Papers, XVII: James Porterfield to Governor Samuel Johnston, August 15, 1788, p. 4; Hugh Williamson to Governor Samuel Johnston, September 26, 1788, p. 21; Governor Samuel Johnston to James Porterfield, October 1, 1788, p. 25. For statistics on public tobacco possessed by the state at the end of 1788, see Clark, ed., *State Records*, XXI, 95-97.

40. Clark, ed., *State Records*, XXI, 145-46.

(a total of about $48,745 North Carolina currency).[41] As the recommendations emerged from the committee, however, the report proposed that the law setting aside the impost and other revenues be retained; that each of the three tobacco commissioners receive enough additional money from the treasury to bring the amount in his hands to $25,000 (which would have required a total additional outlay of something over $26,000); and that the remaining revenue from the allocated taxes be held in the treasury "subject to the order of a future General Assembly."[42] The House accepted the committee report as amended. Nine representatives, convinced with the Senate majority that the program should be terminated, protested the House's action on the following bases: first, the principle of government participation in mercantile speculation had pernicious tendencies; second, the tobacco program was inexpedient and oppressive to the public; third, the practice depreciated the state currency; fourth, the program raised the domestic price of tobacco and thereby discouraged outsiders from buying; fifth, the losses involved in converting currency into specie (in conducting the program) were prohibitive; and sixth, the policy enriched a few and oppressed the many by benefiting the purchasers and a portion of the planters at the expense of the general public. A final effort by the program's enemies in the House to terminate the purchase of tobacco by May 1, 1789, was defeated by a vote of forty-three to thirty-four.[43]

Although the House was determined that the purchase of tobacco should continue, the House's proposals did involve curtailment of the program—at least until the next Assembly. Additional evidence that the House was not unmindful of the program's disadvantages and inadequacies (or of public distaste for taxes) was the defeat of a bill proposing to levy a tax in specie or produce toward discharging the state's portion of the foreign debt of the United States. Another bill pro-

41. The original report, with amendments, is found in the Legislative Papers, LXXXII.

42. Clark, ed., *State Records*, XXI, 138.

43. *Ibid.*, pp. 178-79.

posing, for the same purpose, to levy a poll tax payable in tobacco, rice, or flour was never introduced because of the discouraging prospects for approval.[44] The House, furthermore, agreed with the Senate to divert enough of the tobacco needed to discharge the state's debt to Martinique, a decision that, as we have seen, posed a painful dilemma for an Assembly seeking to meet both the state's obligations.[45]

The protracted controversy between House and Senate over whether to continue the tobacco program, and, if so, under what conditions, remained unsettled until the last day of the Assembly session, when, with some decision mandatory, a resolution was passed stating that until the next Assembly the commissioners were to continue their purchases "under the restrictions and regulations of the Act of Assembly respecting that business."[46] Thus, for lack of agreement as to what changes should be made, the existing tobacco program received another year of life.

After receiving several inquiries about the public tobacco, Governor Johnston called a meeting of the council, which, on March 13, 1789, advised him to sell the tobacco, if possible, at not less than $3 specie per hundredweight (thus abandoning the relationship to the Petersburg price) without re-inspection, or not less than $3.33 specie per hundredweight with re-inspection at state expense. In order that the tobacco could be applied against the state's obligation to Martinique and to the United States, the council specified that payment should be made in advance of delivery and should be in specie or bills of exchange upon Philadelphia or New York and acceptable to the United States Treasury.[47] In May, by which time North Carolina possessed about a thousand hogsheads of public tobacco, the treasury recommended as a purchaser the New York firm of Royal Flint and Company. Negotiations between the state and Royal Flint were subsequently under-

44. The bills are in the Legislative Papers, LXXXI.
45. Above, pp. 114-16.
46. Clark, ed., *State Records*, XXI, 186.
47. Journal of the Council of State, March 13, 1789, Governors' Office Papers, CXXI.

taken but were complicated by the fact that Flint wished to purchase all available good-quality public tobacco, and yet he offered as payment a credit that he had with the United States Treasury, a mode of payment that, of course, would prevent the state from discharging its obligation to Martinique as the 1788 Assembly had directed; and also negotiations were complicated by the fact that Flint's maximum offer was only $3 per hundredweight with re-inspection at state expense.[48] Concerned about the mounting storage fees and anxious that the state make payment against its obligation to the United States, Governor Johnston and the council, as we have seen, accepted Flint's offer and thereby sacrificed payment to Martinique.[49] During the fall of 1789 and the spring of 1790 the company loaded a total of 944,128 pounds of tobacco, giving North Carolina a credit with the United States Treasury amounting to $28,323 specie.[50] While the transaction was being implemented, the 1789 Assembly approved Johnston's decision to sell to Royal Flint and, as we have seen, ordered that the tobacco refused by Flint be sold to help discharge the Martinique debt.[51]

As the state's business with Royal Flint was being conducted, the United States Treasury co-operated in the transactions both before and after North Carolina entered the Union. During the ratification debate within the state, the tobacco program in particular and the requisition system in general had come under sharp attack by North Carolina Federalists. At the 1788 Hillsborough Convention the tobacco

48. United States Treasury to Governor Samuel Johnston, July 3, 1789, Clark, ed., *State Records*, XXI, 556; Governor Samuel Johnston to William Littlejohn, July 20, 1789, *ibid.*, p. 558; Royal Flint to Governor Samuel Johnston, July 11, 1789, *ibid.*, pp. 556-57; Journal of the Council of State, July 29, 30, 1789, Governors' Office Papers, CXXI; Governor Samuel Johnston to James Iredell, July 22, 1789, James Iredell Papers, Duke University.

49. Journal of the Council of State, July 30, 1789, Governors' Office Papers, CXXI. Above, p. 116.

50. "General Abstract of the Claims of the State of North Carolina Against the United States," p. 14, Treasurers' and Comptrollers' Papers, Military Papers, LXVIII.

51. Clark, ed., *State Records*, XXI, 421-22. Above, p. 117.

program's leading critic had been none other than Governor Johnston, an ardent Federalist, who had argued that the state had suffered great losses from the program and deserved to be called a swindler for having purchased tobacco at sixty shillings and sold it, after storage and transportation fees, for twenty-four shillings.[52] Even greater controversy had centered upon the requisition system itself, which Federalists had labeled as patently inadequate to meet the needs of the central government. One of the most objectionable features of the proposed constitution, however, had been the tax powers granted to Congress, an attitude engendered to no small degree by the fact that so little of the national domestic debt resided among North Carolinians. Thus, despite the protests of the Federalist minority, the Hillsborough Convention had proposed, for political and financial reasons, a constitutional amendment that the United States should not collect direct taxes or excises in a state that passed legislation to raise and collect its quota of the congressional taxes or excises.[53] With the state's ratification of the constitution at the Fayetteville Convention, however, congressional taxes came at last to North Carolina, and Federalists savored the general triumph that was the constitution.

An evaluation of North Carolina's public tobacco program establishes that the project did indeed entail disadvantages to the state. As its opponents emphasized, state purchase of tobacco above the market price undermined the reputation of the state currency, discouraged private tobacco transactions, contributed to inflation, and benefited comparatively few individuals (the growers who sold to the state and the buyers) at the expense of the general public. Furthermore,

52. Jonathan Elliot, ed., *The Debates, Resolutions and Proceedings, in Convention, on the adoption of the Federal Constitution* (3 vols.; Washington: Jonathan Elliott, 1827-30), III, 80, 88. A temporary shortage of domestic tobacco had driven the price up to sixty shillings for a brief period, and the state did make some purchases at that price before ceasing in order to await the 1789 crop and the subsequent lower prices. Most of public tobacco was purchased below that figure of sixty shillings.

53. *Ibid.*, pp. 32, 77-81, 82-83, 206, 213.

it is true that the program was plagued by administrative difficulties and errors, notably the carelessness of the commissioners regarding their purchases, the improper storing of the tobacco, and the division of authority concerning shipment of tobacco and execution of sale—a division that was probably inevitable since the vital interests of both Congress and North Carolina were involved in the terms and conditions of the sales.

It is true also, however, that the disadvantages and losses connected with the program were not as severe as portrayed by its enemies, especially by Federalists who hated the process because of its association with fiat currency and with the requisition system that they despised and hoped to supplant with congressional taxes. The problems resulting from offering more than the market price—depreciation of the currency, inflation, interruption of private business, inordinate profits at public expense—were terminated after the program's first year as the 1786 Assembly required the commissioners thereafter to offer no more than the local market price for tobacco. Additionally, the losses associated with the program, while not inconsequential, were not much greater than the losses involved in converting fiat currency into specie within the state, an observation that would be of no consolation to hard-money men but would absolve the program of the allegation that it was absolutely disastrous in conception. At an average price of approximately $6.25 (fifty shillings) North Carolina currency, the state purchased a total of 2,164,067 pounds of merchantable tobacco which sold for a total of $68,610 specie, or about $3.2 specie per hundredweight[54]—an exchange rate of approximately 53 per cent between currency

54. Sales to Constable, Rucker and Company totaled 1,106,606 pounds, giving North Carolina a specie credit of $36,887; sales to Royal Flint totaled 944,128 pounds, providing the state a specie credit of $28,323. In addition, North Carolina received credit for $3,400 specie for 113,333 pounds of public tobacco sold to one William Littlejohn as a result of negotiations entered prior to the sale to Royal Flint. "General Abstract of the Claims of the State of North Carolina Against the United States," pp. 13-14, Treasurers' and Comptrollers' Papers, Military Papers, LXVIII.

and specie, or slightly below the average exchange rate within the state after the 1785 currency emission. It must be observed also, of course, that the state suffered considerable expense in transportation, storage, and re-inspection of the tobacco as well as losses from purchase of poor quality tobacco and from damage to purchased tobacco.

The proponents of the tobacco program, while unhappy with certain problems of execution, were well aware of the project's inherent disadvantages and limitations but were prepared to accept them as the price of maintaining the requisition system and thereby Congress' dependence upon the states. Most of these men would be prepared to argue, as has one contemporary historian,[55] that the program was an ingenious one because the Assembly created fiat currency and, at the expense of the public that bore the cost of the currency's depreciation, converted the currency (through produce) into specie. In short, the program involved all of the advantages and disadvantages, all of the arguments and counterarguments associated with fiat policy. As we have seen in Chapter III, hard-money men were unprepared to live with the disadvantages of that policy.

By 1789 the inescapable conclusion of friends and foes alike was that the program—whatever its usefulness or its perniciousness—was completely inadequate to discharge North Carolina's portion of the foreign debt of the United States. This conviction probably more than any specific disadvantages may have helped persuade many North Carolinians that the requisition system could not maintain Congress as a viable government. To give up the requisition system and establish congressional taxes, however—that is, to ratify the constitution—was clearly (except for the impost) to act against the immediate financial interests of the state, because, as we have seen, North Carolina had extinguished the continental debt among its citizens and because the state possessed a smaller domestic debt than a number of other states and there-

55. Forrest McDonald, *E. Pluribus Unum* (Boston: Houghton Mifflin Company, 1965), p. 83.

fore stood to lose should Congress assume state debts and block the final settlement of accounts. Thus ratification proved difficult to achieve in North Carolina, and Federalists were those who were looking at the state's long-range need to be incorporated into a Union combining the states' resources under a dynamic central government.

IX. Conclusion

As this study has emphasized, the financial policies and practices adopted by the government of North Carolina in the post-Revolutionary period should be judged by the economic realities and immediate fiscal options of the eighteenth century rather than by those of the late nineteenth century and the twentieth century. Possessed in the 1780's of an agrarian economy that afflicted the state, as it had throughout the colonial period, with an unfavorable balance of trade, North Carolina faced a drain of specie that was accelerated during the postwar years by heavy purchasing of manufactured imports, overextension of credit, and overproduction of domestic produce that glutted world markets and thereby greatly reduced market prices. Restricted by limited resources, sparse population, and a shortage of investment opportunities other than land, the economy of North Carolina was, for the foreseeable future, inescapably pre-industrial and therefore saddled with its unfavorable balance of trade and its specie shortage. These, then, were the economic realities facing the government of eighteenth-century North Carolina and these are the realities by which, as E. James Ferguson suggests,[1] the government's policies should be evaluated.

Plagued by the severe and inescapable shortage of specie, North Carolina in the 1780's faced many pressing demands, not the least of which was the enormous certificate and fiat currency debt incurred by the state in fighting the Revolution. So large was this debt that its redemption with specie or other tangible property was patently impossible, and it was

1. E. James Ferguson, *The Power of the Purse: A History of American Public Finance, 1776-1790* (Chapel Hill: The University of North Carolina Press, 1961).

acceptance of that fact rather than perniciousness or irresponsibility that led the Assembly to retire the bulk of the debt by devaluation (repudiation) and sinking taxes. In resorting to these fiat redemption modes, North Carolina was continuing colonial redemption policy based, as Ferguson maintains, upon the necessary and widespread conviction that fiat currency and state certificates did not constitute sacred contracts but rather served as a means to finance government at the expense of the public that shouldered, with varying degrees of resignation and with some protests, the burden of the debt's market depreciation and fiat redemption. Those individuals, who from conviction, self-interest, or both, insisted that certificates and fiat currency were indeed sacred contracts involving the government's honor were distinctly a minority, and although they were able to have confiscated property and western land employed against a portion of the debt, this minority—like most—lost more battles than it won. In sum, fiat redemption was employed not because that policy was inherently desirable but because it was unavoidable.

The economic realities of the 1780's, again arguing more persuasively than talk of sacred contracts, prompted the fiat currency emissions of 1783 and 1785. In a time of severe money shortage, the need and the desire to pay the Continental Line and to meet part of the state's obligation to the United States were the foremost—but not the only—considerations behind the emissions, and to some extent, however inadequate, these primary objectives were served without severe currency depreciation when compared to North Carolina's wartime currency emissions. As everyone anticipated, the currency did depreciate, losses were indeed sustained, specie was driven from circulation, inflation did result, trade was discouraged, and the shortage of money was not fundamentally relieved. What must be emphasized is that the difference between advocates and opponents of these fiat emissions was not the difference between perniciousness and virtue or between irresponsibility and soundness but rather between those who were willing and those who were unwilling to incur the predictable disadvantages of emission in order to meet the exigencies of government. Fiat men, while certainly including individuals who sought to discharge their specie debts cheaply, were, for the most part, responsible realists who, for political reasons or otherwise, were prepared to adjust the government's financial policies to existing conditions in eighteenth-century North Carolina—to institute fiat measures. Hard-money men were the idealists who dreamed of things that were not—an industrial economy, a favorable balance of trade, a specie economy, the honoring of contracts—and it is a measure of this conservative minority's deep concern that after years of unsuccessful effort to amend the Articles of Confederation, they undertook the transformation of their dreams into reality by means of the political and financial revolution that was the constitution.

When the economic conditions of eighteenth-century North Carolina and the motivations and considerations behind governmental policies are kept in mind, many of the evaluations of the "Critical Period" made by John Fiske[2] and other Federalist historians become, as recent critics have suggested, erroneous or irrelevant to an understanding of the post-Revolutionary years. Fiske's general contempt for the Articles of Confederation and, more particularly, his indictment of fiat financial measures reflect the nationalism and fiscal conservation of the late nineteenth century rather than a realistic appraisal of conditions existing and policy options available in the eighteenth century, and therefore, as Merrill Jensen maintains, Fiske's evaluation "is at worst false and at best grossly distorted."[3] And if Jensen in his effort to counteract Fiske portrays rather too optimistically the basic economic conditions of the 1780's, Jensen acknowledges—in statements that would apply to North Carolina at least as fully as to any other state—that the economic collapse of 1785 was serious, that the unfavorable balance of trade and specie shortage

2. John Fiske, *The Critical Period in American History* (Boston: Houghton, Mifflin and Company, 1891).

3. Merrill Jensen, *The New Nation* (New York: Alfred A. Knopf, 1950), p. xiii.

were severe, and that the economy faced the inherent limitations of a pre-industrial society.

As we have seen, North Carolina's domestic financial policies were interrelated with the financial and political aspects of state-federal relations. Antifederalism was both a cause and a result of the state's payment of its Continental Line through 1781 and the state's absorption of the continental debt in its citizens' hands, and those policies shaped North Carolina's opposition to a funding of the national debt, either by state payments against congressional requisitions or by congressional taxation. Having redeemed much of its own domestic debt, North Carolina opposed congressional assumption of state debts at least until after final settlement of accounts between the United States and the respective states had been assured. Convinced that North Carolina would be found a creditor to the United States at that final settlement, the state sought to facilitate final settlement by supporting the rule of equity for determining each state's quota of the war expenses of Congress. Having incurred many wartime expenses without prior congressional authorization, and finding that its public records were in deplorable condition, North Carolina strongly advocated the principle of equity regarding expenditures and evidence. The state favored the congressional impost because a uniform tariff system would benefit North Carolina, but except for the brief life of the continental tax, the state opposed congressional taxes and supported the requisition system because such taxes were a threat to the state's sovereignty and because they did not promise to benefit North Carolina nearly so much as to burden her.

It is clear, in summary, that the financial roots of North Carolina Antifederalism were deep, as indeed the opponents of centralization intended them to be. The state's ultimate ratification of the constitution came not primarily because of the fiat measures adopted by North Carolina during the 1780's nor because of the state's difficulties in procuring specie credit outside the state but rather because of the triumph of

Federalism in other states and the events that flowed therefrom. With no realistic alternative to joining the Union, North Carolina did so reluctantly and in full knowledge that ratification would likely be, in a number of respects, financially disadvantageous to the state. North Carolina Federalists were those who were willing to endure those temporary disadvantages in order to procure the long-range benefits to be derived from a strong central government and a more unified national economy.

A number of North Carolina's postwar policies did indeed prove to be disappointing or disadvantageous to the state. The struggle to discharge the Martinique debt and the state's portion of the national foreign debt only displayed the state's handicaps in seeking credit abroad. The funding of the national debt in 1790 benefited few North Carolinians but subjected the state to significant congressional tax demands. The assumption of state debts relieved North Carolina of less a burden than the relief enjoyed by other states, and while North Carolina's fears that final settlement would be blocked proved groundless, final settlement came as a bitter disappointment when the state, even with the principle of equity regarding evidence and authorization, was unable to establish many of its claims against the United States. Furthermore, to facilitate final settlement the state had agreed to the employment of population as the basis for assigning each state's portion of the central government's wartime expenses, and that policy led North Carolina to be assigned a sum far exceeding the actual expenditures made by the United States on behalf of North Carolina. These factors, together with the fact that the state's continental certificates proved unavailing, made final settlement a bitter experience as North Carolina was declared a debtor to the United States. When one considers the disadvantages and disappointments associated with North Carolina's entrance into the Union and with the immediate years thereafter, the Antifederalism that helped shape North Carolina's policies during the 1780's and the consequent lack of enthusiasm for Federalism and its programs may be better understood.

SELECTED BIBLIOGRAPHY

Selected Bibliography

I. PRIMARY SOURCES

A. *Manuscripts*

Edmund Ruffin Beckwith Papers. Southern Historical Collection, The University of North Carolina at Chapel Hill.

Richard Bennehan Papers. Southern Historical Collection, The University of North Carolina at Chapel Hill.

Herman Brimmer Papers. Duke University.

Cameron Family Papers. Southern Historical Collection, The University of North Carolina at Chapel Hill.

David Miller Carter Papers. Southern Historical Collection, The University of North Carolina at Chapel Hill.

Richard Caswell Papers. Duke University.

Richard Caswell Papers. Southern Historical Collection, The University of North Carolina at Chapel Hill.

Mary Farrow Credle Papers. Southern Historical Collection, The University of North Carolina at Chapel Hill.

Cupola House Papers (microfilm). Southern Historical Collection, The University of North Carolina at Chapel Hill.

William Richardson Davie Papers. Southern Historical Collection, The University of North Carolina at Chapel Hill.

John Dickey Ledger. Duke University.

Samuel S. Downey Papers. Duke University.

Leonidas Chalmers Glenn Papers. Southern Historical Collection, The University of North Carolina at Chapel Hill.

Hayes Collection (microfilm). Southern Historical Collection, The University of North Carolina at Chapel Hill.

John De Berniere Hooper Papers. Southern Historical Collection, The University of North Carolina at Chapel Hill.

John Huske and James Hogg Business Ledger. Duke University.

James Iredell Papers. Duke University.

Charles E. Johnson Collection. State Department of Archives and History, Raleigh.

Lenoir Family Papers. Southern Historical Collection, The University of North Carolina at Chapel Hill.

William Lytle Papers. Southern Historical Collection, The University of North Carolina at Chapel Hill.

Macay-McNeeley Papers. Southern Historical Collection, The University of North Carolina at Chapel Hill.

John Nisbet Papers. Southern Historical Collection, The University of North Carolina at Chapel Hill.

Abraham Rencher Papers. Southern Historical Collection, The University of North Carolina at Chapel Hill.

William Ross Papers. Duke University.

Ruffin-Roulhac-Hamilton Papers. Southern Historical Collection, The University of North Carolina at Chapel Hill.

Simpson-Bryan Papers. North Carolina Collection, The University of North Carolina at Chapel Hill.

Strudwick Papers. Southern Historical Collection, The University of North Carolina at Chapel Hill.

Swann Papers. Southern Historical Collection, The University of North Carolina at Chapel Hill.

Abishai Thomas Papers. State Department of Archives and History, Raleigh.

B. *Public and Official Documents*

American State Papers. 38 vols. Washington: Gales and Seaton, 1833-34.

Annals of Congress. 42 vols. Washington: Gales and Seaton, 1834-56.

British Public Records (photostats). Southern Historical Collection, The University of North Carolina at Chapel Hill.

Clark, Walter, ed. *The State Records of North Carolina.* 16 vols. Winston, Goldsboro, and Raleigh: State of North Carolina, 1895-1906.

Governors' Letter Books. State Department of Archives and History, Raleigh.

Governors' Office Papers. State Department of Archives and History, Raleigh.

Governors' Papers. State Department of Archives and History, Raleigh.

Governors' Papers. Second Series. State Department of Archives and History, Raleigh.

Journals of the Continental Congress, 1774-89. 34 vols. Washington: Government Printing Office, 1904-37.

Journal of the Council of State. State Department of Archives and History, Raleigh.

Legislative Papers. State Department of Archives and History, Raleigh.

Saunders, William L., ed. *The Colonial Records of North Carolina.* 10 vols. Raleigh: State of North Carolina, 1886-90.

Treasurers' and Comptrollers' Papers. State Department of Archives and History, Raleigh.

C. *Newspapers*

Fayetteville *Gazette* (microfilm). North Carolina Collection, The University of North Carolina at Chapel Hill.

North Carolina Gazette (Hillsborough) (microfilm). North Carolina Collection, The University of North Carolina at Chapel Hill.

State Gazette of North Carolina (Edenton) (microfilm). North Carolina Collection, The University of North Carolina at Chapel Hill.

D. *Pamphlets*

Anonymous. "To the People of the District of Edenton." *A Plea for Federal Union.* Edited by Hugh Talmage Lefler. Charlottesville: Tracy W. McGregor Library, 1947.

E. *Travel Accounts*

Attmore, William. *Journal of a Tour to North Carolina.* Edited by Lida Tunstall Rodman. ("The James Sprunt Historical Publications," Vol. 17, No. 2.) Chapel Hill: North Carolina Historical Society, 1922.

Hunter, Robert, Jr. *Quebec to Carolina in 1785-1786.* Edited by Louis B. Wright and Marion Tinling. San Marino: The Huntington Library, 1943.

Schoepf, Johann David. *Travels in the Confederation.* Edited and translated by Alfred James Morrison. 2 vols. Philadelphia: William J. Campbell and Company, 1911.

F. *Collected Works*

Boyd, Julian P., and others, eds. *The Papers of Thomas Jefferson.* 17 vols. Princeton: Princeton University Press, 1950-65.

Burnett, Edmund Cody, ed. *Letters of Members of the Continental Congress.* 8 vols. Washington: Carnegie Institution, 1921-36.

Elliot, Jonathan, ed. *The Debates, Resolutions and Proceedings, in Convention, on the adoption of the Federal Constitution.* 3 vols. Washington: Jonathan Elliot, 1827-30.

Fries, Adelaide L., and others, eds. *Records of the Moravians in North Carolina.* 10 vols. Raleigh: North Carolina Historical Commission [State Department of Archives and History], 1922-66.

Keith, Alice Barnwell, and William Henry Masterson, eds. *The John Gray Blount Papers.* 3 vols. Raleigh: State Department of Archives and History, 1952-65.

McPherson, Elizabeth Gregory, ed. "Unpublished Letters from North Carolinians to James Madison and James Monroe," *North Carolina Historical Review*, XIV, No. 2, (April, 1937), 156-87.

McRee, Griffith John, ed. *Life and Correspondence of James Iredell.* 2 vols. New York: D. Appleton and Company, 1867-68.

Wagstaff, Henry McGilbert, ed. *The Papers of John Steele.* 2 vols. Raleigh: North Carolina Historical Commission [State Department of Archives and History], 1924.

Williamson, Hugh. *Letters from Sylvius.* ("Historical Papers of the Trinity College Historical Society," Series 11.) Durham: Trinity College Historical Society, 1915.

II. SECONDARY SOURCES

A. *General Works*

Ashe, Samuel A'Court. *History of North Carolina.* 2 vols. Raleigh: Edwards and Broughton Printing Company, 1925.

Boyd, William Kenneth. *The Federal Period, 1783-1860.* New York: Lewis Publishing Company, 1919.

Connor, Robert Digges Wimberly. *North Carolina: Rebuild-*

ing an Ancient Commonwealth. 4 vols. New York: The American Historical Society, 1929.

Fiske, John. *The Critical Period in American History.* Boston: Houghton, Mifflin and Company, 1891.

Jensen, Merrill. *The Articles of Confederation.* Madison: University of Wisconsin Press, 1940.

———. *The New Nation.* New York: Alfred A. Knopf, 1950.

Lee, Lawrence. *The Lower Cape Fear in Colonial Days.* Chapel Hill: The University of North Carolina Press, 1965.

Lefler, Hugh Talmage. *History of North Carolina.* 2 vols. New York: Lewis Historical Publishing Company, 1956.

———, ed. *North Carolina History Told by Contemporaries.* Chapel Hill: The University of North Carolina Press, 1934.

McDonald, Forrest. *E. Pluribus Unum.* Boston: Houghton Mifflin Company, 1965.

Merrens, Harry Roy. *Colonial North Carolina in the Eighteenth Century. A Study in Historical Geography.* Chapel Hill: The University of North Carolina Press, 1964.

B. Special Studies

Beard, Charles Austin. *An Economic Interpretation of the Constitution of the United States.* New York: Macmillan Company, 1913.

Bullock, Charles Jesse. *Essays on the Monetary History of the United States.* New York: Macmillan Company, 1900.

Crittenden, Charles Christopher. *The Commerce of North Carolina, 1763-1789.* ("Yale Historical Publications," No. 29.) New Haven: Yale University Press, 1936.

Ferguson, E. James. *The Power of the Purse: A History of American Public Finance, 1776-1790.* Chapel Hill: The University of North Carolina Press, 1961.

Fries, Adelaide L. "North Carolina Certificates of the Revolutionary Period, *North Carolina Historical Review*, IX, No. 3 (July, 1932), pp. 229-41.

Gregory, Marion, and Lennon, Donald. "The North Carolina Revolutionary Debt." Unpublished manuscript at the State Department of Archives and History, Raleigh.

McDonald, Forrest. *We the People: The Economic Origins of the Constitution.* Chicago: University of Chicago Press, 1958.

Macon, Hershal Luther. "A Fiscal History of North Carolina, 1776-1860." Unpublished Ph.D. dissertation, The University of North Carolina at Chapel Hill, 1932.

Masterson, William Henry. *William Blount.* Baton Rouge: Louisiana State University Press, 1954.

Trenholme, Louise Irby. *The Ratification of the Federal Constitution in North Carolina.* ("Studies in History, Economics and Public Law," No. 363.) New York: Columbia University Press, 1932.

INDEX

Index